The Theological Vision of Reinhold Niebuhr's *The Irony of American History*

"In the Battle and Above It"

SCOTT R. ERWIN

OXFORD
UNIVERSITY PRESS

OXFORD
UNIVERSITY PRESS

Great Clarendon Street, Oxford, OX2 6DP,
United Kingdom

Oxford University Press is a department of the University of Oxford.
It furthers the University's objective of excellence in research, scholarship,
and education by publishing worldwide. Oxford is a registered trade mark of
Oxford University Press in the UK and in certain other countries

© Scott R. Erwin 2013

The moral rights of the author have been asserted

First Edition published in 2013

Impression: 1

British Library Cataloguing in Publication Data

Data available

ISBN 978-0-19-967837-2

Printed in Great Britain by
the CPI Group (UK) Ltd

Contents

Acknowledgments

There are many people to whom acknowledgment is due.

First is Walter Russell Mead, who introduced me to Reinhold Niebuhr through a seemingly innocent research request and encouraged me to study theology.

As this monograph is a modified version of my doctoral thesis completed at the University of Oxford, I am hugely indebted to many individuals in this community. First, I am indebted to Dr Joel Rasmussen, my DPhil supervisor, for striking a judicious balance between encouragement and challenge in his guidance. I am also grateful to Joel for "godfathering" the process by which I turned my doctoral thesis into a monograph and, more generally, for the steadfast friendship given by him, Tanya, and the boys. Second, I am grateful for the support of Dr Charlotte Methuen, my MPhil supervisor, who saw academic potential in my fascination for Niebuhr's description of Abraham Lincoln as "America's greatest theologian." Third, I would like to thank Professor Nigel Biggar for the sage guidance he provided me throughout my project and to his wife, Ginny, for adopting me into the Christian Ethics community. Fourth, I would like to acknowledge the many other academics whose tutelage had an influence on my work: Professor George Pattison; Professor Sarah Foot; Professor John Barton; Dr Johannes Zackhhuber; Dr Mark Chapman; Dr Jay Sexton; Reverend Charles Brock; Dr Mark Edwards. In particular, I want to recognize Donald Hay for his wise counsel and the spiritual guidance that he and his wife, Elizabeth, have and continue to provide. Finally, I am grateful to the Rhodes Trust not only for the generous financial support of my academic studies but also for exposing me to a truly remarkable community of scholars. Special thanks to Sir Colin Lucas and Professor Don Markwell for their stewardship of the Trust and to Mary Eaton, Sheila Partridge, John Gee, Bob Wyllie, and Colin Page for making Rhodes House such a lovely place to call home in Oxford.

Beyond the Oxford community, I have also benefited from the insights of number of other academics. Dr Martin Halliwell, a Niebuhr scholar at the University of Leicester, taught me a great about the theologian and about the practical aspects of academia as well.

Dr Will Inboden of the University of Texas at Austin provided sound advice as I crafted my sections on Niebuhr's activity during the Cold War. Christian Sahner, a doctoral student at Princeton University, read and commented upon a number of draft chapters. Finally, I am grateful for my undergraduate professors at the University of Richmond, Dr Gary McDowell and Dr Akiba Covitz in particular, for supervising my initial studies of Abraham Lincoln and his religious beliefs.

I am also deeply indebted to a host of dedicated and talented library administrators and researchers without whom I could not have conducted the primary and secondary research necessary to complete this work. I want to thank Jane Rawson and her colleagues at the Rothermere American Institute in Oxford for countenancing my presence in the library on a near daily basis for three years. I am equally grateful to Elizabeth Birchall at the Theology Faculty Library and Janet McMullin and Cristina Neagu at Christ Church Library for their support.

Writing from England about an influential American theologian is not without logistical challenges. This burden was made increasingly lighter thanks to the helpfulness of Joseph Lemelin, Elizabeth Miraglia, and Seth Kasten from The Burke Theological Library at Union Theological Seminary in locating and scanning numerous articles written by Niebuhr. Elizabeth deserves specific praise for her critical research support in the closing stages of this project. I am also grateful to Linda Offineer at Westminster College's Reeves Library for her investigative work that shed light on Niebuhr's Green Lectures that served as the basis for *Irony*. Finally, I want to recognize Bruce Kirby and the entire staff of the Manuscript Reading Room at the Library of Congress where Niebuhr's papers are housed.

I am deeply grateful to the Theological Monographs Committee, chaired by Sir Diarmaid MacCulloch, for giving me the opportunity to publish this work. In addition, I would like to thank Tom Perridge and Lizzie Robottom at Oxford University Press for overseeing the publication process and their valuable assistance more generally.

I want to also recognize my parents, Bob and Karen Erwin. Both are voracious readers and instilled in me a love of learning from a young age.

Finally, I thank my wife, Nita who is as foundational to this work as Niebuhr himself. Without her courage, wisdom, and inspiration, this book would be unwritten.

Scott Erwin

Introduction

Reinhold Niebuhr was following in the footsteps of a giant when he approached the podium and cast his eyes over the crowded gymnasium. Invited by Westminster College in Fulton, Missouri, to give the 1949 John Findlay Green Lectures, Niebuhr, a Missouri native, was the first Green Lecturer since former Prime Minister Winston Churchill. In the same gymnasium three years prior, the "British Bulldog" had issued a clarion call to the Western world with his "Iron Curtain Address." Churchill's warning that the Soviet Union desired "all the fruits of war and the indefinite expansion of their powers and doctrines," had struck some at the time as an act of aggression against a fellow Allied power.[1] The intervening years had proven him correct, however, as the Soviet Union consolidated its control over Eastern Europe and clashed with the countries of Western Europe. Indeed, the week of Niebuhr's address marked the first major setback in Joseph Stalin's breathtaking power grab—the announced end of the Soviet blockade of Berlin. Rather than discuss the Soviet threat, however, Niebuhr focused his address on the United States and specifically on how the Christian faith could help illuminate the country's responsibilities in the new world order. Over the course of two lectures entitled "This Nation Under God," the theologian challenged the country to strike a balance between remaining morally resolute in its defense of Western civilization while maintaining its awareness of the common frailties that bound it to its current foe. The eventual result of these lectures, *The Irony of American History*, published in 1952, was a penetrating exposition on the

---

[1] Winston Churchill, "Mr. Churchill's Address Calling for United Effort for World Peace: TRUMAN AND CHURCHILL IN MISSOURI," *The New York Times*, March 6, 1946, p. 4.

character of the country. The work remains one of the most widely cited meditations on America and its role in the world.

I

Given the range and magnitude of Niebuhr's corpus, any commentary on the theologian will offer only a partial view, and any effort to summarize his thinking will likely be incomplete. This likelihood is no doubt exacerbated by the fact that Niebuhr's writings are notoriously unsystematic. Nevertheless, this book argues that there was a discernible vision animating Niebuhr's writings, especially during the peak years of his influence—beginning with the United States's 1941 entry into World War II and concluding with his 1952 publication of *The Irony of American History*. Best expressed in a frequently overlooked article Niebuhr wrote in the early months of World War II, the highest ideal to which a Christian could strive was to be "in the battle and above it":

> To be in the battle means to defend a cause against its peril, to protect a nation against its enemies, to strive for truth against error, to defend justice against injustice. To be above the battle means that we understand how imperfect the cause is which we defend, that we contritely acknowledge the sins of our own nations, that we recognize the common humanity which binds us to even the most terrible of foes, and that we know also of our common need of grace and forgiveness.[2]

Niebuhr, in this instance, called on Americans to steady their resolve in the struggle against the Axis powers and simultaneously encouraged them to look beyond the immediate battle and remain humble amidst the conflict. More generally, however, this vision—a modernized gloss on St. Paul's affirmation that Christians are to be in but not of the world—was behind Niebuhr's approach to the majority of historical conflicts in which he would engage. This book will explore Niebuhr's vision in detail, make clear the respects in which it is a *theological* vision, and show how it informed his writings on current affairs.

[2] Niebuhr, "In the Battle and Above It," *Christianity and Society*, 7 (Autumn 1942), p. 3. The only commentary that features the article "In the Battle and Above It," is Charles C. Brown, *Niebuhr and His Age: Reinhold Niebuhr's Prophetic Role and Legacy* (Philadelphia: Trinity Press International, 1992), p. 107.

Although almost forty years have passed since he last commented on global affairs, Niebuhr remains at the center of a national conversation about America's role in the world. Commentators with divergent political and religious positions frequently find themselves in a proverbial "tug of war" to claim his legacy.[3] One camp typically presents Niebuhr as a prophetic figure whose greatest contribution was his ability to expose the hubris that resulted from America's hegemony. Boston University historian Andrew Bacevich exemplifies this "above the battle" view. He characterizes the "Niebuhrian perspective" as one which views America's "combination of arrogance and narcissism" as setting it on a course of "willful self-destruction."[4] The opposing "in the battle" camp presents Niebuhr as a paragon of moral engagement who argued for decisive action on the part of the United States against evil threats. Political theorist Joseph Loconte, for instance, ascribes to Niebuhr the belief that "in a world full of sin, civilized nations must strive for justice . . . with 'ambiguous methods'—unsavory alliances, deception, massive military strikes."[5] This phenomenon has played out most recently in debates over U.S. involvement in Libya and Iraq but has been ongoing since Niebuhr's own time. As social critic Sydney Hook observed in 1974, "There must be something extremely paradoxical in the thought of Reinhold Niebuhr to make so many who are so far apart in their own allegiances feel akin to him."[6] While at times scholars seem willing to acknowledge that Niebuhr held a more nuanced view than the competing perspectives ascribed to him today, few appear willing to acknowledge that Niebuhr gave equal weight to being both in and above the battle.[7]

[3] For a useful overview of the recent Niebuhr revival, see Richard Crouter, *Reinhold Niebuhr: On Politics, Religion, and Christian Faith* (Oxford: Oxford University Press, 2010), pp. 9–11.
[4] Andrew Bacevich, *The Limits of American Power: The End of American Exceptionalism* (New York: Metropolitan Books, 2008), pp. 7, 182.
[5] Joseph Loconte, "The War Party's Theologian," *The Wall Street Journal*, May 31, 2002.
[6] Sydney Hook, "The Moral Vision of Reinhold Niebuhr," in *Pragmatism and the Tragic Sense of Life* (New York: Basic Books, 1974), p. 185.
[7] Commentators on both sides of this debate must realize that Niebuhr held a more balanced view than they accord him but seem to lose sight of this fact in the war of words over Niebuhr's legacy. David Brooks, for instance, in a 2002 article on Niebuhr offers a relatively balanced assessment of Niebuhr's dual aims in *The Irony of American History*, "A Man on a Gray Horse," *The Atlantic Monthly*, September 2002, pp. 24–5.

At the center of the current struggle to claim Niebuhr's legacy is his 1952 work, *The Irony of American History*, due in part to its republication in 2008.[8] Written against the backdrop of the emerging Cold War era, *Irony* is a perceptive reflection on the character of the United States. On the one hand, Niebuhr warned against the self-righteous tendencies of an "adolescent" America that was growing into its role as a global leader; on the other hand, he urged the country to continue to defend Western civilization from the intractable threat of the Soviet Union. The primary irony of history which Niebuhr identified was that America, despite being at the height of global influence following World War II, faced greater existential threats than ever before due to the extent of its foreign commitments and the advent of nuclear weaponry. As he observed, "The pattern of the historical drama grows more quickly than the strength of even the most powerful . . . nation."[9] In the context of the Cold War, Niebuhr expressed equal concern that America's standing in the world would suffer from its unwillingness either to take "morally hazardous action" in pursuit of noble ends or to engage in the necessary critical self-evaluation to prevent it from assuming the very characteristics of the Soviet Union it found most reprehensible. Individuals on both sides of the present debate over his legacy can agree one point: *Irony* is one of the most important works ever written on American foreign policy.

What goes unnoticed today—and was also missed by many of Niebuhr's own contemporaries—is that *Irony* is a product of the "in the battle and above it" orientation. The main reason for this oversight is that Niebuhr's clearest communication of his theological vision came through a meditation not on a traditional doctrinal theme, but on a more proximate historical figure, Abraham Lincoln. A lifelong admirer of the sixteenth president, Niebuhr concluded *Irony* by referencing Lincoln's actions during the American Civil War and, more specifically, his ability to take the morally hazardous steps necessary to secure victory for the North, while maintaining a deep sense of magnanimity toward the South. Niebuhr highlighted Lincoln's Second Inaugural Address, given in the waning days of the war, when the president urged those loyal to the Union to act "with

<hr>

[8] Reinhold Niebuhr, *The Irony of American History*, with a new introduction by Andrew Bacevich (Chicago: University of Chicago Press, 2008).
[9] Niebuhr, *Irony*, p. 3.

malice toward none; with charity for all" in their relations with their Confederate brethren and recall that "both sides read the same Bible and prayed to the same God."[10] Niebuhr described Lincoln's approach in terms of his "in the battle and above it" formulation: a "combination of moral resoluteness about the immediate issues with a religious awareness of another dimension" that gave him a "religious vantage point over the struggle."[11] Niebuhr would repeatedly come back to Lincoln in his writings because he regarded him as the best example of an individual taking decisive action to combat evil while simultaneously remaining humble in the understanding that all humanity is equally sinful in the eyes of God.

In what follows, I argue that Niebuhr viewed Lincoln not simply as the paradigm of national leadership but, more importantly, as an exemplar of his most profound theological views. Niebuhr identified Lincoln as "America's greatest theologian" on multiple occasions,[12] but, despite this remarkable fact, scholars have largely chosen to ignore Niebuhr's words and others have discredited them as little more than an historical infatuation.[13] Niebuhr did inherit a love of Lincoln from his father, Gustav, whose decision to immigrate to America was partially "inspired . . . by a schoolboy's admiration of Abraham Lincoln, who was his constant political inspiration during his lifetime."[14] Moreover, the sixteenth president left an indelible imprint

---

[10] As quoted in Niebuhr, *Irony*, pp. 171–2.

[11] Niebuhr, *Irony*, p. 172.

[12] June Bingham, *Courage to Change: An Introduction to the Life and Thought of Reinhold Niebuhr* (New York: Charles Scribner's Sons, 1972), p. 310.

[13] My interpretation is in direct contrast to political commentator Mac McCorckle, who argues, "Niebuhr went no further than characterizing Lincoln as the model statesman," "On Recent Political Uses of Reinhold Niebuhr," in Richard Harries and Stephen Platten, eds, *Reinhold Niebuhr and Contemporary Politics* (Oxford: Oxford University Press, 2010), pp. 38–9. For additional discussion of Niebuhr's reception of Lincoln, see Martin Halliwell, *The Constant Dialogue: Reinhold Niebuhr & American Intellectual Culture* (Lanham, MD: Rowman & Littlefield, 2005), pp. 18, 253–4, 260; Martin E. Marty, "Reinhold Niebuhr and *The Irony of American History*: A Retrospective," *The History Teacher*, 26:2 (February 1993), pp. 170–1; Martin E. Marty, *Religion and Republic: The American Circumstance* (Boston: Beacon Press, 1987), pp. 117–18; Arthur Schlesinger, Jr., "Forgetting Reinhold Niebuhr," *New York Times Book Review*, September 18, 2005, p. G12.

[14] Niebuhr, "Germany," *Worldview*, 16:6 (June 1973), p. 14. Niebuhr, in a letter to June Bingham, further explained that his father had come to appreciate Lincoln through Karl Schurz, a nineteenth-century German revolutionary turned American statesman who had served under Lincoln in the Civil War, Niebuhr to June Bingham,

on Niebuhr's own childhood, in part because Niebuhr grew up in Lincoln, Illinois—the only town named for Lincoln prior to his becoming president—and attended elementary school in the shadow of the courthouse where Lincoln had once practiced law. Niebuhr's lifelong admiration of Lincoln should not be reason to dismiss his body of writings on the sixteenth president—which include five feature pieces or chapter sections and dozens of other references—but rather to examine these particular writings more closely. These writings bring into sharp focus the degree to which Niebuhr's "in the battle and above it" orientation—one he saw embodied by Lincoln—was rooted in Christianity and, moreover, they demonstrate how *Irony*, despite its susceptibility to de-Christianized readings, is a fundamentally theological work.

II

That Niebuhr's Christian commitments had significant bearing on his writings should be clear from a cursory glance at his biography. At an early age Niebuhr decided to enter ministry, thereby following in the footsteps of his father, a well-known preacher in the German Evangelical Synod.[15] Educated at Eden Theological Seminary outside of St. Louis, Missouri, Niebuhr then pursued bachelor's and master's degrees in divinity at Yale University, which he completed in 1917. Following his ministerial training and graduate work, Niebuhr spent thirteen years as a pastor to a small congregation in Detroit before accepting a teaching position at Union Theological Seminary in New

Niebuhr Papers, n.d., Box 26. It is further understandable that Gustav would be naturally drawn to Lincoln. Historian Barry Schwartz makes clear that Lincoln's humble origins and image as a self-made man held great appeal among immigrants—especially German Protestants—looking to establish themselves in America, Barry Schwartz, *Abraham Lincoln and the Forge of National Memory* (Chicago: University of Chicago Press, 2000), p. 138.

[15] Based in the mid-west the Synod was not "evangelical" in the modern religious sense but rather in a traditional German one—it was a transplant of the Union Church of Prussia formed in the 1817 merger by state decree of the Lutheran and Reformed churches. For more information on the German Evangelical Synod and Gustav Niebuhr, see William G. Chrystal, "A Man of the Hour and Time: The Legacy of Gustav Niebuhr," *Church History*, 49 (1980), pp. 416–32.

York City that he would retain until the last decade of his life. Theology was a family affair for Niebuhr. His wife, Ursula, was the first woman to graduate with first-class honors in theology from Oxford University and later founded the religion department at Barnard College in New York. Niebuhr's younger brother, Richard, taught Christian ethics at Yale for three decades.[16] Reinhold was selected to give the prestigious Gifford Theological Lectures in 1939–1940, an honor he described as second only to his receipt of the Presidential Medal of Freedom in 1964. These lectures were published as two separate works, *Human Nature* and *Human Destiny*, in 1941 and 1943 respectively. While Niebuhr may be better known for his political advocacy during these years of global conflict and the ones that followed, it is important to note that the vast majority of his articles on American foreign policy appeared in Christian magazines, most notably, *Christianity and Crisis*, the magazine he founded in 1941.[17]

Despite these biographical facts, many modern commentators appear unaware of—or do not care to acknowledge—Niebuhr's theological background. Indeed, Bacevich perpetuates this misconception today by failing to address even in passing Niebuhr's religious presuppositions and commitments in the introduction he authored for the 2008 republished edition of *Irony*.[18] While Bacevich's oversight is particularly egregious, his efforts to isolate Niebuhr's political writings place him in good company. Already during Niebuhr's own lifetime, there were those who attempted to draw important conclusions from Niebuhr's political analysis without accepting most, if any, of his theological premises. These individuals, coined "Atheists for

---

[16] Hulda, Niebuhr's older sister, worked in religious education at a number of academic institutions in New York. Compared to Richard, she gets short shrift in biographies of Niebuhr although he often called her the most talented theologian in the family and explained that his lone criticism of his father was his assumption that "girls didn't need or want university training," Niebuhr, Columbia Oral History Project, interviewed by Allan Nevins, p. 7.

[17] Keith Hulsether, *Building a Protestant Left: Christianity and Crisis Magazine, 1941–1993* (Knoxville, TN: University of Tennessee Press, 1999), pp. 24–5.

[18] Leon Wieseltier, a literary critic and student of Niebuhr, has criticized his fellow commentators for "skipping all the religious stuff" in their discussions of Niebuhr. He goes further to remind them that Niebuhr was a "professor at Union Theological Seminary not a fellow at the Center for American Progress [a prominent Washington-based think tank]," "Reinie and Woody," *The New Republic*, September 11–18, 2006.

Niebuhr" by philosopher Morton White, included such prominent figures as social critic Sidney Hook, political philosopher Hans Morgenthau, historian Arthur Schlesinger, and Supreme Court Justice Felix Frankfurter.[19] Hook was perhaps the most adamant member of the group as can be seen from his 1956 observation, "Not a single one of the positions that Niebuhr takes on the momentous issues of social and political life is dependent on his theology."[20] Others such as Schlesinger and Frankfurter acknowledge the important role of Niebuhr's theological presuppositions to his own political beliefs but deny their necessity to arrive at similar conclusions. Despite this, their respect for Niebuhr's religious commitments was real, as is evidenced by a 2005 article authored by Schlesinger in which he explained that Niebuhr's theological contributions, more than any other aspect of his thought, made him indispensable in the twenty-first century no matter how "uncomfortable" they made him personally.[21]

Niebuhr bears some responsibility for the failure of many to recognize the importance of the theological basis of his political writings, particularly regarding those works written later in his career. As his public stature increased throughout the 1940s—he graced the cover of *Time* magazine in 1948 as "America's most influential religious figure"—Niebuhr was increasingly able to appeal to a larger and more diverse constituency.[22] As a result, he adjusted the way in which he communicated his views. Larry Rasmussen, professor of Christian Ethics at Union Theological Seminary, notes that Niebuhr increasingly "cast his case in ways which left his Christian presuppositions and convictions unspoken" in his later writings.[23] The company he

---

[19] Morgenthau was explicit both in his indebtedness to Niebuhr's political views and his respectful disregard for the theologian's religious ones. He famously noted that he and Niebuhr "come out pretty much the same on politics, but I do not need all his [theology] to get where we both get." For more information on the dynamic relationship between Niebuhr and Morgenthau, see Daniel Rice, "Reinhold Niebuhr and Hans Morgenthau: A Friendship with Contrasting Shades of Realism," *Journal of American Studies*, 42 (2008) August, pp. 255–91. Historian Perry Miller's review of Niebuhr's *Pious and Secular America* struck a similar chord. He explained he was one of those that "have copiously availed themselves of Niebuhr's conclusions without pretending to share his basic, and to him, indispensable premise," "The Influence of Reinhold Niebuhr," *The Reporter*, 18, no. 9 (1958) pp. 39–40.

[20] Sidney Hook, "A New Failure of Nerve," *Partisan Review*, 10 (January–February 1943), p. 15.

[21] Schlesinger, "Forgetting Reinhold Niebuhr," p. G12.

[22] Whitaker Chambers, "Faith for a Lenten Age," *Time*, March 8, 1948, p. 76.

[23] Larry Rasmussen, *Reinhold Niebuhr: Theologian of Public Life* (New York: Collins Liturgical Publications, 1991), p. 3.

kept also influenced his writing approach. The latter half of the 1940s saw Niebuhr increasingly move beyond the ecclesiastical circles he had inhabited to engage political and social leaders with non-theological backgrounds.[24] These interactions with important decision-makers, many of whom were unmoved by theological appeals, were another reason behind the increasing tendency for Niebuhr to articulate his religiously motivated views in a form that was amenable to a non-religious audience.[25] *Irony* reflects this tendency to a certain extent. Religious scholar Martin Marty acknowledges that the work does not often "put non-believers at a total disadvantage," in part because of the audience for which it was intended.[26]

Nevertheless Niebuhr's guiding theological vision is readily apparent in the pages of his later writings, including *Irony*. Niebuhr clearly states that a non-theological reading of the work would result in an interpretation best described as "'subjective,' 'imaginative,' 'capricious,' 'superimposed'... and 'arbitrary.'"[27] Unsurprisingly, those adjectives are fairly representative of the reception that *Irony* receives today. There has been commentary in recent years supporting the belief that Niebuhr's theology and politics are not readily separable. Most notably, Robin Lovin, a professor of Christian ethics at Southern Methodist University, has shed light on the interplay between the two. Lovin provides the broad outline for how Niebuhr's political views developed from his theological disposition. Although he does

[24] In 1947 he joined with Schlesinger and Democratic Party leaders Eleanor Roosevelt and Elmer Davis to found Americans for Democratic Action, an organization to combat Communism abroad and advance progressive domestic policies. That same year he joined the Council on Foreign Relations, an influential organization in New York that included among its membership cabinet officials and corporate executives. Niebuhr was most active in his advisory role to the State Department, however, which developed out of his relationship with George Kennan, the influential diplomat credited with authoring the containment policy that would define the U.S. approach during the early stages of the Cold War. Kennan, in his capacity as the Director of Policy Planning for the State Department, officially sought Niebuhr's advice on multiple occasions.
[25] Rasmussen, *Reinhold Niebuhr: Theologian of Public Life*, pp. 12–14. For evidence that Niebuhr had a different audience in mind, Niebuhr's correspondence with Schlesinger prior to the publication of *Irony* reveals that he shared a draft of *Irony* with the historian, see Ursula Niebuhr, ed., *Remembering Reinhold Niebuhr: Letters of Reinhold and Ursula M. Niebuhr* (San Francisco: HarperCollins, 1991), pp. 370–91.
[26] Marty, "Reinhold Niebuhr and *The Irony of American History*," p. 169.
[27] Marty, "Reinhold Niebuhr and *The Irony of American History*," p. 166, referring to Niebuhr, *Irony*, pp. vii, 151–2.

not examine this connection in great detail, Lovin's main contribution (given the unsystematic nature of Niebuhr's thought) is primarily to explain what this relationship is not—namely, a direct progression from the theological to the political. Rather, Lovin explains that it is better to understand Niebuhr's theological beliefs as forming a disposition or perspective from which to view the world.[28] Importantly, Lovin uses terms remarkably similar to the "in the battle and above it" formulation in describing this disposition: "retain[ing] the prophetic grasp of 'the total and ultimate human situation' while dealing with immediate problems."[29]

Making this connection between Niebuhr's theological disposition and his political writings is critical, and it is not enough to rely solely on Niebuhr's biography, as many commentators have done.[30] Stanley Hauerwas, a Christian ethicist at Duke University, picks up on this point in his observation, "Niebuhr thought that everything he said was in someway grounded in his theological concerns . . . But while this may be true biographically Niebuhr was not able to show conceptually why his particular judgments were necessarily related to Niebuhr's interpretation of Christianity."[31] Hauerwas rightly points out that it is necessary but not sufficient to prove by reference to Niebuhr's life story that he arrived at his political conclusions through his theological beliefs. Clearly articulating the principles at the core of Niebuhr's thought is important, therefore, especially given his tendency to avoid doing so himself. For this reason, we now turn to the

---

[28] Lovin explains what he means by the term "disposition": "[Niebuhr's] political choices, however, are not deduced directly from theology. Theology forms habits of judgment and observation. It supports a certain way of attending to people and their interests," "Reinhold Niebuhr: Impact and Implications," *Political Theology*, 6:4 (2005) p. 465. Lovin is not the first scholar to describe Niebuhr's theological foundation as a disposition. James Gustafson explained that for Niebuhr the "revelation of God's grace" provides a "stance or basic disposition toward the world" in which "one can be realistic and hopeful at once . . ." *Christ and the Moral Life* (Chicago: University of Chicago Press, 1968), p. 142.

[29] Robin Lovin, "Prophetic Faith and American Democracy," in Daniel Rice, ed., *Reinhold Niebuhr Revisited: Engagements with an American Original* (Grand Rapids, MI: Eerdmans, 2009), p. 225.

[30] Paul Merkley, *Reinhold Niebuhr: A Political Account* (Montreal: McGill-Queen's University Press, 1975), p. ix. See, on this point, Speaking of Faith with Krista Tippett, "Moral Man and Immoral Society: An Interview with Richard Wightman Fox," *National Public Radio*, December 8, 2004. Fox acknowledges that he failed to sufficiently account for Niebuhr's *Nature and Destiny of Man*, his main theological work.

[31] Stanley Hauerwas, "The Search for the Historical Niebuhr," *The Review of Politics*, 38:3 (July 1976), p. 453.

distinction between immediate and ultimate judgment in history at the core of Niebuhr's theological vision.

III

Niebuhr's theological writings were imbued with the desire to "search for an adequate description of the situation which will allow for discriminate judgments between good and evil on the one hand, and which will, on the other, preserve the Biblical affirmation that all men fall short before God's judgment."[32] His first mature meditation on this question is found in his 1937 work, *Beyond Tragedy*. In a chapter entitled "The Ark and the Temple," Niebuhr commented on the biblical story of King David's desire to build a temple in Jerusalem to house the Ark of the Covenant, which had accompanied him through many successful battles. David believed the Ark had represented the bestowal of divine blessing on his military triumphs. As a result, he was taken aback when God denied his request on the basis of David's involvement in those triumphs.[33] Niebuhr portrayed David's problem as having significance for modern Christians, stating, "How can . . . [one] involved in the conflicts of life build a temple to a God who transcends those conflicts and who judges the sins involved in our highest values?"[34] How humanity could remain deeply engaged in the moral struggles in history while simultaneously appreciating the imperfection of its cause was the animating question behind Niebuhr's theological inquiries. He believed the beginnings of an answer could be found in David's "uneasy conscience" resulting from his "recognition of the sinfulness of all human goodness."[35]

Sin was a fundamental building block of Niebuhr's theology. Such was Niebuhr's preoccupation—and the degree to which many

---

[32] Niebuhr, "Reply to Interpretations and Criticisms," in Charles W. Kegley and Robert W. Bretall, eds, *Reinhold Niebuhr: His Religious, Social, and Political Thought* (New York: Macmillan, 1956), p. 437.

[33] The relevant biblical passage is: "But God said unto me, Thou shalt not build a house for my name, because thou has been a man of war and shed blood," I Chronicles 28:3.

[34] Reinhold Niebuhr, *Beyond Tragedy: Essays on the Christian Interpretation of History* (London: Nisbet, 1938), p. 56.

[35] Niebuhr, *Beyond Tragedy*, p. 60.

contemporary theologians dismissed the doctrine—that *Time* magazine labeled him as the pastor who brought sin "back in fashion." Niebuhr viewed sin primarily as prideful egoism—the tendency on the part of humans to usurp God and place themselves at the center of the universe. Human beings exist at the paradoxical junction of finitude and freedom, or what he often referred to as "standing in and above nature." Humans, like all creatures, are subject to the vicissitudes of their environment. Yet humans, made in the image of God, are also able to transcend their surroundings, take stock of their situation and look beyond the immediate for meaning. While possible to live in balance as creature and a creator, individuals inevitably attempt to escape the ambiguity of this condition through prideful self-assertion. Niebuhr, building on the work of Danish philosopher Søren Kierkegaard, believed that this escape represented a "qualitative leap" into sin.[36] Niebuhr did not view finiteness in and of itself as the basis of sin; rather he pointed to human unwillingness to accept the determinate character of one's existence. An individual, according to Niebuhr, falls into sin when he seeks to raise his "contingent existence to unconditioned significance."[37]

Niebuhr, again like Kierkegaard, was less concerned with the theological exposition of sin than with how it discloses the situation of humanity in the modern context. An acknowledgment of one's fallen state, in his estimation, was a prerequisite for becoming a responsible actor on the world's stage. Only then could individuals overcome the self-righteousness that obscures the difference between immediate and ultimate judgments in history. As Niebuhr explained, accepting sinfulness was a "religious achievement which requires that the human tendency to claim a final position of judgment" be overcome.[38] If this "religious achievement" was necessary to navigate the course of human events, he nonetheless believed it was not sufficient—a sound interpretation of history also was required. History, for Niebuhr, was not merely the study of past events; rather it was the appreciation of our present surroundings given our existence as creatures involved in—but not controlled by—the world around us.

---

[36] Reinhold Niebuhr, *The Nature and Destiny of Man, Volume I: Human Nature* (London: Nisbet, 1941), p. 270, cited hereafter as *Human Nature*.

[37] Niebuhr, *Human Nature*, p. 198.

[38] Reinhold Niebuhr, *Discerning the Signs of the Times: Sermons for Today and Tomorrow* (London: SCM Press, 1946), pp. 19–20.

As philosopher Richard Crouter perceptively notes, for Niebuhr, "[H]istory is the stage upon which the drama of our human nature plays out."[39] An understanding of history is therefore the mechanism by which humans interpret and make intelligible the events through which they live or, as Niebuhr explained, "discern the signs of the times." And it is the Christian faith, according to Niebuhr, that best equips individuals with a "system of order and coherence" to interpret these times and respond accordingly.

A Christian interpretation of history derives its structure and meaning from God, an actor both in and beyond the boundaries of history. In contrast, secular interpretations of history focus solely on the course of events, leaving them ill-equipped to address what Niebuhr saw as the contradiction at the center of human affairs: the need to distinguish between good and evil while acknowledging the universal corruption of all humanity. Ultimately, for Niebuhr, only a Christian interpretation makes sense of this paradox; God's redemptive action in history provides clear direction through the mediating figure of Jesus Christ and, in particular, His death on the Cross. Niebuhr writes, "It is God who suffers for man's iniquity. He takes the sins of the world upon and into Himself. That is to say the contradictions are resolved in history; but they are only ultimately resolved on the level of the eternal and divine."[40] Just how did the "vicarious suffering of the representative of God" resolve the contradictions of history? God's necessary intervention at Calvary attests that historical actions carry serious consequences. The way in which God intervenes, however, reveals the false distinction humans wish to make between the righteous and unrighteous. God conquers the brokenness of the world by taking on Himself the punishment that humanity deserved, thus confirming the universality of sin. As Niebuhr summarized, "[T]he judgment of God preserves the distinction of good and evil in history; and the mercy of God finally overcomes the sinful corruption in which man is involved..."[41]

If the death of the suffering servant reveals how we could maintain moral responsibility in a fallen world, Niebuhr believed the Resurrection gave people the hope to do so. Jesus Christ's victory over death

---

[39] Crouter, *Reinhold Niebuhr*, p. 20.
[40] Reinhold Niebuhr, *The Nature and Destiny of Man, Volume II: Human Destiny* (London: Nisbet, 1943), p. 47, cited hereafter as *Human Destiny*.
[41] Niebuhr, *Human Destiny*, p. 71.

pointed to a divine fulfillment of history in which the Kingdom of God would emerge out of the broken world of humanity. The future promise contained within this understanding of history emboldened Christians to live out their lives in the present with a great faith and security. As Niebuhr explained in the powerful conclusion to his 1945 work, *The Children of Light and Darkness*, the Resurrection means that God will "complete what even the highest human striving must leave incomplete, and . . . purify all the corruptions which appear in even the purest human aspirations."[42] Niebuhr viewed such hope as not only the bedrock of the Christian faith but also a "prerequisite for the diligent fulfillment of our historic tasks."[43] How else could individuals continue to make immediate judgments in history while also being aware of the sinful tendencies that ultimately clouded all human judgments? Indeed, he explained that without Christian hope, humanity was destined for despair and a tragic view of history. What distinguishes the Christian interpretation of history, for Niebuhr, is that it "understands the fragmentary and broken character of all historic achievements and yet has the confidence in their meaning because it knows their completion to be in the hands of a Divine Power."[44]

Niebuhr's critics, as well as his many supporters, do not typically associate such Christocentric beliefs with Niebuhr. For example, theologian Sam Wells criticizes Niebuhr for his "unwillingness to take seriously . . . the full humanity and the full divinity of Christ."[45] Such readings appear misguided in light of Niebuhr's theological and homiletic writings, which, when read selectively, appear to place him firmly within the camp of historic orthodox Protestantism. To do so, however, would fail to acknowledge that Niebuhr's view of Christian doctrine—most notably his symbolic understanding of central Christian events—was profoundly influenced by liberal Protestantism.[46]

---

[42] Reinhold Niebuhr, *The Children of Light and the Children of Darkness: A Vindication of Democracy and a Critique of its Traditional Defense* (London: Nisbet, 1945), p. 128, cited hereafter as *Children of Light and Darkness*.

[43] Niebuhr, *Children of Light and Darkness*, p. 128.

[44] Niebuhr, *Children of Light and Darkness*, p. 128.

[45] Samuel Wells, "The Nature and Destiny of Serious Theology," in Harries and Platten, eds, *Reinhold Niebuhr and Contemporary Politics*, p. 75.

[46] In this view, I am largely following the interpretation laid out by Langdon Gilkey in *On Niebuhr: A Theological Study* (Chicago: University of Chicago Press, 2001). Gilkey makes clear that Niebuhr's symbolic interpretation of traditional elements of

Taken literally, the Crucifixion and Resurrection of Christ, according to Niebuhr, were absurd to the modern mind. A symbolic or mythical appraisal, however, was able to "paradoxically" disclose aspects of the human character and the nature of history that other philosophies tended to obscure. Niebuhr never fully explained what exactly he meant by a symbolic interpretation of biblical events. He did, however, express caution at claiming too much knowledge of eternal mysteries or forgetting, to paraphrase St. Paul, we see through a glass darkly regarding such matters. In this position he was typical of post-Kantian Protestant liberalism, for which such speculative theological questions were simply beyond the epistemic reach of human understanding. He also frequently explained that such inquiries were of little "practical" concern.[47] Fueled by the desire to convince his countrymen of the usefulness of the Christian faith to the challenges facing the modern age, Niebuhr explained he had little time to address challenges from "stricter sets of theologians."[48]

This book will argue that inquiring into the meaning of Niebuhr's symbols is a practical concern. An understanding of how he employs the symbolic themes of Christian doctrine is central to understanding his guidance for faithful action in human history. Niebuhr said as much himself. On multiple occasions he identified a deep and abiding faith in the "symbol" of the Resurrection as the only means "by which we can seek to fulfill our historic tasks without illusions and without despair."[49] Niebuhr clearly struggled to strike the right balance in his discussion of the relationship between the otherworldly elements of the Christian faith and the current world. He certainly made a compelling case for the applicability of Christian symbols to contemporary experience and, by doing so, believed he was validating those classic tenets of the faith. An open question, however, is to what degree Niebuhr "refashioned" those Christian symbols in the

---

the faith was a reflection of his indebtedness to the liberal Protestant tradition. Yet the "Biblical faith" in which Niebuhr placed those symbols was grounded in the "classical message of the historic Christian faith." Niebuhr's aim, according to Gilkey, was not only to recontextualize Christian symbols in a contemporary context but to pursue "an act of recovery, a recovery of the Biblical tradition over against what he thought of as modern culture," *On Niebuhr*, p. 226.

[47] Kegley and Bretall, eds, *Reinhold Niebuhr*, p. 3.
[48] Kegley and Bretall, eds, *Reinhold Niebuhr*, p. 3.
[49] Niebuhr, "Christian Otherworldliness," *Christianity and Society* (Winter 1943), p. 12.

process.[50] Indeed Niebuhr acknowledged the challenges inherent in "correlating" the revelatory events of the Christian faith with the questions raised by human existence in a 1952 article on theologian Paul Tillich's efforts to this end. Niebuhr judged that Tillich walked the tightrope between the otherworldly and the this-worldly "with the greatest virtuosity, but not without an occasional fall," but the verdict he rendered on his own efforts was more telling.[51] He explained, "The fall may be noticed by some humble pedestrians who lack every gift to perform the task themselves."[52]

Niebuhr's theological approach remains divisive today, as leading theologians have starkly different opinions of Niebuhr's effort to exercise responsibility in the present age. Hauerwas, in one camp, takes a dim view of Niebuhr's tendency to validate his theological beliefs on the basis of their relevance to ongoing historical events. Such an approach is insufficient, in his estimation, because it reduces the faith to another philosophy—albeit one that uses theological categories—that conforms to, rather than unsettles, what people already believe.[53] Niebuhr's mode of interaction, in his estimation, too often results in a capitulation of faith rather than in its "confident and unapologetic" assertion. Lovin, on the other side, insists that Christians have a critical role to play in shaping decisions in the contemporary world and that Niebuhr's example is one to follow.[54] Unlike Hauerwas, he views positively Niebuhr's willingness to ground

[50] Gilkey, *On Niebuhr*, p. 226.
[51] Reinhold Niebuhr, "Biblical Thought and Ontological Speculation," in Charles W. Kegley and Robert W. Bretall, eds, *The Theology of Paul Tillich* (New York: Macmillan, 1952), p. 227.
[52] Niebuhr, "Biblical Thought and Ontological Speculation," p. 227.
[53] Stanley Hauerwas, *With the Grain of the Universe: The Church's Witness and Natural Theology.* (Grand Rapids, MI: Brazos Press, 2001), pp. 139–40. For instance, Hauerwas points to Niebuhr's frequent description of original sin as an empirically verifiable doctrine in order to question, "But if original sin is but a name for a reality that can be known separate from the Christian view of the self and God, then how are we to understand the status of Niebuhr's theological claims?" *With the Grain of the Universe*, p. 121.
[54] Lovin, "Reinhold Niebuhr: Impact and Implications," p. 463. That this debate is about more than Niebuhr is evidenced by the fact that Lovin and Hauerwas's earlier debates on the relationship between theology and politics do not focus on the theologian. See, on this point, Stanley Hauerwas, *The Peaceable Kingdom: A Primer in Christian Ethics* (Notre Dame, IN: University of Notre Dame Press, 1983); Robin Lovin, *Christian Faith and Public Choices: The Social Ethics of Barth, Brunner, and Bonhoeffer* (Philadelphia: Fortress, 1984); and a joint review of the two books, Harlan Beckley, "Book Review," *Theology Today*, 42:1 (April 1985), pp. 123–5. For more

his theology in the world around him and credits this approach with allowing him to make such insightful proximate judgments. This book builds on the views of both theologians to argue that Niebuhr was most persuasive in his proximate judgments when he was also willing to speak "unapologetically" about the eternal. After all, as Niebuhr himself observed, "[The] more Christians seek to commend their faith as the source of the qualities and disciplines required to save the world from disaster, the less does that kind of faith prove itself to have the necessary resources."[55] Niebuhr's theological vision for faithful action in history was most convincing during those periods in his life when he was less concerned with its temporal relevance and more concerned with its eternal truthfulness.

The strengths and weaknesses of Niebuhr's distinctive theological approach are evidenced by his reliance on Lincoln as the vehicle by which to express his "in the battle and above it" viewpoint in *Irony* and elsewhere. Fittingly, Niebuhr made reference to Lincoln in his first mature meditation on his theological vision in *Beyond Tragedy*. After observing that David's "uneasy conscience" allowed him to distinguish appropriately between proximate and ultimate judgments, Niebuhr explained "America...had at least one statesman, Abraham Lincoln, who understood exactly what David experienced."[56] Niebuhr went on to write that Lincoln provided the best "example of a consummate interweaving of moral idealism and a religious recognition of the imperfection of all human ideals."[57] Niebuhr's reliance on Lincoln, an iconic historic figure in American history, is representative of his ability to make his theological vision relevant to a broader audience. Nevertheless, Niebuhr was clear in *Beyond Tragedy* that it was not the memory of Lincoln that allowed an individual to pass "through the sense of the tragic to a hope and assurance which is 'beyond tragedy'" but rather assurance received

---

information on this debate, see Scott Paeth, "Being Wrong and Right: A Response to Larry Rasmussen and Robin Lovin," *Political Theology*, 6:4 (October 2005), pp. 473–86; Mark Haas, "Reinhold Niebuhr's 'Christian Pragmatism': A Principled Alternative to Consequentialism," *The Review of Politics*, 61:4 (Autumn 1999), pp. 605–36; and David True, "Embracing Hauerwas? A Niebuhrian Takes a Closer Look," *Political Theology*, 8:2 (2007), pp. 197–212.

[55] Niebuhr, "Utilitarian Christianity and the World Crisis," *Christianity and Crisis*, May 29, 1950, p. 66.

[56] Niebuhr, *Beyond Tragedy*, p. 66.

[57] Niebuhr, *Beyond Tragedy*, p. 67.

through God's triumph over sin through Jesus Christ.[58] In later works such as *Irony*, however, Lincoln takes on an increasingly central role as the embodiment as opposed to an exemplar of Niebuhr's theological vision. The lack of theological context serves to diminish Niebuhr's discussion of Lincoln as exemplar. Rather than appreciating the full stature of Lincoln's importance in relation to Niebuhr's theological vision, Niebuhr's acolytes today have largely overlooked both aspects of Niebuhr's thought.

IV

In order to develop a holistic picture of Niebuhr's theological vision and how he applied it to the historical events of his time, this book relies on historical research, close textual analysis, and theological interpretation. This book spans disciplinary categories by combining archival research from Niebuhr's Papers at the U.S. Library of Congress in Washington D.C.; Union Theological Seminary in New York; and Westminster College in Fulton, Missouri (the location where Niebuhr gave the lectures that would form the basis for *Irony*) with exegesis of his full-length theological works. The archival work was necessary because Niebuhr acknowledged that his theological vision was deeply intertwined with the remarkable world events that he experienced. Niebuhr's personal correspondence and journalistic writings, often written in quick response to the changing global landscape, best reveal how he applied his theological vision to current affairs. The exegesis of Niebuhr's theological works is likewise important because his theological vision developed from engagement with fundamental Christian truths. Niebuhr's "in the battle and above it" orientation was rooted not in day-to-day events but rather the foundational narrative of the Christian interpretation of history centered on the life and death of Jesus Christ. A familiarity with the historical and theological elements of Niebuhr's thought is necessary for this study to reveal to his present-day admirers the way in which both converge in *Irony*.

---

[58] Niebuhr, *Beyond Tragedy*, p. x.

The Theological Vision of Reinhold Niebuhr's The Irony of American History: *"In the Battle and Above It"* shows how Niebuhr's theological vision, derived from his Christian understanding of history, served as the foundation for his analysis of the world around him. *Irony*'s theological basis can be seen in the fact that *This Nation Under God* was the book's working title until shortly prior to its publication. Perhaps the most compelling evidence, however, is that the analysis in *Irony* is similar to that which can be found in his previous theological works. In order to show the extent to which this is the case, I will begin my analysis at the beginning of the 1930s where we can already observe the influence of Niebuhr's developing view of history on his general outlook and, in turn, his interpretation of America and its role in the world. By the outbreak of World War II, Niebuhr had largely formed the basic disposition that would inform his political views over the remainder of his career. Niebuhr would develop the theological basis for this disposition in numerous journalistic articles and such works as *Human Nature* and *Human Destiny* in addition to *Faith and History*, published in 1948. Nevertheless, the real challenge for Niebuhr would be to maintain this "in the battle and above it" orientation in the face of the political challenges facing the United States during and following the war. For guidance in this effort, Niebuhr looked to the life and writings of Abraham Lincoln as early as 1937 and began to assert in the beginning of the 1950s that Lincoln was the personification of the very disposition he advocated. This was certainly evident in *Irony*, as Niebuhr relied on Lincoln as the primary conduit by which to communicate his theological vision.

My first chapter traces Niebuhr's theological development during the 1930s and the direct influence it had on the formation of his "in the battle and above it" disposition at the end of the decade. Specifically, I will focus on Niebuhr's maturing views of human nature and God's role in history, and the interplay between the two. Niebuhr, at the beginning of the decade, held an optimistic view of human nature and showed little interest in the interpretation of history. Over the course of the 1930s, however, Niebuhr began amending these beliefs in such published works as *Moral Man and Immoral Society*, *Reflections on the End of an Era*, and *An Interpretation of Christian Ethics*. In this decade we see Niebuhr beginning to engage seriously in theological study, which led him to focus on the fallen human condition and to accept a more active role for God in the historical realm. Critical to this transformation are Niebuhr's personal relationships with his brother, Richard, and German theologian Paul Tillich, as well as historical developments such as the economic depression in the United States and the rise of fascism in Germany. Most important, however, was Niebuhr's theological study during this period, which he later identified as his first serious engagement with the discipline. Niebuhr's mature beliefs can be first identified in *Beyond Tragedy*, published in 1937, in which he identifies the crucifixion of Christ on the cross as the defining event in the history of humanity. In this work, Niebuhr sheds the cynical outlook with which he opened the decade and replaces it with a more balanced disposition. Moreover, Niebuhr here references Abraham Lincoln for the first time in the context of the constructive role that America can play in the world.

My second chapter explores the role that Niebuhr's Gifford Lectures played in the continued development of his theological outlook and explores his mixed success in remaining in and above the battle during World War II. Although most scholars have portrayed *The Nature and Destiny of Man* as a largely academic work, it is no coincidence that Niebuhr explicitly acknowledged his "in the battle and above it" orientation between the 1941 publication of the work's first volume, *Human Nature*, and the 1943 publication of the second, *Human Destiny*. Indeed, the key to understanding *Nature and Destiny* is examining its two volumes separately and in the context of the wartime events occurring at their time of publication. Niebuhr was a strong advocate for U.S. involvement in World War II in the years immediately preceding the country's eventual entry after Pearl Harbor, going so far as to found the journal *Christianity and Crisis* to achieve this end. Published mere months prior to the Japanese surprise attack, *Human Nature* can be read as a theological justification for Niebuhr's advocacy for the United States to enter the war, based on its insistence that humanity was required to make morally difficult distinctions in history. By the second year of American involvement in the war, however, Niebuhr focused primarily on remaining above the fray, or, on warning his country against its own self-righteousness and excessive demonization of the German population. To this end, *Human Destiny* makes a case for the common humanity of all combatants and the universal need for

God's grace. In *Human Nature* and *Human Destiny*, we see Niebuhr forging the two aspects of his "in the battle and above it" formulation in the respective works. Niebuhr's uneven application of this formulation into policy advice both prior to and during the war reveals the practical challenges associated with bringing his theological vision to bear on current events.

My third chapter explores Niebuhr's efforts in the years immediately preceding the publication of *Irony* to apply his outlook to the rapidly escalating Cold War between the United States and the Soviet Union. Niebuhr's Christian understanding of history was largely established following *Nature and Destiny*, but he would further solidify his conception in two additional works, *Discerning the Sign of the Times* and *Faith and History*, both published in the late 1940s. With his theological foundation secured, Niebuhr became far more concerned with asserting its relevance in political affairs. This means that Niebuhr at this point focused, as he did in *Irony*, on the compound commitment of remaining politically engaged in opposing Soviet aggression and maintaining a perspective on the shared failings of both countries that perpetuated the conflict. In his effort to reach an appropriate equilibrium, Niebuhr was forced to come to terms with the challenges posed by his own increasingly active role in the historic struggle. Niebuhr, as an adviser to the U.S. State Department, was a central actor as opposed to a commentator on events, or, to paraphrase his words, was bobbing in the current of history as opposed to sitting safely on its banks.[59] As a result, the issue of perspective became even more of a central focus for Niebuhr during this period and led to the ironic viewpoint that he applied to current affairs in *Irony*.

My fourth chapter turns to *Irony*, where Niebuhr, more than in any other work, relied on his theological vision to address the American conflict with the Soviet Union. Niebuhr develops from this vision an ironic perspective that he would wield throughout the course of the work to warn the United States against its own illusions on one hand while pointing out the injustices perpetuated by the Soviet Union on the other. Niebuhr was not explicit in *Irony* about the Christian basis for his ironic perspective, however, so this chapter will broaden its scope to include his writings both prior to

---

[59] Niebuhr, "Sermon on the Wheat and Tares," Niebuhr Papers, n.d., Box 41.

and following the work's publication in order to reveal the pertinence of his specific religious beliefs and overall Christian disposition. In particular, I will explore a frequently overlooked chapter in *Discerning the Signs of the Times* entitled "Faith and Humor," in which Niebuhr made clear how his ironic perspective grew out of his Christian interpretation of history. Equally important, he explained in *Discerning* how efforts to divorce his ironic perspective from its Christian moorings would inevitably lead to cynicism and despair. I also look to Niebuhr's complete writings on Abraham Lincoln, many of which were published in the late 1950s, to reveal the theological significance of Niebuhr's identification of Lincoln as the historical figure exemplifying his perspective of Christian irony. Niebuhr reveals the true extent of how Lincoln personified his highest theological ideals in personal letters and unpublished essays, in addition to articles published on the centenary anniversary of the Civil War. This context, along with the developments of the previous three chapters, establishes both the centrality and religious significance of Niebuhr's "in the battle and above it" formulation to *Irony* and his thought overall.

In turning now to the first chapter, we should acknowledge the looming question of whether Niebuhr would have approved of this effort to uncover the theological basis of *Irony*. I think the answer is undoubtedly yes. In a letter toward the end of his career, Niebuhr explained that the "significance" of his life lay in his "rigorous criticism of the presuppositions of modern culture" and his argument that "the classical expression of the Christian faith is...truer than modern substitutes."[60] He went on to explain somewhat wistfully that he had not "fully elaborated my thesis" and to the extent that he had, "people agree with me on political matters, if they do, without in any way taking my religious convictions seriously."[61] Establishing the theological basis of Niebuhr's thought is even more important today given Niebuhr's significant influence on subsequent generations and the fact that many of these avowed admirers are woefully unaware of his foundational Christian disposition. The result is that much of what is labeled "Niebuhrian" today amounts to little more than banalities about world affairs or, at best, a diluted form of his actual message. Peter Viereck, in his 1952 review of *Irony*, was

[60] Niebuhr to Bingham, Niebuhr Papers, n.d., Box 26.
[61] Niebuhr to Bingham, Niebuhr Papers, n.d., Box 26.

remarkably prescient about what the future held for the legacy of the theologian. He explained, "The Middle Ages stopped a prophet by burning him. Today the forces of mere prestige make their victim chic. Fashionableness is the ambush endangering the noble and beautiful spiritual message of Reinhold Niebuhr."[62]

[62] Peter Viereck, "Freedom is a Matter of Spirit," *The New York Times*, April 6, 1952, p. 24.

1

From Tragedy to Beyond Tragedy: The Development of Niebuhr's Christian Understanding of History

The 1930s were a remarkable period of intellectual development for Niebuhr. At the end of the decade he would tilt against many of the beliefs he had held in its beginning.[1] Numerous commentators have noted the singular importance of this period to the formation of Niebuhr's mature beliefs. Too many, however, have relied on vague generalizations such as describing Niebuhr as moving from the ranks of liberal to orthodox Protestantism.[2] This is not a particularly useful description because Niebuhr never fit comfortably into either category at any point of his career.[3] Langdon Gilkey, in *On Niebuhr*, provides us with the best avenue to understand this development by stressing Niebuhr's maturing view on the character of history and its indebtedness to "his Biblically shaped reflections on human nature."[4] Gilkey does not tease out the "extremely close and very complex"

---

[1] Niebuhr, "Ten Years that Shook My World," *The Christian Century*, April 26, 1939, p. 542.

[2] See, on this point, Paul Carter, *The Decline and Revival of the Social Gospel: Social and Political Liberalism in American Protestant Churches, 1920–1940* (Ithaca, NY: Cornell University Press, 1956), pp. 152–162.

[3] Debates over how to categorize Niebuhr's thought were as pervasive in his own day as they are today. Niebuhr addressed the issue in multiple publications and letters to friends. In one such letter to John C. Bennett, Niebuhr explained his dissatisfaction with both traditions but continued by explaining he "never thought of himself in [the neo-orthodox] category" but, if he had to choose, "belonged to the liberal tradition . . . ," Letter from Niebuhr to John Bennett, March 1943, Niebuhr Papers, Box 42.

[4] Gilkey, *On Niebuhr*, p. 144.

relationship between the two subjects, but does identify Niebuhr's primary development to be the move away from a tragic view of history to a more hopeful one that acknowledged the redeeming involvement of God in temporal affairs. This chapter will argue that it is from this development that Niebuhr derived the "in the battle and above it" orientation discussed in the introduction. As we shall see, Niebuhr's acknowledgment of human brokenness perhaps counterintuitively contributed to a more hopeful vision of history.

My survey will commence with Niebuhr's 1932 debate with his brother in the pages of *The Christian Century* over the Manchurian crisis and conclude with the 1937 publication of *Beyond Tragedy*. These parameters have been chosen because the fraternal debate highlights Niebuhr grappling with his understanding of human nature and history for the first time, and *Beyond Tragedy*, a mere six years later, signifies the emergence of Niebuhr's mature views toward these two subjects. Niebuhr developed his theological vision in the intervening years as seen in such works as *Moral Man and Immoral Society*, *Reflections on the End of an Era*, and *An Interpretation of Christian Ethics*, in addition to numerous journalistic writings.[5] This period of intellectual growth for Niebuhr is also inextricably tied to the Great Depression in the United States and

[5] Niebuhr, *Moral Man and Immoral Society* (New York: Charles Scribner's Sons, 1932); Niebuhr, *Reflections on the End of an Era* (New York: Charles Scribner's Sons, 1934); Niebuhr, *An Interpretation of Christian Ethics* (London: SCM Press, 1936). These works will hereafter be referred to as *Moral Man*, *Reflections*, and *Interpretation*. It should be said at the outset that this chapter is not a detailed exegesis of Niebuhr's writings during the 1930s. This is, in part, a result of Niebuhr's rapidly changing thought during this period but also stems from the sheer volume of his output. Although the 1940s may have been Niebuhr's most prolific from a journalistic perspective, the period between 1932 and 1937 contains the greatest density of his full-length works—five in six years. The most important reason, however, is the transitional nature of Niebuhr's writings addressed in this chapter, especially when considered against his complete authorship. Although Niebuhr's mature thought begins to come into focus in the 1930s, the period also sees him engaging with political theories he would later reject and utilizing theological categories he would ultimately disavow. Given the overall focus of this thesis, Niebuhr's writings in the 1930s are most important for where they reveal his thought to be going.

the rise of Communism and fascism abroad.[6] Niebuhr assigned a significant importance to the influence of these global affairs, explaining at the end of the decade, "Since I am not so much a scholar as a preacher, I must confess that the gradual unfolding of my theological ideas has come not so much through study as through the pressure of world events."[7]

It is important to acknowledge at the outset that Niebuhr honed his political and theological ideas in conversation with others. Martin Halliwell's *The Constant Dialogue* captures the essential role that dialogue played in Niebuhr's intellectual development. This chapter argues that Niebuhr's brother, H. Richard, and the German theologian, Paul Tillich, played especially significant roles. For instance, it was Richard who challenged his brother's understanding of history during their Manchurian exchange and pushed Niebuhr toward his developed views on history and human nature.[8] Tillich's influence on Niebuhr has received less attention but may have been of greater importance.[9] Niebuhr was shaped, initially, by Tillich's writings and

---

[6] The economic downturn following the stock market crash in October 1929 that led to high unemployment and widespread poverty throughout much of America was at the forefront of Niebuhr's mind throughout the first half of the 1930s. As Rasmussen has noted, Niebuhr turned to Marxism in search of a "coherent meaning" to the calamity around him and became active in Socialist politics during much of the decade, *Reinhold Niebuhr*, p. 10. Niebuhr's focus on economic inequality in the United States only abated in 1936 with his growing realization of the threat to Western civilization posed by Adolph Hitler and his Nazi party in Germany. Gilkey is representative of many commentators who have described Niebuhr's transition as "shift[ing] from the domestic struggle against capitalism to . . . the rise of . . . European fascism and international Communism," *On Niebuhr*, p. 42. This explanation is correct, but also a bit misleading, as it insinuates that Niebuhr's domestic struggle against capitalism was not influenced by world events in the early part of the decade. This chapter will argue the exact opposite and highlight the degree to which events occurring in Russia and Germany, in particular, determined Niebuhr's outlook over the course of the entire decade.

[7] Niebuhr, "Ten Years that Shook My World," p. 546.

[8] Richard's influence on Niebuhr has been widely documented, most notably by Fox, where he is depicted as wielding great sway over Niebuhr in the 1930s, Richard Wightman Fox, *Reinhold Niebuhr: A Biography* (New York: Pantheon Books, 1985), pp. 143–7.

[9] Though the friendship between these two formidable figures has been written about extensively, Tillich's role in Niebuhr's theological development requires additional study. Halliwell's *The Constant Dialogue* provides the best picture of the friendship between the two men, but does not focus in detail on their theology, pp. 79–103. For a brief, but more analytical, discussion of the relationship between Tillich and Niebuhr by a former student of both, see Roger L. Schinn, "Reinhold Niebuhr as Teacher, Colleague, and Friend," in Rice, ed., *Reinhold Niebuhr Revisited*,

then, following the German's theologian's arrival at Union Theological Seminary, through their conversations as well.

POLITICAL CYNICISM AND A TRAGIC
VIEW OF HISTORY

While Reinhold and Richard did not hesitate to criticize each other's work in private correspondence, the brothers held a mutual agreement throughout the course of their respective careers not to publicize their debates.[10] An exception to this steadfast rule was occasioned by the Japanese invasion of Manchuria in 1932. The inability of the League of Nations and world powers such as the United States to constrain Japanese aggression through existing international treaties and diplomatic overtures led many Christian pacifists in America to reevaluate whether their country should forcefully respond to international offensives. Occurring in the pages of C. C. Morrison's *The Christian Century*, the fraternal exchange provides a useful departure point for our examination of Reinhold's understanding of history, as Richard was uniquely able to call into question his brother's core beliefs.[11]

Richard's article, "The Grace of Doing Nothing," was the opening salvo, and, as the title would suggest, advocated against American involvement in the conflict. He based this stance on the basic belief that mankind was incapable of constructive action in history. As a result, the most useful contribution would be to acknowledge humanity's complete dependence on "God of things as they are" in order to bring about change in this world. This perspective made Richard especially aware of the hypocrisy inherent in any efforts to judge

pp. 10–13. Gary Dorrien provides the most insightful account of this subject in isolated references throughout the chapter, "Revolt of the Neo-Liberals," in *The Making of American Liberal Theology, Volume 1: Idealism, Realism, & Modernity* (Louisville, KY: Westminster John Knox Press, 2003), pp. 435–521.

[10] I will refer to Richard Niebuhr as "Richard" and Reinhold Niebuhr as "Reinhold" in this section.

[11] I am not the only observer to have identified the significance of this exchange. See, on this subject, Hauerwas, *The Peaceable Kingdom*, pp. 135–41; Fox, *Reinhold Niebuhr*, pp. 132–4; and John D. Barbour "Niebuhr vs. Niebuhr: The Tragic Nature of History," *The Christian Century*, November 21, 1984, pp. 1096–9.

the actions of others. With regard to the Manchurian crisis, Richard called for American Christians to realize "that Japan is following the example of the [United States] and that it has little real ground for believing America to be a disinterested nation."[12] The proper American response was to ignore Japan and engage in the "inaction of those who do not judge their neighbors because they cannot fool themselves into a sense of superior righteousness."[13] Richard did advocate for action but in the form of repentance. American Christians should commence rigorous self-analysis of their country's own motivations and actions in preparation for "a different kind of world with lasting peace."[14]

In his response, "Must We Do Nothing?," Reinhold concurred with his brother that national interest was the primary motivation behind America's concern over Japanese aggression but disagreed that such considerations should preclude the country from engaging in the conflict. Not only did Niebuhr advocate for U.S. involvement, but he also supported the country's use of less than ethical means to dissuade Japan from its military venture. While Reinhold admitted that his brother's position was more in line with Christian teaching, he nevertheless argued that individuals and nations, regardless of their impure intentions and unethical means, were required to act to best of their abilities. As justification, he cited his understanding of history revealed that all social struggles involved the "assertion of right against right and interest against interest until some kind of harmony is achieved."[15] Given such reality, Reinhold explained that a responsible Christian approach to the problems of society was one of "ethically directed coercion," which he explained in rather ambiguous terms entailed a "judicious use of the forces of nature in service of the ideal."[16] Despite his advocacy for U.S. action in the Manchurian conflict, Reinhold harbored little optimism as to the result of its involvement or any involvement in the struggles of history. In multiple places throughout the piece he commented that the "tragic" nature of human existence did not allow for achievement

---

[12] Richard Niebuhr, "The Grace of Doing Nothing," *The Christian Century*, March 23, 1932, p. 379.

[13] Richard Niebuhr, "The Grace of Doing Nothing," p. 380.

[14] Richard Niebuhr, "The Grace of Doing Nothing," p. 379.

[15] Niebuhr, "Must We Do Nothing?," *The Christian Century*, March 30, 1932, p. 416.

[16] Niebuhr, "Must We Do Nothing?," pp. 416–17.

of the ends mankind envisaged. Such a conclusion was not dissimilar from that of his brother. Where Richard looked to God's grace to bring about the necessary changes in this world, however, Reinhold did not. Instead, he could only make vague reference to—but not take solace in—a point beyond history where the unobtainable might be obtained.

One can see the vague outlines of Niebuhr's "in the battle and above it" orientation in this article despite the fact its first clear formulation came years later.[17] This is evident in the overriding assertion that an individual or nation must act to the best of its abilities despite the impurity of its motives. What is strikingly different between Niebuhr's writings of 1932 and those of the following decade is the despair that permeates the former. Niebuhr may have called for the United States to engage in the Manchurian crisis, but it is hard to understand his intentions given he saw no prospect of success. In order to understand the cynicism evident in much of Niebuhr's writings on the United States during this period, commentators have pointed to the influence of World War I. Niebuhr fully supported the U.S. entry into the war and actually spent the majority of its duration as leader of a commission in the German Evangelical Synod created to reassure a skeptical domestic population of the denomination's loyalty. Niebuhr's actions and writings during this period reveal his strong patriotism.[18] Reflecting on America's involvement in the conflict, Niebuhr remarked, "I do not believe that any nation ever tried more diligently and honorably to avoid conflict than our nation did, and, being forced finally to enter, that any nation has ever placed the issues of a conflict upon a higher moral plane than

---

[17] From this point forward I will return to referring to Reinhold Niebuhr primarily as "Niebuhr."

[18] Niebuhr, "The Present Day Task of the Sunday School," as found in *Young Reinhold Niebuhr: His Early Writings, 1911–1931*, ed. William G. Chrystal (St Louis: Eden Publishing House, 1977), pp. 88–95. Niebuhr's first action as leader of the commission was to remove the word German from the masthead of all publications of the Synod for the stated purpose of protecting those receiving the material on military bases from discrimination, William Chrystal, "Reinhold Niebuhr and the First World War," *Journal of Presbyterian History*, 55 (1987), p. 289. Shortly thereafter, he began campaigning against what he saw as the sympathizing elements in the Synod's main mouthpiece, *The Evangelical Herald*, and ultimately passed a commission resolution "urging the adoption of an editorial policy of unqualified patriotism," p. 290. Niebuhr's advocacy on behalf of the Synod took him to military bases and town halls around the country.

ours."[19] Niebuhr's idealism was short-lived, however, as the post-war failures at Versailles led him to view President Woodrow Wilson's justifications for American involvement as self-righteous moralizing. Niebuhr commented on this change of perspective in 1928, explaining, "When the War started I was a young man trying to be an optimist without falling into sentimentality. When it ended and the full tragedy of its fratricides had been revealed, I had become a realist trying to save myself from cynicism."[20]

While Niebuhr's pessimistic tone in "Must We Do Nothing?" certainly was related to his dissatisfaction with the U.S. government both during and after World War I, there was an underlying factor of greater importance that Richard picked up in the final installment of this exchange. Richard explained that the most important difference between the brothers was not their policy views but rather their perspectives on God's presence in history. As he acknowledged, for Reinhold, "God is outside the historical processes," while, for him, "God... is always in history."[21] Richard went on to explain that he could not separate the two because God was "the structure in things, the source of all meaning."[22] For this reason, he believed history could not ultimately be tragic, but rather saw it as a long and arduous path to redemption.[23] Richard was correct in his observation that his brother's tragic view of history was at the root of their policy disagreement and, more generally, his overly cynical outlook. Where did Reinhold's viewpoint come from, however? In order to answer this question we must look to the rise and fall of the social gospel movement in the 1920s. The dominant movement in theology at the beginning of the twentieth century, the social gospel was predicated on the belief that the Kingdom of God would ultimately be

---

[19] Niebuhr, "The Present Day Task of the Sunday School," p. 91. He went on to explain in the same article, "For the first time in the history of the world we have the inspiring spectacle of a nation making every sacrifice of blood and treasure for aims which do not include territorial ambitions or plans for imperial aggrandizement," p. 91.

[20] Niebuhr, "What the War Did to My Mind," *Christian Century*, September 27, 1928, p. 1161.

[21] Richard Niebuhr, "The Only Way Into the Kingdom of God," *The Christian Century*, April 6, 1932, p. 447.

[22] Richard Niebuhr, "The Only Way Into the Kingdom of God," p. 447.

[23] Richard argued that since humanity could only detract from the "the divine creative process" in history, its "task is not that of building utopias, but that of eliminating weeds and tilling the soil so that the kingdom of God can grow," "The Only Way Into the Kingdom of God," p. 447.

achieved in this world through profound societal change. This view of Christianity and human progress as one and the same led social gospel advocates to interpret political and economic advancements during this period as both the proof and the result of God's historical immanence. Niebuhr was firmly under the influence of the social gospel in his early years, going so far as to identify it as the defining element of his thought upon his departure from Yale.[24]

World War I proved to be not merely a political crisis but a religious one for adherents to the social gospel as they struggled to explain God's involvement in this horrific turn of events. Many Europeans, responding to the "death and carnage on their doorstep," followed the lead of German historian, Otto Spengler, in his 1924 *Decline of the West* and adopted a pessimistic view of the future of Western civilization.[25] Others, particularly those in America, maintained much of their pre-war optimism on the basis of the country's continued economic prosperity and isolation from the fighting. Such optimism ended for Niebuhr and many others with the onset of the Great Depression in the 1920s, however. Indeed, he had a clear view of the destruction wrought by the economic collapse as a pastor in Detroit's industrial core. The widespread unemployment, homelessness, and undernourishment Niebuhr observed led him to conclude that his past religious beliefs were "irrelevant . . . to the complex social issues of an industrial city."[26] More fundamentally, he also came to reject the central premise that the Kingdom of God could ever be approximated in history. God, instead of being immanent in history, was now, in Niebuhr's opinion, a largely absent figure in a tragic world. If adherence to the main tenets of the social gospel had largely defined Niebuhr's beliefs in the 1920s, the rejection of those same tenets was the dominating influence on his thought at the time of the fraternal debate.

This fact was not lost upon Richard, who proved prescient in pinpointing the origins of his brother's cynical attitude. Another one of Reinhold's weaknesses that Richard did not press, however, was the uselessness of his policy advice. While criticizing his brother for the political irrelevancy of his moral perfectionism, Reinhold offered a roadmap that was extraneous to the current political debate.

[24] Neibuhr, "Detroit in the Twenties," n.d., as found in Neibuhr Papers, Box 57.
[25] C. T. McIntire, ed., *God, History, and Historians: An Anthology of Modern Christian Views of History* (Oxford: Oxford University Press, 1977), p. 9.
[26] Niebuhr, "Intellectual Autobiography," in Kegley and Bretall, eds, *Reinhold Niebuhr*, p. 6.

His explanation of "ethically-driven coercion" was lacking in prescriptive quality:

> [We] must use coercion to frustrate her designs if necessary, must reduce coercion to a minimum and prevent it from issuing in violence, must engage in constant self-analysis in order to reduce the moral conceit of Japan's critics and judges to a minimum, and must try in every social situation to maximize the ethical forces and yet not sacrifice the possibility of achieving an ethical goal because we are afraid to use any but purely ethical means.[27]

Such advice contained little of the purposefulness that made his later political commentaries indispensable reading to foreign policy elites such as George Kennan and Arthur Schlesinger, Jr. All was not lost, however. The most important result of the exchange was Richard's offer to serve as a partner in his brother's intellectual development. He conveyed as much in a letter he wrote to Reinhold in the days following the public exchange. He explained, "Though I don't see eye to eye with you I think I understand you and that in your battle I am an ally if not a soldier in the same division."[28]

Before Richard would have the chance to influence Reinhold's Christian understanding of history, Reinhold would take some small steps on his own. This would occur, like much of Niebuhr's intellectual development, from the rejection of another viewpoint—the Marxist understanding of history. Niebuhr had become interested in more radical political solutions to the problems facing society following his disillusionment with the social gospel in the early 1930s. Although sympathetic to certain aspects of Communism, Niebuhr chose instead to become actively involved in the Socialist Party.[29] The reason for this can be found in the dispatches Niebuhr wrote in the pages of *The Christian Century* during his travels to the Soviet Union in the summer of 1930. Niebuhr, like other political radicals of the period, was interested in seeing firsthand the political manifestation of a doctrine he knew only in theory. Whatever romantic views Niebuhr had held about Communism were dispelled upon

---

[27] Niebuhr, "Must We Do Nothing?," p. 417.

[28] Richard to Reinhold Niebuhr, n.d., Niebuhr Papers, Box 58.

[29] Niebuhr's early involvement in the Socialist Party included editing one of its organs, *The World Tomorrow*, and running for political office himself. He was defeated soundly in the race for a New York State Senate seat in 1930 and, two years later, for a Congressional seat in the Nineteenth District of New York.

his arrival in Russia, however.[30] In one of his first dispatches home, he wrote, "There is justice in revolution when seen from a distant and historical perspective, but seen in the immediate instance, the brutality of revolutions freezes the soul."[31] While Niebuhr was admittedly impressed with the ambition of the country's economic programs, he was dismayed by the universal poverty he observed throughout as well as the violent and oppressive nature of the state.[32] These systemic problems led him to dismiss the Marxist view of history given the reality he saw failed to conform with its utopian prophecies regarding post-revolutionary life. Niebuhr's next work, *Moral Man*, while certainly influenced by Marxist elements, also contains a more extended critique of its historical viewpoint.

Moral Man primarily concerns the difference between individual and group morality, and the associated implications for addressing class conflicts in an industrial society. While Niebuhr believed that an individual was capable of acting in a virtuous manner through checking his natural impulses and considering the needs and desires of others, the theologian was clear that collections of individuals did not share this trait. Incapable of self-consciousness, groups were captive to their collective egoism, and, thus, concerned solely with the acquisition of power. Given the fact a group was unlikely to cede its authority voluntarily if in a dominant position, coercion and even violence on select occasions were to be employed to unseat the comfortable classes of the bourgeoisie. The collective that received Niebuhr's most pessimistic assessment in *Moral Man* continued to be the nation-state and America, in particular. Nations, Niebuhr argued, were constitutionally self-righteous and acted purely in their own self-interest. Given the nation's need to secure the approbation of its own citizenry and other countries, however, it necessarily cloaked its narrow pursuits in the garb of "universal values

---

[30] Fox offers a different perspective on the lessons Niebuhr derived from his travels to the Soviet Union. He argues that while Niebuhr recognized the problems unleashed by Communism, the theologian was nevertheless "captivated by the 'energy' and 'vitality' of the revolutionary effort," *Reinhold Niebuhr*, pp. 123–4. This appears to be a selective reading, at best, as the citations Fox relies on are often the lone positive observations Niebuhr offers in otherwise critical pieces on Russian life.

[31] Niebuhr, "The Church in Russia," *The Christian Century*, September 24, 1930, p. 1146.

[32] In particular, Niebuhr was critical of the persecution of the priests by Russian officials in the course of their effort to secularize the country, "The Church in Russia," pp. 1144–6.

and ideals."[33] Niebuhr found this hypocrisy particularly apparent in American history, and made multiple derogatory references to Woodrow Wilson and World War I. This revealed his continued resentment over backing a conflict he believed, in retrospect, to be an exercise in national self-righteousness. If there was a country that was capable of doing "justice to wider interests than its own," it certainly was not the United States.[34]

Perhaps, in part, due to the provocative nature of Niebuhr's political claims in *Moral Man*, his discussion on the philosophy of history has been largely overlooked.[35] Niebuhr established through his discussion of history's "ominous tendency" toward "perfect tragedy" that he continued to hold similar views to those he advanced in the fraternal debates.[36] Despite this fact there did appear to be a growing awareness on Niebuhr's part of just how influential an understanding of history could be to a religion or ideology. He revealed this much in his critique of Marxist philosophy and its "confident prophecy of the future."[37] He found absurd the notion that a revolution of the proletariat would bring about redemptive change in history—largely as a result of his own observations in Russia. Identifying views of history he found inadequate was a critical step in the development of his own. If the Marxist view of history was mistaken, however, its attitude toward social problems and the ultimate goal of equal justice for all were both to be applauded. This was particularly true in comparison to the "orthodox Christian view," which he categorized as so concerned with the contrast between divine and human that "all lesser contrasts between good and evil on the human and historic level are obscured."[38] Echoing his criticism of Richard in the fraternal debates, he derided Christians for the fact that their belief in mankind's fallen nature often rendered them politically indifferent toward the problems of society.

If some reviewers of *Moral Man* fixated on its "hue of cynicism" and "unrelieved pessimism," Richard reproached his brother for

---

[33] Niebuhr, *Moral Man*, p. 95.   [34] Niebuhr, *Moral Man*, p. 108.
[35] Gilkey detects early signs of Niebuhr's interest in the philosophy of history and understanding of human nature in *Moral Man*, or, as he says, the genesis of ideas that "will themselves be thoroughly 'transmuted' in his later theology," *On Niebuhr*, p. 36.
[36] Niebuhr, *Moral Man*, p. 2.
[37] Niebuhr, *Moral Man*, p. 155.   [38] Niebuhr, *Moral Man*, p. 67.

being too optimistic in his portrayal of human nature.[39] While Reinhold believed that there was little hope for interactions between groups, he did hold that individuals could one day overcome their self-centeredness to achieve greater social justice on a small scale.[40] Sin did exist in Reinhold's estimation; however, he believed it to be a selfish attitude that could be overcome through the development of more rational faculties. Questioning his brother's premise that man could actually be moral, Richard wrote, "I am convinced that there is quite as much hypocrisy in this idealization of our personal relationships as there is in our collective behavior."[41] Richard's words seem to have had an immediate effect as can be seen in an article Reinhold wrote in February 1933 to combat the forceful criticisms of *Moral Man*. In defending his beliefs in the tragic nature of history, Niebuhr not only cited the immorality of groups but also acknowledged the insurmountable "force of human sin." In words seemingly taken straight from his brother's letter, he castigated those who held utopian beliefs for their "romantic conception of human nature and its perfectibility."[42]

While it may initially seem counterintuitive, Niebuhr's exploration of human sinfulness would ultimately lead to a more hopeful view of history that accorded God an active role in its progress and completion. In order for this transformation to take place, however, Niebuhr would need further guidance than Richard was able to provide. For all of Richard's success in bolstering Reinhold's theological beliefs, he could not come to terms with his brother's political and social activity.[43] In the same letter in which he questioned Reinhold's view

---

[39] Theodore C. Hume, "Prophet of Disillusion," *Christian Century*, January 4, 1933, p. 18. See Fox, *Reinhold Niebuhr*, pp. 142–3 for a summary of the reception of *Moral Man* as well as Niebuhr's response.

[40] Niebuhr, *Moral Man*, p. 34.

[41] Richard to Reinhold Niebuhr, n.d., Niebuhr Papers, Box 58. Richard, continuing in terms similar to the modern-day critique of Niebuhr, told his brother, "You are speaking of humanistic religion so far as I can see. You come close to breaking with it at times but you don't quite do it."

[42] Niebuhr, "Optimism and Utopianism," *World Tomorrow*, February 22, 1933, p. 180. Richard had opened an earlier letter to his brother by stating, "My first criticism is that you are still too romantic about human nature in the individual," Richard to Reinhold Niebuhr, n.d., Niebuhr Papers, Box 58.

[43] The obvious question is what caused this significant shift in Niebuhr's thought? Fox attributes it solely to Richard, whom he rightly sees as a formidable influence on Niebuhr. While this may be correct, other influences were likely at play, not the least of which was the natural progression of his thought. Niebuhr, in 1956, explained in a

of human nature, Richard urged his brother to stop "constantly . . . interfering in events" and predicted that he would soon "break with that activism."[44] This proved to be one of Richard's worst predictions in light of Reinhold's lifelong engagement with the political realm. For Reinhold to acknowledge God's involvement in history, he would have to see the divine as working alongside, rather than in place of, mankind. Richard could not serve as a model for this, but, fortuitously for Reinhold, there were others that could.

PAUL TILLICH AND THE CATEGORY OF MYTH

Niebuhr was not the only theologian fighting a two-front battle against orthodoxy and utopianism.[45] Paul Tillich, a German theologian, described a similar struggle in *The Religious Situation*, translated into English by Richard in 1931.[46] On the one hand, Tillich's experiences in World War I had led him to reject what he characterized as the "bourgeois belief in progress": that a more equitable social order would gradually reveal itself in history. On the other hand, Tillich had

letter to philosopher Morton White that he retained his optimistic appraisal of human nature longer than he actually should have largely because he associated a more pessimistic outlook of man with an unwillingness to engage in the struggles of this world, Letter from Niebuhr to Morton White, May 17, 1956, Niebuhr Papers, Box 53.

[44]   Richard to Reinhold Niebuhr, n.d., Niebuhr Papers, Box 58.

[45]   Niebuhr's interest in Tillich can be seen as part of his overall tendency to look overseas for a broader perspective on the political and economic challenges confronting the United States. We already have observed, for instance, how Niebuhr had turned to Russia at the beginning of the decade only to reject the ideology of Communism upon closer inspection. The political situation in Germany, likewise, had always been at the forefront of Niebuhr's mind. This can be attributed not only to his ethnic heritage but also to the ascendancy of the Social Democratic Party in Germany, whose political platform was similar to that of Niebuhr's marginalized Socialist Party in the United States.

[46]   Tillich, later in his career, reflected on his frustrations in Weimar Germany in terms similar to those Niebuhr used with regard to America of the 1930s. Tillich described his efforts as finding "the way between the old Social Democratic utopianism on the one hand, which was unaware of the human situation . . . and the ecclesiastical, the Lutheran transcendentalism, on the other hand, which was aware, certainly, of the human situation but did not believe that this situation allows any transformation," "Sin and Grace in the Theology of Reinhold Niebuhr," in Harold R. Landon, ed., *Reinhold Niebuhr: A Prophetic Voice in Our Own Time* (Greenwich, CT: Seabury Press, 1962), p. 31.

condemned elements of orthodox Christianity that he perceived to lead to an attitude of indifference toward the temporal world. In *The Religious Situation*, Tillich advanced a synthesis, radical socialism, which he believed capable of "overcom[ing] the unbelieving element in Utopian socialism" while pushing the religious into engaging in "this worldly-activity."[47] Such an approach was desperately needed given the rare opportunity God had provided Germany following the war to fundamentally reorient its society. Tillich explained that the period in which his country now found itself was one of *kairos*, or "fulfilled time . . . time which is invaded by eternity."[48] Acknowledging the irrationality of this concept, Tillich explained the best way to understand this phenomenon was through the category of myth. Considered by Tillich to be "symbolic of the eternal," myth provided a form of expression by which to understand "the appearance of the religious element in the individual spheres of meaning."[49] In his introduction to the work, Richard pointed to Tillich's notion of kairos as an important concept for anyone interested in a Christian understanding of history.[50]

This was not lost on Niebuhr, who, in his review of *The Religious Situation*, described Tillich's thought as the key to combating the "realities of our decaying civilization and culture."[51] Indeed, Niebuhr began striking similar chords to Tillich in his next work, *Reflections*. Niebuhr began the work by explaining that only "a more radical political orientation and more conservative religious convictions" could adequately address the growing economic and political challenges facing mankind today.[52] From a political perspective, *Reflections* was quite similar to *Moral Man* with its Marxist undertones and

---

[47] Paul Tillich, *The Religious Situation*, trans. H. Richard Niebuhr (New York: Henry Holt, 1932), p. 138.

[48] Tillich, *The Religious Situation*, p. 139.

[49] Tillich, *The Religious Situation*, p. 12; Tillich, *What is Religion?*, trans. James Luther Adams (New York: Harper & Row, 1969), pp. 101–2.

[50] See, for more detail on the practical aspects of Tillich's thought, Mary Ann Stenger and Ronald H. Stone, *Dialogues of Paul Tillich* (Macon, GA: Mercer University Press, 2002), pp. 67–8. They explain that the philosophy of history represented by Tillich's religious socialism was paradoxical in that kairos combines the biblical notion that each moment is meaningful with the modern notion that each moment offers a new opportunity for mankind to bring about something new in history.

[51] Niebuhr, "Eternity and Our Time," *World Tomorrow*, December 15, 1932, p. 596. In a sign of his eagerness to learn more from the German theologian, Niebuhr sought out Tillich when in Frankfurt in July 1933.

[52] Niebuhr, *Reflections*, p. ix.

fulminations on the crumbling capitalist system. In *Reflections*, however, Niebuhr was far more preoccupied with the importance of
history.[53] In particular, Niebuhr faulted modern-day liberalism for
its view of history as unending progress. He explained this "new
philosophy of history conceived under the influence of the youthful
exuberance of a past era" failed to adequately represent the tragic
character of contemporary life.[54] Not only did the reality of collective
interactions serve to discredit confidence in the perfectibility of society, but, in a departure from *Moral Man*, the corruption of individuals also rendered it unobtainable. Moreover, Niebuhr indicated that
the two were connected. He explained, "An optimistic interpretation
of human nature leads to an optimistic interpretation of human
history in which the inertia of natural impulses to moral life, particularly in man's collective life, is obscured."[55]

Niebuhr next turned his critical eye on what he referred to as
orthodox Christianity. If the liberal belief in progress was an inadequate account of history, then, Niebuhr explained, the orthodox
were equally mistaken in their judgment of all history as "unre-
deemed and unredeemable chaos."[56] Niebuhr explained his main
problem with this understanding of history was its associated social
quietism; just as with liberalism, the orthodox Christian view of
history largely stemmed from its understanding of human nature.
More specifically, if the liberal belief in progress was built on an
assuredness as to the perfectibility of human nature, orthodox Christianity's indifference to the temporal world was largely the result of its
belief in the sinfulness of mankind. Given this fact, the former held
that mankind's efforts to improve civilization could only perpetuate
its fallenness. Niebuhr's criticisms of both liberalism and orthodox
Christianity reveal him beginning to explore the relationship between
the philosophy of history and views of human nature. Whereas his
earlier works had briefly dealt with the aforementioned separately or,
at best, together in a haphazard manner, Niebuhr, in *Reflections*,

---

[53] As Gilkey explains, "Both . . . were present in *Moral Man*, but served more as the
implicit background for Niebuhr's analyses of the domestic social struggle . . . I believe
that in *Reflections* they now appear as the explicit subjects of the volume," *On
Niebuhr*, p. 42. Gilkey proposes that Niebuhr's shifting focus from domestic economic
struggles to international crises could possibly be the cause, but as we have seen in this
chapter, Niebuhr was always deeply moved by world affairs.
[54] Niebuhr, *Reflections*, p. 48.
[55] Niebuhr, *Reflections*, p. 113.   [56] Niebuhr, *Reflections*, p. 135.

unequivocally asserted the two were inextricably tied. More important to Niebuhr than the connections between history and human
nature in liberalism and orthodox Christianity was the reality that
neither was able to "give guidance and direction to a confused
generation."[57] Niebuhr spent the latter pages of *Reflections* attempting to synthe-
size the two into a Christian interpretation that could prove relevant
to the human situation. It is here that the outlines of Niebuhr's
mature views begin to emerge. Humanity, Niebuhr explained, was
enmeshed in the conflicts and passions of history, yet despite understanding the contingent nature of its existence, was still required to
make judgments on good and evil, as if from a vantage point above
the conflicts and passions of history. This "paradoxical existence"
could only be solved, in Niebuhr's estimation, by the Christian
"conception of a transcendent-immanent God . . . which does justice
both to the moral necessities of human life and to the actual facts of
human experience."[58] Niebuhr, in describing this "conception of a
transcendent-immanent God," like Tillich, looked to the category of
myth: "For only in the concepts of religious myth can an imperfect
world mirror the purposes of the divine Creator and can the mercy of
God make the fact of sin and imperfection bearable without destroy-
ing moral responsibility for the evil of imperfection or obscuring its
realities in actual history."[59] This struggle to align the universal
sinfulness of humanity and the need for moral responsibility would
play an especially prominent role in *Nature and Destiny*, as we shall
see in Chapter 2. What distinguished most of Niebuhr's writings in
Reflections from those of a decade later was his tragic view of history
or, as he explained, the "doleful realities of human life" in "an age,
facing its doom."[60]

Given the fact that Niebuhr did not explicitly reference Tillich
in *Reflections*, it is difficult to determine whether he was actually
influenced by the German theologian. What we can say is that
Niebuhr was certainly aware of Tillich's work, and there are
similarities between *Reflections* and Tillich's *Socialist Decision*.
That said, this would surely be the case with any two people
writing about religion, socialism, and politics in the early 1930s.
Any doubt as to the degree of Tillich's influence upon Niebuhr,

[57] Niebuhr, *Reflections*, p. ix.   [58] Niebuhr, *Reflections*, pp. 200–1.
[59] Niebuhr, *Reflections*, p. 292.   [60] Niebuhr, *Reflections*, p. 48.

however, is resolved by the former's assumption of an academic post at Union Theological Seminary in November 1933. Niebuhr actually facilitated Tillich's emigration from Germany, which was a necessity following his publication of *The Socialist Decision*, a controversial work that reformulated his notion of radical socialism to combat the rise of Nazism.[61] When reflecting on the origins of their relationship, Niebuhr would often refer to the "providential political vicissitudes" that brought Tillich into his intimate circle at Union. By all accounts the two were almost inseparable from the beginning due, in part, to the fact that Tillich spoke little English and, thus, was completely reliant upon Niebuhr to communicate with others. But as this chapter has asserted, Niebuhr was dependent upon Tillich as well and, as we shall see, that would only increase upon his arrival in New York.[62]

The first fruits of this partnership can be seen in Niebuhr's increased criticism of Swiss theologian Karl Barth, who emerged as the most influential theologian in Europe following World War I.[63] Although initially an adherent of the liberal theological tradition, Barth left the fold as a result of the tragedy of the conflict along with the religious sanction that many of his mentors had provided for the Kaiser's military aims. Initially he pursued a path similar to Tillich and Niebuhr in that he searched for ways to combine his religious beliefs with domestic socialist movements in his capacity as a pastor in an economically depressed Swiss industrial town. It was the failure of the Democratic Socialist Party in Germany, in part, that,

---

[61] For a good account of Tillich's departure from Germany as a result of his publication of *The Socialist Decision*, see Stenger and Stone, *Dialogues of Paul Tillich*, p. 54. Tillich, according to James Luther Adams, would later say of the work, "If I am proud of anything I have written, this is the one," as found in James Luther Adams, *Paul Tillich's Philosophy of Science, Culture and Religion* (New York: Schocken, 1965), p. 76.

[62] See Stenger and Stone, *Dialogues of Paul Tillich*, p. 48. The mutual dependency between Niebuhr and Tillich was fully evident in animated conversations the two famously engaged in during strolls throughout Riverside Heights, the neighborhood surrounding Union Theological Seminary. Given the conversational nature of their relationship, however, it is impossible to trace with certainty today how Tillich's ideas filtered into Niebuhr's thought.

[63] For more information on the relationship between Tillich and Barth, see Douglas J. Cremer, "Protestant Theology in Early Weimar Germany: Barth, Tillich, and Bultmann," *Journal of the History of Ideas*, 56:2 (April 1995), pp. 289–307. Cremer establishes that Tillich's aforementioned concept of kairos was developed in response to Barth's otherworldly theology, p. 298.

led Barth to conclude, "The religious socialist thing (*Sache*) is out, taking God seriously begins..."[64] what followed was his ground-breaking second edition of *The Epistle to the Romans*, in which Barth urged Christians to understand revelation and salvation as a divine act of God as opposed to a process that unfolded through the changing and transitory temporal world.[65] As part of this reorientation, Barth appeared to insinuate that theology should occupy a space separate from the social and political sphere. Tillich and Niebuhr certainly interpreted it as such and identified Barth in the late 1920s as an exemplar of the political quietism they associated with orthodox Christianity.[66]

Barth's growing influence in America and Britain as a result of the translation of *Romans* into English in 1933 led Niebuhr to conclude that he needed to address him directly. In raising problems with the Swiss theologian's thought, Niebuhr looked to Tillich's *Socialist Decision* as a robust model to follow. In the work, Tillich had argued that Barth's efforts to disassociate theology from the public realm allowed Nazism to develop unchecked into a dangerous form of political romanticism that played upon national mythologies. While Tillich acknowledged Barth's own opposition to the Nazi party, he maintained that the approach nonetheless had the unfortunate tendency to either become "accommodated to the demands of the ruling groups, or else become so transcendent that it allows the social forces to work unhindered, and therefore serves their interest."[67] Tillich had argued that radical socialism could counter the political romanticism of the Nazi party by incorporating the method of prophetic criticism found

---

[64] As found in Joseph L. Mangina, *Karl Barth: Theologian of Christian Witness* (Louisville: Westminister John Knox Press, 2004), p. 10.

[65] Karl Barth, *The Epistle to the Romans*. Translated from the sixth edition by Edwyn C. Hoskins (Oxford: Oxford University Press, 1933), the first English translation of the revised German edition. The first German edition of *Der Romerbrief* appeared in 1919.

[66] Niebuhr's first critical engagement with Barth dates back to 1928, see Niebuhr, "Barth—Apostle of the Absolute," *The Christian Century*, December 13, 1928, pp. 1523–4.

[67] Paul Tillich, *The Socialist Decision*, trans. Franklin Sherman (New York: Harper & Row, 1977), pp. 35–6. Tillich discussed at length the political and cultural effects of what he calls the political romanticism of Barth's followers with a particular focus on what he sees as their deification of the state. Tillich largely included Barth in this assessment with the caveat that the Swiss theologian had in the past criticized the ruling National Socialist Party, *The Socialist Decision*, pp. 36–44, 166.

in the Old Testament.[68] In optimistic terms, Tillich explained that his approach would not only serve to combat the growing influence of Nazism but also highlight his own political program as an attractive alternative for the German population. He explained that if the prophets of the Old Testament could cast judgment on Israel on one hand while invoking a clear vision for a promised future on the other, Christian theologians such as himself should be able to do the same in the present age.[69]

A comparison of two of Niebuhr's articles on Barth, one six months following Tillich's arrival in New York and the other a year later, appears to point to the incremental way in which Niebuhr built on Tillich's arguments. Niebuhr's June 1934 article in *Century* restated his old arguments regarding the Barthian complacency toward social justice. In a new line of attack, however, Niebuhr argued that aspects of Barth's thought were also being interpreted in such a way as to lead to a religious deification of existing social institutions. Niebuhr explained how Nazis were benefiting from Barth's theological beliefs: "In one moment the world is a world of sin which cannot be redeemed. In the next moment it represents a 'God-given' order that must not be violated."[70] If the first article revealed Niebuhr relying on Tillich to broaden his criticisms of Barth, the second showed Niebuhr countering Barth as Tillich had done. Niebuhr explained, "A Christian socialism in our day could find an adequate theology and an adequate political strategy by a return to the dialectic of prophetic religion."[71] He further explained that believing in a transcendent God and in the meaningfulness of history as the Hebrew prophets had done would have "direct relevance to modern social problems."[72]

Given the frequency and intensity of Niebuhr's criticisms of Barth in the middle part of the 1930s, it is worth exploring whether his primary attack of political quietism was warranted. In Niebuhr's defense, Barth did categorize all political revolutions as transgressions

---

[68] Tillich describes this approach as natural given he had come to see socialism as a form of "prophetism on the soil of an autonomous, self-sufficient world," *The Socialist Decision*, p. 101.

[69] Tillich, *The Socialist Decision*, pp. 102–4.

[70] Niebuhr, "Barthianism and Political Reaction," *The Christian Century*, June 6, 1934, p. 757.

[71] Niebuhr, "Marx, Barth and Israel's Prophets," *The Christian Century*, January 30, 1935, p. 140.

[72] Niebuhr, "Marx, Barth and Israel's Prophets," p. 139.

against God in *Romans* since a revolutionary necessarily "usurps a position which is not due him, a legality which is fundamentally illegal, an authority which . . . soon displays its essential tyranny."[73] Many interpreted this view to mean that citizens had to accept the existing political order in Germany, regardless of how it treated them. Barth did not explicitly disabuse his readers of this notion, even in the immediate wake following Hitler's ascension to power in 1933. In a published work shortly thereafter, Barth explained that he "endeavor[ed] to carry on theology, and only theology, now as previously, and as if nothing had happened."[74] Against Niebuhr's allegations, however, Barth did stand firmly against the Nazi party on multiple occasions, most notably as the principal author of the 1934 Barmen Declaration. Written to deny the Nazi party the theological sanction from German churches, the declaration, according to some commentators, was part of a larger strategy of Barth's to "ideologically starve the state" by disassociating it from the church.[75] However, Barth's writings were certainly ambiguous on this point, and he acknowledged later in life that he could have done far more to combat the events of the late 1920s and early 1930s.[76] While Niebuhr's early criticisms of Barth's otherworldliness appear warranted, as we will see, he failed to appreciate the degree to which Barth's mature theology did ultimately provide greater practical guidance for political engagement.[77]

Regardless of the accuracy of Niebuhr's criticisms of Barth, they were representative of a larger intellectual development, namely, a

---

[73] Barth, *Romans*, p. 480.

[74] Barth, *Theological Existence Today! A Plea for Theological Freedom*, trans. R. Birch Hoyle (London: Hodder & Stoughton, 1933), p. 9.

[75] Arne Rasmusson, "Deprive them of their 'Pathos': Karl Barth and the Nazi Revolution Revisited", *Modern Theology*, 23.3 (July 2007), p. 371. Rasmusson makes a compelling case for interpreting Barth's efforts to separate the theological from the political in his writings as an intentional effort to subvert Nazi efforts to co-opt the Christian church. Particularly convincing is Rasmusson's reference to the personal correspondence of Barth in which the theologian mentions the existence of more overtly political messages in the earlier drafts of his works such as *Theological Existence Today* that he was required to remove for fear of prosecution by the Nazi officials: Rasmusson, "Deprive them of their 'Pathos': Karl Barth and the Nazi Revolution Revisited," p. 376.

[76] As found in Rasmusson, "Deprive them of their 'Pathos': Karl Barth and the Nazi Revolution Revisited," p. 376.

[77] For instance, Nigel Biggar has argued convincingly that Barth's later works do contain a positive contribution to the field of individual ethics that has been largely ignored as a result of the "reputation that Barth acquired during the early 'dialectical' period of his thinking, when the stress on divine judgment seemed such as entirely to devalue human activity," *The Hastening that Waits: Karl Barth's Ethics* (Oxford: Clarendon Press, 1993), p. 1.

growing comfort with and interest in theological discourse.[78] If Niebuhr's past works had been criticized for being more sociological than theological, *Interpretation*, published in 1935, was recognized to strike a better balance. After formally acknowledging for the first time Tillich's influence on him in the introductory chapter, Niebuhr turned to their shared concept of prophetic religion which was capable of bringing "illumination to its age, so sadly in need of clues to the meaning of human nature and the logic of contemporary history."[79] If *Reflections* had revealed Niebuhr beginning to explore the connections between human nature and philosophies of history, *Interpretation* found him bringing his views of the two into alignment through deeper theological inquiry. Niebuhr mediated between these realms by applying the category of myth to biblical events. Niebuhr explained that, taken literally, the divine creation, fall of mankind, the crucifixion and resurrection of Christ were absurd. A mythical appraisal, however, was able to disclose aspects of the human character and the nature of history that more "consistent philosophies" tended to obscure.[80]

Eager to develop this concept of prophetic religion, Niebuhr, like Tillich, grounded his use of the category of myth in Hebraic thought. By doing so, however, he attempted to recover the category from its recent use in theological circles. Since David Friedrich Strauss's publication of the controversial *Life of Jesus* in 1835, many theologians had begun to reject the literal truth of the Gospels in favor of a mythical interpretation. This process, known as demythologization, was, ostensibly, an effort to separate the philosophical concepts of the Bible from their representation as fantastical events in order to defend the former in an age that increasingly found the latter an offense to reason.[81] As Gary Dorrien explains, Tillich and Niebuhr both believed demythologization to be a poor defense of the faith, or, more specifically, less about preserving the timeless truths of Christianity and more about ridding the faith of its "marginal and dispensable"

---

[78] See Fox, *Reinhold Niebuhr*, pp. 164–5.

[79] Niebuhr, *Interpretation*, p. 14. He thanked Tillich in the introduction for "many valuable suggestions in the development of [his] theme, some of them made specifically and others the by-product of innumerable discussions on the thesis of this book," *Interpretation*, pp. 7–8.

[80] Niebuhr, *Interpretation*, p. 93.

[81] I am indebted to lectures given by Joel Rasmussen in the Exam Schools during Hilary Term, 2009 for my understanding of this subject.

elements to align it with prevailing sensibilities.[82] Niebuhr, in *Interpretation*, was highly critical of such "uncritical accommodation to modern culture" and explained it inevitably resulted in a superficial religion based on little more than "complacent optimism."[83] Following Tillich, Niebuhr explained that mythical thought was not merely "pre-scientific" thought in need of repudiation but also "supra-scientific" in that it understood reality with a wholeness that could not be achieved solely with reason. In support of this claim, Niebuhr turned to the Christian myth of the Fall to show how it informed his view of human nature and history.

If Niebuhr's view of history appeared to be merely a restatement of his previous tragic interpretation, his understanding of human nature did reflect a new perspective. As we have seen in this chapter, Niebuhr, in his writings on human nature, had depicted sin as a selfish impulse in need of control. If reexamining the subject following *Moral Man* led Niebuhr to conclude that the impulse was more powerful than he previously thought, the overall paradigm remained the same. In *Interpretation*, however, Niebuhr adopted a radically different viewpoint in that he depicted sin as the fundamental corruption of mankind's existence. What the rebellion by Adam and Eve in the Garden of Eden made clear, according to Niebuhr, was that sin was the prideful human pretension to make oneself God.[84] Elaborating on this point, Niebuhr explained that humans, as creatures made in the image of God, had been endowed with a capacity for self-transcendence. This capacity was the source of all human flourishing but inevitably also resulted in attempts to overcome this creatureliness. The paradoxical relationship between

---

[82] Dorrien, *The Making of American Liberal Theology*, p. 534. Dorrien is effective in his analysis of the use of myth by Tillich and Niebuhr but describes the development as more collaborative than it appears on closer examination. For instance he states, "Tillich and Niebuhr . . . developed this theory of the mythic nature of religion and its accompanying concept of religion as a dimension of depth in life," *The Making of American Liberal Theology*, p. 455.

[83] Niebuhr, *Interpretation*, pp. 22, 25. Tillich had asserted the mythic nature of the Hebrew faith in his 1930 *Religiöse Verwirklichung*, a work that Niebuhr regarded as important, since he called for its translation into English in his review of *The Religious Situation*, "Eternity and Our Time," *World Tomorrow*, December 21, 1932, p. 596. The complete *Religiöse Verwirklichung* remains unavailable in the English language, but the work's central chapter has been translated, "The Religious Symbol," trans. James Luther Adams, *Daedalus*, 87:3 (Summer 1958), pp. 3–21.

[84] Niebuhr, *Interpretation*, p. 83.

one's finiteness and freedom that formed the basis for Niebuhr's newfound understanding of sin clearly was influenced by his newfound appreciation for the Christian myth of the Fall.[85]

Given the importance that Niebuhr attached to the category of myth, he was surprisingly evasive in *Interpretation* about his definition of this category. Indeed, his primary explanatory approach appeared to be avoidance, as he brushed aside the subject through such observations as, "The metaphysical connotations of the myth of the Fall are, however, less important for our purposes than the psychological and moral ones."[86] The most direct explanation he offered was comparing the difference between his mythical interpretation and a literal one to that between a portrait and a photograph. He proposed that while a photographer was limited in the extent he could capture the physical nature of a subject, a portraitist could represent an individual's "transcendent unity and spirit of personality."[87] Myths, for Niebuhr, had the unique capability to capture the heights and depths of human existence. But, given their inexact nature, a mythic representation of the ultimate truth inevitably contained a degree of falsification. Returning to the metaphor of the painter, Niebuhr described "vagueness of the boundary line between the art of portraiture and that of caricature" to acknowledge "how difficult it is to distinguish between deception in the interest of higher truth and deception which falsifies the ultimate truth."[88]

Niebuhr may have thought he was being intellectually honest in acknowledging the "vague" nature of this important aspect of his theology; however, he clearly realized that further explanation was required, especially as to how his understanding of myth differed from the most prominent contemporary "demythologizer," German theologian Rudolph Bultmann. Niebuhr attempted to answer this question in an article published a few months after *Interpretation*, entitled "The Truth in Myths." The primary means by which Niebuhr attempted to distinguish his view from "the modern protagonists of religion" was through a discussion of primitive and permanent

---

[85] Although *Interpretation* marked the first time Niebuhr described this paradoxical relationship in terms of sin, it was not the first time he had noticed it as a part of human nature. In *Reflections*, for instance, Niebuhr observed that mankind was constantly engaged in a "self-defeating" effort "to overcome its arbitrary and capricious character by universalizing itself," p. 6.

[86] Niebuhr, *Interpretation*, p. 86.

[87] Niebuhr, *Interpretation*, p. 94.   [88] Niebuhr, *Interpretation*, p. 94.

myths.[89] On the one hand, Niebuhr was in agreement with the likes of Bultmann that Christianity was on questionable ground when asserting those aspects of the faith that failed to withstand scientific scrutiny. For this reason, he explained that he supported the dismissal of primitive myths. On the other hand, Niebuhr claimed to be different from the demythologizers in that he believed myths had a permanent quality in that they contained unique insights into "the ultimate value of a thing in a total scheme of purpose."[90] Gilkey explains Niebuhr's distinction as an effort to remove the "outworn shell of primitive literalism and to present . . . as necessary for contemporary human understanding the permanent myths of the Christian faith enshrined in these accounts, a clearly different enterprise from that of Bultmann."[91] Niebuhr's reliance on myth may have made sense to Gilkey, but, as we shall see in the remainder of this book, many of his contemporaries remained perplexed as to the meaning behind the category.

THE CROSS AND A VIEWPOINT BEYOND TRAGEDY

Niebuhr's focus turned to practical affairs at the end of 1935, as he and Tillich founded a Christian journal, *Radical Religion*. In the inaugural issue Niebuhr affirmed that if his theological beliefs had developed since *Moral Man*, his political observations remained much the same: the capitalistic system was disintegrating and the management of this transformation was the most pressing issue facing the global order.[92] After the first issue, however, these well-worn concerns receded to the background as the growing threat of Nazi Germany came to the fore. In the second issue of *Radical Religion*, Niebuhr explained, "The historic situation in western nations does not offer the possibility of breaking through to a new society. It only offers the immediate possibility of defending democratic institutions, however corrupted, against the peril of

---

[89] Niebuhr, "The Truth in Myths," in *The Nature of Religious Experience: Essays in Honor of Douglas Clyde Macintosh*, ed. Julius Seelye Bixler (London: Harper & Brothers, 1937), p. 118.

[90] Niebuhr, "The Truth in Myths," p. 119.

[91] Gilkey, *On Niebuhr*, p. 68.

[92] Niebuhr, "Radical Religion," *Radical Religion* (Fall 1935), pp. 4–5.

fascism."[93] While he would remain a member of the Socialist Party until after World War II, it was in name only, as his concerns from this point in his career forward were almost solely focused on defending democratic institutions as opposed to calling for their wholesale overhaul as he had previously.[94] Just as Niebuhr's mature theological beliefs were beginning to emerge during this period, the contours of Niebuhr's future political preoccupations were coming into focus as well. The interaction between the two would have quite profound and surprising consequences.

The first glimpses of this came in Niebuhr's address before the Oxford Conference on Church, Community and State in 1937. The ecumenical gathering was dominated by conversations regarding the appropriate role for Christians in resisting the growing Nazi aggression in Germany as well as the militant nationalism ascendant in Spain and Italy.[95] Against this backdrop, Niebuhr, according to the majority of commentators, spoke compellingly on the subject of sin in one's life.[96] The forcefulness of Niebuhr's commentary, which was largely a restatement of his discussion in *Interpretation*, served to overshadow the most novel portion of his hour-long address. Despite the darkening clouds on the international horizon, Niebuhr offered his most optimistic portrayal of history to date. In a thinly veiled reference to Germany, Niebuhr explained the futility of deifying the state and, instead, assured the audience that hope could only come from belief in the tenets of the Christian faith. In a stark departure from his earlier statements, Niebuhr explained, "[T]he ultimate question is not whether life has a meaning...but whether or not the meaning is tragic...Christianity is a faith which takes us through

---

[93] "United Front," *Radical Religion* (Winter 1935), p. 4. Although the article is an unsigned editorial piece, its tone and content indicate that Niebuhr was the likely author.

[94] It should be noted that it was not only the specter of international conflict but also the influence of his changing theological views, particularly his conception of sin, which pulled Niebuhr away from his prior leanings. As Niebuhr would acknowledge later in life, "I expressed socialist political convictions long after my basic presuppositions seemed to contradict those convictions," Niebuhr to Morton White, May 17, 1956, Niebuhr Papers, Box 53.

[95] David McCreary, "John Bennett on Oxford '37," *The Christian Century*, October 28, 1987, pp. 942–4. For the most comprehensive summary of the conference proceedings, see J. H. Oldham, *The Oxford Conference: World Conference on Church, Community and State (Official Report)* (New York: Willett, Clark, 1937), esp. pp. 25–7 for a summary of Niebuhr's speech.

[96] See Fox, *Reinhold Niebuhr*, pp. 180–1.

tragedy to beyond tragedy, by way of the cross to a victory in the cross."[97] Niebuhr did not expand on this revelation in his thought, but the brief mention of humanity's salvation foreshadowed the distinct shift in his next work, *Beyond Tragedy*, with regard to his view of history.

Beyond Tragedy, as is clear from its original title, *God and History*, was Niebuhr's first work dedicated primarily to the Christian understanding of history.[98] Just how far Niebuhr's thinking had developed on this subject was evident at its outset. Niebuhr explained, "It is the thesis of these essays that the Christian view of history passes through the sense of the tragic to a hope and assurance which is 'beyond tragedy.'"[99] What appears to have prompted Niebuhr's more hopeful appraisal of history was his greater appreciation for human sinfulness or, more specifically, its profound consequences. If Niebuhr had previously focused on the contemporary social problems resulting from sin, he now gave primacy to the central theological repercussion—the ultimate sacrifice of Jesus Christ on the cross. The atoning death of Christ not only represented the intractability of sin to Niebuhr, but also, more importantly, it offered hope by showing the lengths to which God would go to overcome the brokenness of humanity. This appreciation had profound consequences on Niebuhr's understanding of history. He explained, "Christianity's view of history is tragic insofar as it recognizes evil as an inevitable concomitant of even the highest spiritual enterprises. It is beyond tragedy insofar as it . . . regard[s] [evil] as finally under the dominion of a good God."[100] Perhaps more telling was Niebuhr's description of what resulted from a failure to acknowledge God's entry into history to redeem the sins of humanity. In words that could have been used to describe his own beliefs at the beginning of the 1930s, Niebuhr explained, "Without the Cross men are beguiled by what is tragic . . . [in human existence] into despair."[101]

Many commentators have agreed that, of all Niebuhr's works, *Beyond Tragedy* contains some of the most positive affirmations of

---

[97] Niebuhr, "The Christian Church in a Secular Age," reprinted in *The Essential Reinhold Niebuhr*, ed. Robert McAfee Brown (New Haven, CT: Yale University Press 1986), p. 85.

[98] Niebuhr to Ursula Niebuhr, summer 1937, Niebuhr Papers, Box 58.

[99] Niebuhr, *Beyond Tragedy*, p. x.

[100] Niebuhr, *Beyond Tragedy*, pp. x–xi.

[101] Niebuhr, *Beyond Tragedy*, p. 20.

his Christian convictions.[102] If his previous writings had been weighed down by concern over the "the contradictions of human existence," Niebuhr, in *Beyond Tragedy*, expressed palpable relief and wonder over how those contradictions were "swallowed up in the life of God Himself."[103] Niebuhr hinted at this transformation much later in life in correspondence with Morton White, explaining, "[A]n examination of the whole nature of man's historical freedom led me to an espousal of more of the Christian faith than I possessed in the beginning (I mean the whole range of realities comprehended in the ideas of responsibility, sin, and grace)."[104] Despite the obvious differences between *Interpretations* and *Beyond Tragedy*, however, critics continued to question the exact nature of Niebuhr's faith as a result of his continued reliance on the category of myth.[105] Niebuhr argued for a mythical understanding of Christ's death on the cross, arguing that a literal interpretation would obscure its present relevance to man's historical condition. Nevertheless, Niebuhr's most insightful critic, Richard, reacted far more favorably to *Beyond Tragedy* than he had to any of his brother's previous works. His wait for Reinhold to acknowledge God's redeeming presence in history was over. With a hint of relief, Richard observed, "There is more positive assurance, more faith, hope and love in this book than in anything I've seen in a long time."[106]

More important for the purposes of this study, it was in *Beyond Tragedy* that Niebuhr's "in the battle and above it" formulation began to take shape. Specifically, he relied on the biblical story of "The Ark and the Temple" we first encountered in the Introduction to this work to apply his emerging theological vision to the United

---

[102] Cyril Richardson, a former colleague of Niebuhr's at Union Theological Seminary, stated that *Beyond Tragedy* contained "a deeper religious discernment than anything [Niebuhr] had previously written," "Review of *Beyond Tragedy*," *Review of Religion*, 12 (March 1938), p. 331.

[103] Niebuhr, *Beyond Tragedy*, p. 19.

[104] Niebuhr to Morton White, May 17, 1956, Niebuhr Papers, Box 53.

[105] Theologian Cyril Richardson criticized Niebuhr for portraying the doctrines of the Incarnation, Atonement, and Resurrection as myths given the centrality of these events to the Christian faith. "Review of *Beyond Tragedy*, n.d., Neibuhr Paper, Box 20." Edwin T. Buehrer in a review in *The Christian Century* similarly criticized Niebuhr with regard to his use of myth, comparing Niebuhr's interpretation to that of David Friedrich Strauss, "The Mythology of Theology," *The Christian Century*, March 2, 1938, pp. 277–8. In a letter to the editor-in-chief, Clayton Morrison, Niebuhr criticized *The Christian Century* for what he perceived to be an unfair review. Letter from Winifred Garrison to Neibuhr, March 4, 1938, Niebuhr Papers, Box 3.

[106] Richard to Reinhold Niebuhr, November 1937, Niebuhr Papers, Box 58.

States. According to Niebuhr, just as Solomon was only able to build the temple as a result of David's shedding of blood, America's present prosperity was the result of its past transgressions. Niebuhr offered a litany of complaints similar to those he had advanced in *Moral Man*. Moreover, he went on to add that where Solomon had at least remained aware of his father's past transgressions, America was a "Solomonic civilization that denies or forgets it ever had a David preceding a Solomon."[107] It was this fact more than any other that contributed to "the self-righteous pride" that Niebuhr often detected in America's interactions with the world. For all the similarities between Niebuhr's cynical assessment of America and those previously, there was one significant difference—he now believed the possibility existed that his country could act responsibly on the world stage because "America... had one statesman, Abraham Lincoln, who understood exactly what David experienced."[108] What drew Niebuhr to this conclusion were Lincoln's actions during the Civil War and, specifically, his Second Inaugural Address in which he humbly acknowledged a God whose will transcended that of both the North and South. That said, Niebuhr equally admired Lincoln's commitment to ending slavery, because it proved that his "religious insight into the inscrutability of the divine does not deter Lincoln from making moral judgments according to his best insight."[109] Indeed, Niebuhr found that Lincoln provided the best "example of consummate interweaving of moral idealism and a religious recognition of the imperfection of all human ideals."[110] Just as Niebuhr would in *Irony*, he identified Lincoln as the illustration of his "in the battle and above it" orientation, which, beginning with the publication of *Beyond Tragedy*, would emerge as the dominant theme in his writing.

The appearance of Niebuhr's "in the battle and above it" orientation can be directly related to his developing theological beliefs. This is particularly clear as we remember how Niebuhr's previous denial of God's involvement in history in the fraternal debates had limited his ability to understand how anything constructive could be achieved in the temporal realm. He explained as much in the fraternal debates, holding: "the history of mankind is a perennial tragedy; for the highest ideals which the individual may project are ideals which he

[107] Niebuhr, *Beyond Tragedy*, p. 58.   [108] Niebuhr, *Beyond Tragedy*, p. 66.
[109] Niebuhr, *Beyond Tragedy*, p. 67.   [110] Niebuhr, *Beyond Tragedy*, p. 67.

can never realize in social and collective terms."[111] In the early 1930s Niebuhr saw no need to balance moral idealism with the imperfection of all human ideals because he had no appreciation of the former. As Niebuhr's understanding of human nature and history developed over the course of the decade, however, this belief began to change. Niebuhr's deeper engagement with human sin ultimately allowed him to pass through the tragic and toward a more hopeful view of history as he realized that, through the cross, God was at work in this world. Niebuhr came to the conclusion that what was necessary in order to reach proximate ideals in history was not an assertion of goodness but rather acknowledgment of sinfulness. As he explained in *Beyond Tragedy*, "Man's contrition is the human foundation... but God's grace is its completion."[112] This theological understanding, as well as Niebuhr's "in the battle and above it" orientation on which it was based, would be severely tested in the coming months as World War II approached.

---

[111] Niebuhr, "Must We Do Nothing?," p. 417.
[112] Niebuhr, *Beyond Tragedy*, p. 61.

2

"In the Battle and Above It": Niebuhr's *Nature and Destiny of Man* and World War II

In the last chapter we saw Niebuhr begin to articulate his "in the battle and above it" viewpoint. In this chapter we will observe him developing the underlying theological foundations and interpreting the events of World War II through its lens. Niebuhr clearly established—in full-length works as well as hundreds of articles published between 1938 and 1945—that his overarching political and theological concern was the need for individuals to discriminate between good and evil in history on one hand, and acknowledge the common sinfulness of all humanity on the other. If these two aspects were essential pillars of Niebuhr's thought, their relative importance shifted with the motion of events and, specifically, America's entry into the war. This much is evident in two articles written by Niebuhr, one six months preceding the December 1941 bombing of Pearl Harbor by the Japanese and another six months after the event. In urging America to enter the conflict prior to the attack, Niebuhr observed, "We are well aware of the sin of all the nations, including our own . . . yet we believe the task of defending the rich inheritance of our civilization to be an imperative one."[1] Alternatively, in warning the nation against self-righteousness once at war, Niebuhr observed, "Beyond all moral distinctions in history, we must know ourselves as one with our enemies . . . by a common guilt by which that humanity

---

[1] Niebuhr, "The Christian Faith and the World Crisis," *Christianity and Crisis*, February 10, 1941, p. 6.

has been corrupted."[2] The contrasting emphases of these statements reveal that whereas Niebuhr was dedicated to being in the battle while remaining above the fray until America began combat operations, his focus shifted for the remainder of the war to being "above the battle" while remaining in the fray.

This subtle movement in Niebuhr's thought is perhaps best evidenced in the two volumes that comprise his seminal work, *The Nature and Destiny of Man*. *Human Nature*, published in March 1941, centers on the need to make moral judgments in a corrupted world, while *Human Destiny*, published in January 1943, highlights the sinfulness of all humanity and the universal need for God's divine mercy. Both volumes provide clear windows into the underlying theological foundations driving Niebuhr's political beliefs at their specific time of publication. Commentators, however, have misjudged the contemporary relevance of both works. This is because the works are often read as a whole given their origins in two related lecture series that comprised Niebuhr's 1939 Gifford Lectures.[3] Accordingly, this has led many commentators to look more to the context surrounding the lectures as opposed to that surrounding their dates of publication for insights.[4] This is particularly problematic with regard to *Human Destiny* given the four-year period between the lectures and

---

[2] As found in Paul Elie, "A Man for All Reasons," *The Atlantic*, November 2007, <http://www.theatlantic.com/magazine/archive/2007/11/a-man-for-all-reasons/6337/> (accessed August 9, 2012).

[3] Established in 1888 by Scottish judge Adam Lord Gifford, the Gifford Lectures remain to this day the most prestigious theological lecture series in the world. Niebuhr was offered the lectureship primarily through the influence of former Union colleague, John Baillie, who had become the Principal of New College at the University of Edinburgh. Niebuhr's decision to explore the topic of "The Nature and Destiny of Man" was a simple one. He explained later in life, "I chose the only subject I could have chosen because the other fields of Christian thought were beyond my competence," "Intellectual Autobiography," p. 245. Given the fact that by "human destiny" Niebuhr meant his philosophy of history, the focus of Niebuhr's lectures clearly supports the argument that an understanding of human nature and history had become the primary subjects of Niebuhr's theological inquiry at this point in his career.

[4] See, on this point, Ronald H. Stone, *Professor Reinhold Niebuhr* (Louisville, KY: John Knox Press, 1992), pp. 131–52. His compression into a few pages of Niebuhr's preparation, delivery, and publication of the lectures leaves the reader confused as to the basic chronology of the process, much less the influence that historical events played on the process that transpired over the course of five years. As to biographical treatments that follow a similar pattern, see also Merkley, *Reinhold Niebuhr*. Almost without exception, *Human Nature* and *Human Destiny* are conceived as a complete whole when addressed in non-biographical treatments of Niebuhr's thought.

publication date. This has caused confusion, for instance, as to how Niebuhr could have been so sanguine about the Allied war prospects at one of its darkest periods.[5] Such a reading of *Human Nature* and *Human Destiny* is most problematic, however, because it fails to account for their actual development. While both works did originate in the Gifford Lectures, those in attendance confirmed that Niebuhr spoke extemporaneously and had only a few "skeleton notes" on the lectern before him.[6] Indeed, Niebuhr explained in letters to friends that the actual writing of *Human Destiny*, in particular, occurred following the lectures series and in the midst of his ongoing political advocacy.[7]

Other commentators have failed to appreciate the relevance of *Human Nature* and *Human Destiny* to Niebuhr's political thought by largely ignoring the surrounding context of the two works altogether.[8] They have justified this approach by pointing to their academic nature as well as the paucity of direct references to World War II in their pages.[9] Given the prestige surrounding the Gifford

[5] Stone, *Professor Reinhold Niebuhr*, pp. 148–9.

[6] John Baillie, "Niebuhr's Gifford Lectures," *Union Seminary Quarterly Review*, 2 (March 1941), p. 7, as found in Niebuhr Papers, Box 57.

[7] *Human Destiny* was largely written after the Gifford Lectures because Niebuhr's preparations for the second series, especially in comparison to his efforts for the first, were limited. Indeed, they occurred in the few months between the first and the second series when Niebuhr remained in England with his family to vacation and attend conferences throughout Europe. While Niebuhr's colleagues at Union marveled at the number of hours he spent in the library preparing for the first lectures, he did not even have regular access to a library where he was staying in Sussex. Fox, far better than any other biographer, documents the difficulties Niebuhr faced with the second series and, in general, depicts with a fair degree of accuracy how the actual writing of *Human Nature* and *Human Destiny* occurred, *Reinhold Niebuhr*, pp. 189–92.

[8] The clearest example of this is Brown, as he takes the development, delivery, and publication of *Nature and Destiny* completely out of its surrounding context by placing it in its own chapter, *Niebuhr and His Age*, pp. 68–94. The detachment is all the more striking given how effective Brown is in the rest of the book at exploring the interaction between Niebuhr's politics and theology.

[9] The most perceptive students of Niebuhr's thought, such as Halliwell, have questioned why he did not seem to explicitly apply his ideas "more closely to the unfolding events in Europe," *The Constant Dialogue*, p. 126. A plausible reason numerous commentators have mentioned was a desire to prove his mettle as an academic theologian in addition to a powerful writer on current events, see, on this point, Cornel West, *The American Evasion of Philosophy: A Genealogy of Pragmatism* (Madison, WI: University of Wisconsin Press, 1989), pp. 150–64. If West exaggerates the extent to which Niebuhr felt intellectually insecure, it is likely that, without a Ph.D., Niebuhr viewed the Gifford Lectures as an opportunity to establish his credentials in a more academic community, p. 150. Indeed, a more academic approach is

Lectures, Niebuhr would have clearly seen them as an opportunity to develop a work that would stand the test of time. However, as the last chapter made clear, current events were always at the forefront of Niebuhr's mind. Thus it is inevitable that *Human Nature* and *Human Destiny* were written to shape and, indeed, were shaped by the ongoing global conflict. Niebuhr clearly viewed his insistence in *Human Nature* that mankind was required to make partial judgments on the basis of the division between good and evil in history as a call for America to join the Allied forces in resisting the "demonic" aggression of Nazi Germany. Likewise, Niebuhr certainly intended his discussion in *Human Destiny* of the common sinfulness of all individuals and nations before God to temper the self-righteousness he perceived in how the United State and the Allied forces conducted the war. As this chapter shall reveal, the question is not whether Niebuhr's theological writings in *Human Nature* and *Human Destiny* informed his political writings of the period but whether Niebuhr's political writings went far enough to reflect the theological positions developed in both works.

THE GATHERING STORM

We mentioned in the last chapter that Niebuhr's concern with the rise of the Nazi party in Germany was only heightened by his travels to England for the Conference on Church, Community and State. While across the Atlantic Niebuhr wrote a series of letters to social critic Waldo Frank expressing his firm belief that Hitler was intent on bringing much of Europe under his influence through military aggression.[10] Equally as troubling to Niebuhr was what he perceived to be the unwillingness of Europe to resist this growing threat. Niebuhr predicted with remarkable prescience that Europe's accession to

---

precisely what was hinted at in Niebuhr's invitation to give the lectures. In a February 1937 letter of congratulation accompanying the invitation, John Baillie hinted that Niebuhr, the self-professed "preacher-journalist," was expected to meet the rigorous academic standard of the lectureship, or as Baillie diplomatically explained, "the more theological the better," Letter from John Baillie to Ursula Niebuhr, March 22, 1937, Niebuhr Papers, Box 46.

[10] See Fox, *Reinhold Niebuhr*, pp. 179–84 for a discussion of Niebuhr's letters to Frank.

Hitler's demands, rather than placating the dictator, would only embolden him, thereby making military confrontation more likely. He summarized in an article written in early 1938, "The democratic nations of the world are involving themselves more inexorably in world catastrophe by their very efforts to avert or avoid it."[11] The events of 1938 only served to confirm Niebuhr's worst fears, as the Nazis entered unopposed into Vienna that March to complete the bloodless unification of Germany and Austria. Far more troubling to Niebuhr was the news from Munich in September that European leaders, led by English Prime Minister Neville Chamberlain, assented to German demands for Czechoslovakia's Sudetenland in exchange for Hitler's word that he would cease territorial expansion. Chamberlain's heroic reception upon his return to England and his famous appraisal of the Munich agreement as securing "peace for our time" revealed to Niebuhr the extent to which the continent was unprepared for war.

If Niebuhr was critical of Neville Chamberlain's role in the appeasement of Germany, his harshest judgments were reserved for the duplicity of the (London) *Times*. Influential in the elite circles of Britain during the period, the *Times* consistently obfuscated the threat posed to the country by Nazi Germany. Indeed, the paper described the unification of Germany and Austria as an event to be celebrated comparable to the joining of England and Scotland. Moreover, the *Times* actually proposed prior to Munich that the Sudetenland really belonged to Germany and should thus be returned. What bothered Niebuhr more than the spurious nature of these claims was the "cynicism" with which the *Times* attempted to obscure the actual political consequences of these events. For instance, the *Times* portrayed Chamberlain's peaceful accession to Hitler's demands as a heroic victory of peace over war. As the newspaper explained in an editorial, "at the moment when the current racing toward the precipice seemed irresistible, it was the leadership of the British Prime Minister that showed how immense were the forces ranged on the side of reason against violence."[12] This approach of overlooking the actual political outcome of Munich and, instead, framing the events as an unequivocal triumph of peace over violence was, according to

---

[11] Niebuhr, "Greek Tragedy and Modern Politics," as found in *Christianity and Power Politics* (New York: Charles Scribner's Sons, 1940), p. 96.
[12] As found in Niebuhr, "The *London Times* and the Crisis," *Radical Religion* (Winter 1938), pp. 30–1. For the original, see "A New Dawn," *The Times*, October 1, 1938, p. 13.

the *Times*, clearing "the moral issue . . . of all its irrelevancies."[13] Rather than "irrelevancies," Niebuhr believed the consequences of Munich to be "a tremendous shift in the balance of power in Europe that . . . opened the gates to a German expansion and . . . changed the whole course of European history."[14]

In a series of articles written in the early months of 1939 against the backdrop of Germany's complete annexation of Czechoslovakia, Niebuhr repeatedly portrayed the *Times* as the symptom of a much more significant problem.[15] In his mind what led many individuals to celebrate the Munich Agreement and then express surprise at Germany's unchecked hostility was their fundamental "faith in the essential goodness of man and the possibility of completely rational behavior."[16] Such beliefs lead to an abdication of moral responsibility when its adherents came into contact with a foe that valued aggression above reason. What was necessary to alert modern society to the Nazi threat was an ability to "understand the coercive element in all political life, and to appreciate the 'ideological' taint in all human reason."[17] Thus it should come as no surprise that his first series of Gifford Lectures, given in April, addressed these very characteristics in human nature. Remaining in England to prepare for his second lecture series that fall, Niebuhr became aware of the country's growing resolve to resist further Nazi aggression.[18] This was revealed when Britain declared war on Germany in September following Hitler's invasion of Poland. As if Niebuhr required any more convincing as to the Nazi threat prior to his return to the United States, Luftwaffe bombs falling on a nearby British naval base were audible during his final Gifford lectures on human destiny.[19]

Upon his return to the United States, Niebuhr attempted to generate backing amongst his fellow countrymen to support Allied resistance of German offensives in Scandinavia, France, and the Low

---

[13] As found in Niebuhr, "The *London Times* and the Crisis," p. 30. For the original, see "The Issue Defined," *The Times*, September 28, 1938, p. 11.

[14] Niebuhr, "The *London Times* and the Crisis," p. 32.

[15] Niebuhr, "Peace and the Liberal Illusion," *The Nation*, January 28, 1939, pp. 118–19, as found in Niebuhr, *Christianity and Power Politics*, pp. 83–93; Niebuhr, "Synthetic Barbarism," *The New Statesman and Nation*, September 9, 1939, pp. 390–1, as found in Niebuhr, *Christianity and Power Politics*, pp. 117–30.

[16] Niebuhr, "Peace and the Liberal Illusion," as found in *Christianity and Power Politics*, p. 84.

[17] Niebuhr, "Peace and the Liberal Illusion," p. 89.

[18] Niebuhr, "The British Conscience," *The Nation*, August 26, 1939, p. 220.

[19] Fox, *Reinhold Niebuhr*, p. 191.

Countries.[20] He knew this task would be challenging given the same "moral illusions" he had railed against in European culture were more firmly entrenched in America. Although Niebuhr primarily blamed the country's wealth and geographic isolation for this fact, he expressed in a number of articles his wariness of certain elements of society that he believed particularly responsible for its unhealthy prejudices. First, Niebuhr criticized his own Socialist Party for its unwillingness to view Nazi tyranny as anything more than a predictable consequence of the global capitalist economy.[21] Second, Niebuhr bemoaned the widespread pacifism he observed throughout American churches, viewing it as a misguided rejection of human sinfulness or disillusionment stemming from World War I. Such beliefs led Niebuhr to associate pacifist Christians with a third, and, in Niebuhr's estimation, more influential group, "secular moralists," in the tradition of the *Times* readership in England. Far greater in number than either the Socialists or true pacifists, these individuals were cynical toward the current conflict as a result of a fundamental misreading of human nature as well as the failure of Versailles.[22] The most influential member of this group, in Niebuhr's estimation, was American philosopher John Dewey.

Niebuhr's arrival at Union Theological Seminary brought him into the orbit of Dewey, who was then nearing the end of his distinguished career as an emeritus professor at neighboring Columbia

[20] Following the fall of France and the Low Countries in May 1939, Niebuhr assumed a position of leadership in William Allan White's Committee to Defend America by Aiding the Allies. This organization advocated American provision of material support to Britain in direct opposition to the Neutrality Acts passed by the Congress, Brown, *Niebuhr and His Age*, p. 98.

[21] Niebuhr actually resigned his membership of the Socialist Party with a published letter that confirmed he had largely transformed from critic to the defender of democratic institutions in less than two years, Niebuhr, "Idealists as Cynics," *The Nation*, January 20, 1940, p. 74. He explained when "one is not so certain what lies on the other side of social breakdown . . . one does not lightly hope for the breakdown of any social system in which there is a degree of freedom and the possibility of achieving better social and economic adjustments," "Idealists as Cynics," p. 74. This fact was perhaps best reflected in his newfound support for Roosevelt in the 1940 presidential elections. Despite Niebuhr's close friendship with Socialist candidate Norman Thomas, he fully supported the incumbent on the grounds of his foreign policy and, more specifically, his advocacy for U.S. engagement overseas.

[22] Niebuhr, "Idealists as Cynics," p. 74.

University.[23] What led many to consider Dewey the foremost intellectual of his time were his efforts to render philosophy useful to specific societal challenges. His summarized this in a 1917 essay in which he observed, "Philosophy recovers itself when it ceases to be a device for dealing with the problems of philosophers and becomes a method, cultivated by philosophers, for dealing with the problems of men."[24] Dewey did this by extending the application of the scientific method—a process that tested the validity of a proposition on the basis of its consequences—to the social realm. He believed that the majority of society's problems, no matter how intractable they might appear, could be resolved through the processes of rational inquiry. The extent of Dewey's belief in mankind's capabilities was revealed in his belief that, "Faith in the power of intelligence to imagine a future which is the projection of the desirable in the present, and to invent the instrumentalities of its realization, is our salvation."[25] Not content with merely inventing theoretical instrumentalities, Dewey utilized his consequence-based approach to bring about the realization of reforms targeted at modernizing the American educational system and creating a more equal distribution of society's resources.

Niebuhr first set his sights on Dewey in *Moral Man* for what he described as Dewey's misguided belief that the experimentalism of the physical sciences could be applied to the social realm in order to resolve inequality between individuals and groups. Such an approach, in Niebuhr's estimation, failed to "do justice to the complexity of human behavior," because it was based on the belief that rational intelligence could be shielded from the temptations of self-interest.[26] He expressed increased skepticism of Dewey's understanding of human nature in *Reflections* and *Interpretation* as he gained a greater appreciation for the pervasiveness of sin.[27] Throughout the 1930s Niebuhr criticized intellectuals such as Dewey for "shrink[ing] from the conclusions to which a realistic analysis of history forces the careful student" in an effort to preserve their belief in society's potential for

---

[23] Daniel F. Rice, *Reinhold Niebuhr and John Dewey: An American Odyssey* (Albany, NY: State University of New York Press, 1993), pp. 14–15.
[24] John Dewey, "The Need for A Recovery of Philosophy," in Dewey, ed., *Creative Intelligence: Essays in the Pragmatic Attitude* (New York: Holt, 1917), p. 65.
[25] Dewey, "The Need for a Recovery of Philosophy," p. 69.
[26] Niebuhr, *Moral Man*, p. 35.
[27] Niebuhr, *Reflections*, pp. 127, 132; Niebuhr, *Interpretation*, pp. 218, 234.

growth and development.[28] Case in point for Niebuhr was Dewey's view on U.S. involvement in World War II, which he established succinctly in 1938, "No matter what happens, stay out."[29] Niebuhr was not opposed to the rational lens through which Dewey claimed to view the world. Rather he took issue with what he perceived as the "absolute faith in the purity of reason in all situations" evident in Dewey's writings.[30]

Many commentators have criticized the accuracy of Niebuhr's attacks. Most recently, Fox and Rice have accused him of failing to acknowledge that Dewey's writings did account for the conflict inherent in human interactions.[31] John Diggins finds this may have been the case with the early Dewey, but asserts that Niebuhr's criticisms—especially those in the late 1930s—were justified given Dewey's repeated assertions that he would fight fascism through the "method of discussion."[32] Regardless, Niebuhr's portrayal of Dewey, like that of Barth, was in keeping with what Daniel Day Williams identifies as Niebuhr's tendency to caricature an individual in order to "go swiftly to the heart of a vast and complex cultural movement [and] lift out the central idea which gives it its drive."[33] Niebuhr acknowledged as much when he explained in a 1938 article that the simple moralism he attributed to Dewey was representative of a much larger cultural phenomenon "informed by cultural presuppositions that had their rise in eighteenth-century rationalism."[34] Appreciating this fact is central to understanding the continuity between Niebuhr's interventionist writings and *Human Nature*, much of which is dedicated to placing views he attributes to Dewey into a larger intellectual tradition in order to prove their inadequacy. Commentators may acknowledge that an appreciation of Niebuhr's political writings during the period can provide a "helpful corrective to a decontextualized reading of the *Nature and Destiny of Man*."[35] They fail to

---

[28] Niebuhr, "After Capitalism—What," *The World Tomorrow*, March 1, 1933, pp. 204–5.

[29] As found in John Patrick Diggins, *The Promise of Pragmatism: Modernism and the Crisis of Knowledge and Authority* (Chicago: University of Chicago Press, 1994), p. 274.

[30] Neibuhr letter to Morton White, Niebuhr Papers, 4 July 1956. Box 53.

[31] See Fox, *Reinhold Niebuhr*, pp. 136–7 and Rice, *Reinhold Niebuhr and John Dewey*, pp. 29–41.

[32] As found in Diggins, *The Promise of Pragmatism*, p. 286, see also pp. 285–91 for a comprehensive discussion of Niebuhr's critique of Dewey.

[33] Daniel Day Williams, "Niebuhr and Liberalism," in Kegley and Bretall, eds, *Reinhold Niebuhr*, p. 195.

[34] Niebuhr, "Greek Tragedy and Modern Politics," *The Nation*, January 1, 1938, as found in Niebuhr, *Christianity and Power Politics*, p. 103.

[35] Stone, *Professor Reinhold Niebuhr*, p. 133. Immediately prior to the publication of *Human Nature*, Niebuhr published a compilation of many of his journalistic articles, *Christianity and Power Politics*. The proximity of the two works' publication

appreciate the extent, however, to which Niebuhr viewed his efforts in *Human Nature* as central to strengthening the resolve of those that were, and those that needed to be, involved in resisting Hitler's advances.

HUMAN NATURE

The first chapters of *Human Nature* presented the fallacies of those accounts of human nature Niebuhr perceived to be in conflict with the Christian viewpoint. This theme is one that can be found in Niebuhr's writings in one form or another dating back to *Moral Man*. The main difference in *Human Nature*, however, is the lengths to which Niebuhr went to justify his criticisms of what he viewed as competing accounts of the Christian faith. For instance, while Niebuhr continued his well-worn criticisms of Dewey's belief that a general advance in human knowledge could eliminate social discord, he went further to trace the origins of this belief to the writings of such intellectuals as Bacon, Rousseau, Descartes, Kant, Hegel, and Freud. Niebuhr explained that regardless of the disputes between naturalists, rationalists, and romanticists since the Enlightenment, each represented an overly optimistic appraisal of human nature.[36] He explained that each considered man "as essentially good" and thought it "only necessary for man either to rise from the chaos of nature to the harmony of mind or to descend from the chaos of spirit to the harmony of nature in order to be saved."[37] Dewey was merely the latest in a long line of thinkers unable to fully understand mankind's capacity for good and evil. Only a biblical perspective, in

dates leads Stone to believe that politics was on Niebuhr's mind in the writing of *Human Nature*. That said even Stone seems to undervalue just how central *Human Nature* was to Niebuhr's political advocacy, as he mentions current events once in his section dedicated to the work, pp. 134–42.

[36] Analyzing Niebuhr's wide-ranging critiques is difficult, as rather than engaging philosophically with intellectuals, he takes a more polemical approach by placing them into what seems at times to be arbitrary categories. Gilkey describes this as Niebuhr arguing "theologically," or in a fashion more concerned with "different schemes of meaning" that animate these philosophers than their actual systems, *On Niebuhr*, p. 59.

[37] Niebuhr, *Human Nature*, p. 25.

Niebuhr's estimation, was capable of adequately capturing the depths, along with the heights, of human existence.

If Niebuhr provided some additional context to his critique of the view represented by Dewey, he dedicated the majority of his effort to explaining the broader intellectual heritage he relied upon in formulating his Christian interpretation of human nature. Specifically, Niebuhr identified the importance of Augustine for his understanding of the self-transcendent freedom and creaturely finitude that constituted the human self. It was Augustine who explained how this combination both stemmed from our creation in the image of God and rendered individuals only able to find ultimate contentment in God. Niebuhr cited Augustine's observation in *The City of God* that humanity, unwilling to accept its absolute indebtedness to, and sole fulfillment in, God, instead, "abandons Him to whom it ought to cleave as its end and becomes a kind of end in itself."[38] Herein lay Augustine's most significant contribution to the Christian understanding of human nature, according to Niebuhr. Rather than considering the fragmentary character of human life as sinful, Augustine established that "sin has its source . . . in man's willful refusal to acknowledge the finite and determinate character of his existence."[39] Niebuhr explained that Augustine's view of sin as mankind's universal rebellion against God had a profound influence on his understanding of human nature.[40]

Niebuhr's overall desire in *Human Nature*, however, was not only to assert the universality of sin but also to emphasize the necessity of making moral judgments in history. As we saw in the last chapter, Niebuhr's criticisms of Barth revealed he did not believe the two went hand in hand. Niebuhr reiterated in *Human Nature* his opposition to "theologies, such as that of Barth, which threaten to destroy all relative moral judgments by their exclusive emphasis on the religious fact of the sinfulness of all men."[41] The second half of *Human Nature*, as a result, was primarily concerned with how distinctions could be made between the oppressors and the victims in history, keeping in mind their shared sinfulness. In tackling this problem, Niebuhr viewed Augustine not as the solution but rather a primary part of the problem. Specifically, Niebuhr pointed to Augustine's understanding of sin as literal inheritance.[42] Augustine established

[38] As found in Niebuhr, *Human Nature*, p. 199.
[39] Niebuhr, *Human Nature*, p. 189.   [40] Niebuhr, *Human Nature*, p. 165.
[41] Niebuhr, *Human Nature*, p. 234.   [42] Niebuhr, *Human Nature*, pp. 256–8.

that sin originated in Adam's initial transgression and had since been transmitted to all of humanity from generation to generation through physical heredity. He thus conceived of sin as engrained in an individual's nature from birth. This tradition, according to Niebuhr, had the tendency to undermine moral accountability among many Christians, because it was difficult to hold others responsible for actions that resulted from an inherited corruption. Niebuhr believed that the only way to combat this "crude" form of determinism was to stress the existential dimensions of sin over its historic transmission.[43] To this end, Niebuhr turned to Danish philosopher, Søren Kierkegaard, whom he identified as the Christian thinker that best captured the "paradox of inevitability and responsibility" contained within sin.[44]

Specifically, Niebuhr focused on Kierkegaard's *The Concept of Anxiety*, which advanced a symbolic interpretation of original sin counter to the Augustinian notion of literal inheritance.[45] Kierkegaard explained that the Fall, rather than depicting a historic event, represented a move from innocence that occurred in the lives of every individual: "Through the first sin, sin came into the world. Precisely in the same way it is true of every subsequent man's first sin, that

[43] Niebuhr, *Human Nature*, p. 278.
[44] Niebuhr, *Human Nature*, p. 278. It appears that Niebuhr was drawn to Kierkegaard by Swiss theologian Emil Brunner. Niebuhr and Brunner first become acquainted at the Oxford Conference on Church, Community and State, where they were immediately struck, according to those in attendance, by the similarities between their understandings of mankind's sinful nature. Indeed Brunner published his own wide-ranging survey on the Christian understanding of human nature and history in 1937, later translated into English as *Man in Revolt: A Christian Anthropology*, trans. Olive Wyon (London: R. T. S. Lutterworth, 1939). After Niebuhr read the work he wrote a long letter to Brunner conveying the deep impression it was having on his own thought. Niebuhr explained, "I have studied the book with mingled feelings, partly because I learned so much from it and partly because it took the wind out of my sails as it dealt with some matters like the 'historicity of the fall . . . ,' which I had expected to deal with in the Gifford lectures on which I am working," as found in Brown, *Niebuhr and His Age*, p. 69. It is no coincidence that Brunner was heavily reliant on Kierkegaard for his understanding of the Fall. Specifically, it was Kierkegaard's rejection of the traditional view of sin as literal inheritance that informed Brunner's efforts to assign mankind at least partial responsibility for his sinful nature, *Man in Revolt*, p. 63. Niebuhr must have identified Brunner, or, more specifically, Brunner's reliance on Kierkegaard, as a legitimate theological basis for his own efforts to this end.
[45] While it does not appear that Niebuhr looked to Kierkegaard before reading Brunner's *Man in Revolt*, he did shortly thereafter. Brown establishes that Niebuhr familiarized himself with *The Concept of Anxiety*, reading the German translation prior to the publication of *Human Nature*, *Niebuhr and His Age*, pp. 72–3.

through it sin comes into the world."[46] Niebuhr argued through Kierkegaard that what united humanity to Adam was not a process of genetic transmission but rather shared psychological factors that led everyone to sin. In particular Niebuhr relied on the primary precondition identified by Kierkegaard, anxiety, which was firmly rooted in human consciousness at the juncture of one's finitude and freedom.[47] While possible, in theory, to live in equilibrium between these two poles, individuals, in Kierkegaard's observation, always attempted to escape this anxiety, thereby precipitating a "qualitative leap" into sin.[48] Even though this leap was inevitable, in Niebuhr's estimation, he believed that an individual's responsibility was maintained on account of the feeling of guilt that inevitably accompanied this action. He explained it was the feeling of "remorse and repentance which followed the sinful action" representing "that some degree of conscious dishonesty accompanied the act."[49] In other words, Niebuhr was reiterating the basis for Kierkegaard's observation in

[46] Søren Kierkegaard, *The Concept of Anxiety: A Simple Psychological Orienting Deliberation on the Dogmatic Issue of Heriditary Sin*, trans. and ed. Howard Hong and Edna Hong (Princeton, NJ: Princeton University Press, 1980), p. 31.

[47] If commentators have been quick to acknowledge Niebuhr's indebtedness to Kierkegaard's understanding of anxiety, they have largely ignored his dependence upon Kierkegaard's understanding of original sin. Rasmussen and Brown, the commentators who most clearly acknowledge Kierkegaard's influence, are guilty of this error, *Reinhold Niebuhr*, p. 290, ff. 61, *Niebuhr and His Age*, pp. 78, 81. This represents a widespread misunderstanding on the part of Niebuhr commentators with regard to the purpose and content of the *Concept of Anxiety*. As the subtitle of the work ("A Simple Psychologically Orienting Deliberation on the Dogmatic Issue of Hereditary Sin") suggests, Kierkegaard invokes anxiety in order to provide the reader with an orientation for the notion of original sin. Kierkegaard had made this distinction largely because he did not think that man had the ability to understand sin. Niebuhr had no such concerns and, as a result, co-opted Kierkegaard's analysis into a solution of his own. Niebuhr clearly was not a student of Kierkegaard in the sense of appreciating the nuance and complexity of his thought. For instance, Niebuhr was not familiar with the full scholarship of Kierkegaard at the time of *Human Nature*, nor did he display a basic understanding of Kierkegaard, such as his use of indirect communication through a reliance on pseudonyms. Pointing to the fallacies in Niebuhr's reception of Kierkegaard is not productive given what has already been said about the way in which Niebuhr addressed previous thinkers—whether in agreement or disagreement with them. A better way to look at Niebuhr's use of Kierkegaard is offered by Roger Badham, who, while acknowledging Niebuhr's flaws, attempts to focus more on "Niebuhr's creative developments of Kierkegaard's thought," "Redeeming the Fall: Hick's Schleiermacher versus Niebuhr's Kierkegaard," *Journal of Religion*, 78:4 (October 1998), p. 566.

[48] Niebuhr, *Human Nature*, p. 270.

[49] Niebuhr, *Human Nature*, p. 270.

The Concept of Anxiety: "It is not in the interests of ethics to make all men except Adam into concerned and interested spectators of guiltiness but not participants in guiltiness . . ."[50]

A testament to the lengths Niebuhr went to affirm the moral accountability of individuals is that he actually went beyond Kierkegaard's existential understanding of original sin.[51] Niebuhr argued the Fall represented not only the first moment in the life of a person when sin is committed, as Kierkegaard had held, but also saw it as a symbol of every moment in which sin occurred thereafter. Niebuhr explained, "When the Fall is made an event in history rather than a symbol of an aspect of *every historical moment* in the life of man, the relation of evil to goodness in that moment is obscured."[52] He not only wanted to prove the overall moral responsibility of mankind for its actions; he wanted to assert the relevance of this fact to every decision that was made in the temporal world. Niebuhr reinforced this point in a separate section of *Human Nature* in which he stressed that while all individuals were sinners, there was, nevertheless, an inequality of guilt in the actualities of history. Niebuhr explained in this context that guilt, along with a feeling of remorse, was the "objective and historical consequences of sin, for which the sinner must be held responsible."[53] Turning to the biblical prophetic tradition, Niebuhr explained that while God condemned all human sinfulness, He also cast judgments based on the degrees of social injustice that result from one's actions. This also applied to nations engaged in the act of war. In discussing the "daemonic" actions of Germany, Niebuhr explained, "While all modern nations . . . have been involved in the sin of pride, one must realize—in this as in other estimates of human sinfulness—that it is just as important to recognize differences in the degree of pride and self-will expressed by men and nations, as it is to know that all men and nations are sinful in the sight of God."[54] Niebuhr may have mentioned the Nazi threat

---

[50] Kierkegaard, *The Concept of Anxiety*, p. 36.

[51] See, on this point, Badham, "Redeeming the Fall," p. 564.

[52] Niebuhr, *Human Nature*, p. 285.

[53] Niebuhr, *Human Nature*, p. 235. Gilkey, in his discussion of these two concepts, offers a useful way to conceptualize Niebuhr's characterization. He explains that "Niebuhr applies the category of sin to the vertical, religious relation to God, and guilt to the horizontal effects of sin in the temporal world," *On Niebuhr*, p. 113.

[54] Niebuhr, *Human Nature*, p. 233.

only in a limited number of places, but it was an underlying theme throughout the entire work.

If *Human Nature* is received largely as an academic work today, Niebuhr's peers also recognized it as concerned with contemporary "events and problems and especially evils."[55] Tillich, in his review of the work, remarked on the profound repercussions that Niebuhr's theology would have on the present conflict in Europe.[56] Robert Calhoun saw it primarily as a prophetic condemnation of the current global situation from "a preacher expounding the Word in line with his own private revelation."[57] Some of the most frequently commented upon sections of the work were those on moral responsibility, as reviewers correctly questioned the ambiguous nature of Niebuhr's understanding of guilt and its relationship to sin. For instance, William John Wolf perceptively questioned, "But may there not be sins for which man feels or should feel guilty that have almost no determinable objective and historical consequences?"[58] Niebuhr subsequently explained that his formulation of the "equality of sin and the inequality of guilt" was in fact a mistaken one. More important than Niebuhr's retraction of the formulation was his explanation of what he was attempting to accomplish with the concept. He explained in familiar terms that it was part of his "search for an adequate description of the situation which will allow for discriminate judgments between good and evil on the one hand, and which will, on the other, preserve the Biblical affirmation that all men fall short before God's judgment."[59]

CHRISTIANITY AND CRISIS

Niebuhr's emphasis on moral accountability was reflected in his founding a new Christian journal, *Christianity and Crisis*, within a

---

[55] Robert L. Calhoun, "A Symposium on Reinhold Niebuhr's *The Nature and Destiny of Man*," *Christendom*, 6 (Autumn 1941), p. 574, as found in Niebuhr Papers, Box 57.

[56] Tillich, "Review of *Human Nature*," *Radical Religion* (Spring 1941), pp. 35–6.

[57] Calhoun, "A Symposium on Reinhold Niebuhr's *The Nature and Destiny of Man*," p. 575, as found in Niebuhr Papers, Box 57.

[58] William J. Wolf, "Reinhold Niebuhr's Doctrine of Man," in Kegley and Bretall, eds, *Reinhold Niebuhr*, p. 240.

[59] Niebuhr, "Reply to Interpretations and Criticisms," p. 437.

month of the publication of *Human Nature*. In promotional materials for *Crisis*, Niebuhr explained the mission of the journal was to address the question: "What is the Christian's Responsibility in the World Conflict?"[60] While there would be no easy answers to this question, Niebuhr explained, "When men or nations must choose between two great evils, the choice of the lesser evil becomes their duty."[61] In the opening editorial of *Crisis*, Niebuhr was not clear what this meant in real terms, merely asserting that any harms associated with U.S. involvement in World War II paled in comparison to the threat posed by Nazi Germany to all of Western civilization. The absence of detail partially can be attributed to the fact that *Crisis* was formed primarily as a corrective to another Christian magazine, *The Christian Century*, which condemned any U.S. involvement in the conflict.[62] Indeed, Mark Hulsether explains in *Building A Protestant Left* that in the first year of *Crisis*, if "the war was the great issue . . . combating *Century* was the overriding concern."[63] As a result, many of Niebuhr's initial articles in *Crisis* were merely reiterations of his familiar attack on how a policy based on avoiding war obfuscated the need for Christians to make important moral distinctions. Eventually, however, Niebuhr and his colleagues at *Crisis* began to focus more on specific policies and strategies regarding how America should actually involve itself in the conflict. The prescriptions were surprising given the magazine's repeated editorials of the disastrous consequences in store for the American population given the westward march of Nazi tyranny.

It seemed natural that when Niebuhr urged Roosevelt to put the full resources of America behind aiding the beleaguered British

---

[60] *Christianity and Crisis* Promotional Flier, n.d., Niebuhr Papers, Box 10.

[61] *Christianity and Crisis* Promotional Flier, n.d., Niebuhr Papers, Box 10.

[62] Hulsether, *Building a Protestant Left*, pp. 25–6. See also Martin E. Marty, *Modern American Religion, Volume III: Under God, Indivisible, 1941–1960* (Chicago: University of Chicago Press, 1996), pp. 51–2 and Fox, *Reinhold Niebuhr*, p. 196. Fox goes so far as to argue, "From the alliterative double *C* of the title to the familiar layout . . . it was plain to all that Morrison's *Christian Century* was both target and model," *Reinhold Niebuhr*, p. 196. It appears that Niebuhr's subscription outreach for *Christianity and Crisis* prior to its first publication targeted readers of *The Christian Century*, many of whom were not receptive to Niebuhr's interventionist slant. One recipient of Niebuhr's pamphlet responded with a scathing criticism that concluded, "Trusting your magazine will encounter the failure it deserves in a peace-loving nation," Rufus Ainsley to Niebuhr, February 4, 1941, Niebuhr Papers, Box 2.

[63] Hulsether, *Building a Protestant Left*, p. 26.

military following the surrender of France and the Low Countries in June 1941, he would sanction military involvement on the part of the United States. This was not the case, however, as *Crisis* rejected the deployment of U.S. forces overseas. Despite the fact Niebuhr observed in July 1941, "The next three months may be the turning point of world history," he was firm in his commitment that the conflict did not "call for an American expeditionary force."[64] Instead he supported the extension of the Lend-Lease Act by which the U.S. supplied war material to Britain and advocated for naval escorts to protect the shipping convoys.[65] Niebuhr justified this incremental approach by explaining that while Western civilization, as a whole, may have been under attack, the United States was not in immediate danger given its geographical location. Given his longstanding belief that American citizens "did not sense ultimate peril with the same urgency as an immediate one," Niebuhr came to the conclusion that it was not politically feasible for the United States to enter the conflict directly.[66] We will recall, however, that Niebuhr had identified American isolationists as the very political group he was determined to win over in his advocacy for the Allied cause following his return from the Gifford Lectures. Now he appeared content to rest the basis of opposition to military involvement on the security the country derived from its geographical advantages.

The other reason behind Niebuhr's hesitancy to recommend U.S. military involvement was his own disillusionment over World War I and, specifically, his concern over giving religious sanction to another military conflict. Niebuhr would frequently describe the position he advocated as the *via media* between the unhealthy alternatives of "fanaticism and inaction," with inaction being the policy of *Century* and fanaticism being the proclamation of "holy war." By projecting his thinking in such a way, Niebuhr seemed to insinuate that any support for military intervention—regardless of the extent to which it was undertaken with a proper sense of contrition— amounted to sanctification of the cause. As Hulsether explains, attacks from writers at the *Century* exacerbated Niebuhr's concern along these lines, as they would identify the smallest policy prescription offered by *Crisis* as confusing "U.S. military policy for a crusade

---

[64] Niebuhr, "The Crisis Deepens," *Christianity and Crisis*, May 5, 1941, p. 2.
[65] Niebuhr, "The Crisis Deepens," p. 2.
[66] Niebuhr, "The Lend Lease Bill," *Christianity and Crisis*, February 10, 1941, p. 2.

for Christianity."[67] Niebuhr's journalistic writings during this period reflect an actual struggle on his part to work out the practicalities of what he had been examining more generally in *Human Nature*, namely, how to make partial judgments between good and evil, while preserving the biblical affirmation that all men fall short before God's judgment.

If Niebuhr was torn over how best to engage in the current struggle, Barth had no such problem. Instead of arguing against involvement, as one might expect given his past writings, Barth was adamant that all Christians should take part in the war. Indeed, this was the message of Barth's "A Letter to Great Britain from Switzerland," which Niebuhr printed in the October 1941 issue of *Crisis*. Expelled from Germany as a result of his opposition to the Nazi regime, Barth wrote the letter in order to steady the resolve of a British population struggling through nightly bombing raids. Given the nature of its contents, however, Niebuhr must have read it as a message written directly to him. Barth commenced the letter by attacking the parallels made between this conflict and World War I. The difference, in his opinion, was "we do not just accept this war as a necessary evil, but that we approve of it as a righteous war, which God does not simply allow, but which He commands us to wage."[68] Such was his belief in the need to resist Hitler's aggression, Barth went so far as to portray the Allied case as one and the same with God's will, thereby providing precisely the religious sanction that Niebuhr was intent to avoid. In explaining the basis for his opposition to Hitler, Barth seemed also to criticize Niebuhr and his justifications. He classified the standard ones offered, such as the preservation of "Western civilization," for not "sufficiently indicat[ing] the distance between us and Hitler" and not being "genuinely Christian."[69] Instead, Barth held that "resistance to Hitler would be built on a really sure foundation only when we resist him unequivocally in the name of a peculiarly Christian truth, unequivocally in the name of Jesus Christ."[70] In what must have been a bitter realization for Niebuhr, the very theologian whom he had accused of political quietism was arguing with greater force on this

---

[67] Hulsether, *Building a Protestant Left*, p. 27.
[68] Barth, "A Letter to Great Britain from Switzerland," *Christianity and Crisis*, October 20, 1941, p. 6.
[69] Barth, "A Letter to Great Britain from Switzerland," p. 7.
[70] Barth, "A Letter to Great Britain from Switzerland," p. 7.

decisive issue and doing so in such a way that seemed to reveal the weaknesses of his own approach.

As was to be expected, *Century* took note of Barth's letter in *Crisis* and interpreted its publication as a declaration of "a crusade against the Germans" by the magazine. Niebuhr countered these accusations in the next issue of *Crisis*, explaining that if he had disagreed with Barth "when he refused to make any distinctions between the relative achievements of justice in history," he disagreed with him "now . . . when he tends to make these distinctions too absolute."[71] His primary concern was to reiterate his criticism of the false choice between religious fanaticism and religious inaction presented by *Century* and to present his approach as the viable alternative. In order to reinforce this point, Niebuhr turned to Lincoln, whom he explained to be the embodiment of decisive, yet contrite, action. Specifically, he cited Lincoln's ardent condemnation of slavery combined with his declaration in his Second Inaugural Address, "But let us judge not that we be not judged," as evidence that a middle road was possible.[72] Niebuhr explained, "It was precisely because [Lincoln] found a way between inaction and self-righteous fanaticism that . . . he was superior to many theologians of his day, whether they were perfectionists or political relativists, and remains superior to many theologians of our day."[73] In Niebuhr's estimation, it was Lincoln, not Barth or the editors at *Century*, that "[drew] upon the full resources of the Christian faith."[74]

Debate over American involvement in the conflict was largely silenced by the fateful events of December 7, 1941. The Japanese surprise attack on Pearl Harbor, home to the U.S. Navy's Pacific fleet, resulted in 2,402 American deaths and served to convince even the staunch non-interventionists at *Century* that military response was required.[75] The subsequent joint declaration of war from

---

[71] Niebuhr, "Just or Holy," *Christianity and Crisis*, November 3, 1941, p. 1.

[72] Niebuhr, "Just or Holy," p. 2.

[73] Niebuhr, "Just or Holy," p. 2.

[74] Niebuhr, "Just or Holy," p. 2.

[75] Morrison, the foil for many of Niebuhr's past critiques of non-interventionism, now threw his support behind American military engagement. Morrison authored a book in the middle of 1942 in which he justified his conversion by explaining the exigencies of wartime trumped whatever freedom of choice with regard to conflict Christians were allowed in times of peace. In other words, the attacks on Pearl Harbor gave pacifists no choice but to acknowledge the "existential reality" of war and support their country in battle. Niebuhr reviewed the work in *Crisis*, and, while commending

Germany, Italy, and Japan against the United States further ensured that the country would soon be engaged in both the Pacific and European theaters. In his first article following the attack on Pearl Harbor, Niebuhr expressed disappointment that events rather than decisive leadership had ultimately overcome the country's resistance to "assum[ing] the obligations to which history pointed."[76] Niebuhr was especially critical of his own inability to grasp the fact that since Munich it was not a question of if, but when, the United States would be forced to take military action. Putting the past behind him, Niebuhr explained that the United States would no longer attempt to escape its moral responsibilities toward the Allied nations. He explained that it was his responsibility, as well as that of all Christians, to "help our nation live through this ordeal with fortitude, and above all, with freedom from hatred and bitterness."[77] For guidance on how to accomplish this Niebuhr pointed to the "words of our greatest American," a well-known passage from Abraham Lincoln's Second Inaugural Address: "With malice toward none and charity toward all, with firmness in the right as God gives us to see the right."[78] If Niebuhr had been mistaken in his political advice in the months immediately preceding the war, the fact that he now appeared to have found his guide made this period quite significant.

Morrison's new political stance, roundly rejected the logic by which he arrived at support for American military involvement. Specifically, Niebuhr found fault with Morrison's "absolute distinction between war and peace," which he believed to be nothing more than a convenient construction thereby allowing Morrison to avoid "discriminating between the comparative justice of embattled causes," "The Christian and the War," *Christianity and Crisis*, November 16, 1942, p. 6. Niebuhr believed Morrison's transformation into a "pure nationalist" was more a result of his unwillingness to engage in the partial moral judgments required in history. The logical extension of Morrison's argument was that in times of peace no cause was of sufficient justice to engage in battle and in times of war any action, however immoral, was justified by use of force. Niebuhr's most telling critique of Morrison's "neat formula" was his description of it as a misguided effort toward the noble goal "to find some guarantee against the persistent tendency of all human beings to an inordinate self-righteousness," "The Christian and the War," p. 7.

[76] Niebuhr, "Christmas Light on History," *Christianity and Crisis*, December 29, 1941, p. 2.

[77] Niebuhr, "Christmas Light on History," p. 3.

[78] Niebuhr, "Christmas Light on History," p. 3.

IN THE BATTLE AND ABOVE IT

The common theme unifying Niebuhr's writings in the years preceding the war had been that Christians had a moral responsibility to make difficult judgments in history while maintaining humility with regard to the shared fallibility of humanity. Following America's entry into the war, however, the common theme unifying Niebuhr's writings would increasingly switch to the moral responsibility of Christians to maintain humility with regard to the shared fallibility of humanity, while remaining resolved to make difficult judgments in history. This distinction, while slight, was nevertheless important to Niebuhr as he moved from championing the righteousness of the Allied cause to warning against American hubris in the conduct of the war. This movement was already underway a month following Pearl Harbor, as seen in an article Niebuhr published on the one-year anniversary of the founding of *Crisis*. In laying out the duties of the readership in the coming year, Niebuhr stressed the importance of supporting the war effort. His overriding message, however, was, "Beyond all moral distinctions in history, we must know ourselves one with our enemies... by a common guilt by which that humanity has been corrupted."[79] Niebuhr saw this self-righteousness manifesting itself in two specific ways throughout the war: a categorical demonization of all Germans and a conflation of God's will with America's. As a result, many of his writings and activities during the war were dedicated to countering both trends.

Niebuhr remained dedicated during and following the war to disabusing Americans of the uniformly negative view of all Germans he perceived as dominant throughout the country. To this end Niebuhr founded and served as the chairman of the American Friends of German Freedom, a group dedicated to raising awareness about and providing support to German citizens involved in active resistance within their country. Niebuhr took a particular interest in one member of the German underground, a theologian named Dietrich Bonhoeffer, who had been a visiting student at Union in the early 1930s. Niebuhr had secured Bonhoeffer a teaching post at the seminary shortly before the war began, which the German theologian filled

---

[79] As found in Paul Elie, "A Man for All Reasons," *The Atlantic*, November 2007, <http://www.theatlantic.com/magazine/archive/2007/11/a-man-for-all-reasons/6337/> (accessed August 9, 2012).

for 26 days before returning home to face the Nazi menace with his fellow citizens. In a letter to Niebuhr explaining his decision, Bonhoeffer wrote, "I shall have no right to participate in the reconstruction of Christian life in Germany after the war if I do not share the trials of this time with my people."[80] Tragically, Bonhoeffer would not live to see the end of the war, as he was executed in 1945 for his role in an assassination plot against Hitler. Following the war, Niebuhr authored an introduction to an anthology of writings by Germans like Bonhoeffer who had formed the resistance against Hitler. In describing the purpose for the work, Niebuhr wrote, "Non-German readers will be instructed by reading these letters that it is impossible to indict a whole nation and that there were spiritual resources in the same nation which generated and succumbed to Nazism, which made these heroic lives and deeds possible."[81] To those who saw all Germans to blame for the current crisis, Niebuhr pointed out, "Millions of Germans offered resistance to Hitler, went to concentration camps and to death, while the so-called democratic world bargained with him."[82] Niebuhr's overall message was, "No theory of complete German depravity squares with the complex facts of history."[83]

Niebuhr's other focus during the early stages of the war was to counter the certainty of religious figures that God's purposes were readily discernible. One theme that Niebuhr detected from individuals on both sides of the conflict was that God was punishing all of humanity for its lack of faith. Niebuhr considered this little more than a ploy to increase church attendance but, nevertheless, found such thoughts less harmful than the frequent claims from all combatants that God was on their side. Niebuhr observed, "The frank assertions of confidence in God's favoritism for a particular nation on the part of the belligerents . . . strike neutral ears with the unholy ring of hypocrisy."[84] The hypocrisy, in Niebuhr's mind, was that the hollow

---

[80] Dietrich Bonhoeffer, *A Testament to Freedom: The Essential Writings of Dietrich Bonhoeffer*, ed. Geffrey B. Kelly and F. Burton Nelson (New York: Harper One), 1995, pp. 479–80.

[81] Niebuhr, "Forward," n.d., Niebuhr Papers, Box 10. Details of the published work: *Dying We Live: The Final Messages and Records of the German Resistance*, ed. Helmut Gollwitzer, Kathe Kuhn, and Reinhold Schneider, introd. Reinhold Niebuhr (New York: Pantheon), 1956.

[82] Niebuhr, "Forward," n.d., Niebuhr Papers, Box 10.

[83] Niebuhr, "The Christian Faith and the German Problem," *The Student Movement*, October 1944, p. 8.

[84] Niebuhr, "The War and Religion," n.d., Niebuhr Papers, Box 17.

attempts of nations to enlist God's support in times of crisis rarely were followed by piety in the resultant times of peace and prosperity. Rather than look to God "as a ready ally for any end which man desires to attain," Niebuhr suggested that greater consideration be given to the "question whether the end is sufficiently moral and spiritual to be worthy of God's support."[85] Niebuhr frequently asserted that the aim of American Christians should not be to identify their purposes with God's will but be "of good conscience that our cause is in line with His righteousness."[86]

The result of Niebuhr's increased focus on America's self-right-eousness was a newfound tension in his writings during the war that was less evident in his earlier work. Niebuhr certainly continued to stress the justness of the Allied cause in combating the spread of totalitarianism across the globe. But he now appeared equally con-cerned, if not more so, with how America's own prejudices were having a detrimental effect on its conduct of the war. By way of clarification, Niebuhr stated that his position was not one of unques-tionable devotion to the "patriotic preoccupations of war-time"; nor, however, was it one of detached disregard for the immediate duties and urgencies the conflict required. Rather Niebuhr explained that his uniquely Christian approach was one that took positive elements of each in striving to be "in the battle and above it." As we already discussed in the introduction, Niebuhr elaborated:

> To be in a battle means to defend a cause against its peril, to protect a nation against its enemies, to strive for truth against error, to defend justice against injustice. To be above the battle means that we under-stand how imperfect the cause is which we defend, that we contritely acknowledge the sins of our own nations, that we recognize the common humanity which binds us to even the most terrible foes, and that we know also of our common need of grace and forgiveness.[87]

Niebuhr acknowledged that it was difficult to combine these two strategies but doing so was necessary. America not only had to worry about external threats but also the self-imposed damage that often occurred in its efforts to respond to acts of aggression. Niebuhr made clear that "[i]f a resolute foe seeks to rob us of our dignity as

[85] Niebuhr, "The War and Religion," n.d., Niebuhr Papers, Box 17.
[86] As found in Hulsether, *Building a Protestant Left*, p. 27.
[87] Niebuhr, "In the Battle and Above It," p. 3.

human beings, we might capitulate to his power if only we ourselves are involved in the degradation."[88] That said, the United States, in Niebuhr's estimation, would most clearly lose its dignity if it "allow [ed] the enslavement of our fellowmen."[89] While Niebuhr called for an equal emphasis on being both "in the battle and above it" in the article, his other writings of the period reveal his emphasis to be placed on the latter.

One important element lacking from Niebuhr's discussion of maintaining a view above the battle while remaining in its midst was how one was to achieve such a position. Niebuhr began to address this, however, in the summer of 1942 while rewriting the second set of Gifford Lectures. In an article entitled, "A Faith for History's Greatest Crisis," Niebuhr offered a preview of *Human Destiny* by presenting the Christian understanding of history as the only view "sufficiently profound to be able to transcend both the political and moral confusion and to give a vantage point from which the errors, which brought it on, can be corrected."[90] Niebuhr justified this, in part, by echoing his argument from *Beyond Tragedy* that only Christianity could acknowledge and move past a tragic view of history as a result of its belief in a divine mercy that redeemed this fallen world. That Christianity was able to derive its meaning beyond history enabled it, in Niebuhr's estimation, to offer the most profound perspective of what was occurring in history, especially in comparison to the purely progressive or tragic views. Indeed, Niebuhr explained that if the former viewed history as a "realm of infinite possibilities" and the latter "understood that all historic achievements are limited and precarious," the biblical viewpoint was unique in that it saw history as revealing both.[91] While the article did not elaborate on the exact means by which Christianity was better able to define the possibilities of human creativity in history along with the limits of human

[88] Niebuhr, "In the Battle and Above It," pp. 3–4.
[89] Niebuhr, "In the Battle and Above It," p. 4.
[90] Niebuhr, "A Faith for History's Greatest Crisis," *Fortune*, July 1942, p. 100.
[91] Niebuhr, "A Faith for History's Greatest Crisis," p. 131. Niebuhr offered his typical critique of the progressive view of history and the tragic view of history, but also included a discussion of what he called the Renaissance and Reformation intellectual movements from which each had developed. Developed in response to the teachings of the medieval Christian church, the Renaissance adopted a more optimistic approach to human nature and history while the Reformation took the diametrically opposite stance. This is precisely the same argument Niebuhr would make in *Human Destiny*.

possibility, it did provide the perfect segue to *Human Destiny*, in which Niebuhr would develop his argument in greater detail.

HUMAN DESTINY

Niebuhr commenced *Human Destiny* by asserting that an individual's view of history was a clear indicator of his general outlook on life because it encompassed the understanding of one's involvement in the historical process and the end to which he was striving. It was this latter point that most distinguished the Judeo-Christian religions from their secular alternatives in Niebuhr's estimation. Whereas the former regarded history "as potentially meaningful but . . . still awaiting the full disclosure and fulfillment of its meaning," the latter believed fulfillment to occur within history, as Niebuhr held to be the case with Marxism and its materialist viewpoint.[92] Niebuhr explained that a Christ was only expected when individuals became personally aware of problems which they themselves could not solve. In a return to the central theme in *Human Nature*, Niebuhr held that a predicament at the center of history was the need to distinguish between good and evil, on one hand, and to acknowledge the universal corruption of all humanity, on the other.[93] This tension, according to Niebuhr, formed an effective basis for the day-to-day business of history but fell apart when considering the broader question of its consummation. Given the universality of sin, Niebuhr concluded, "The final enigma of history is therefore not how the righteous will gain victory over the unrighteous, but how the evil in every good and the unrighteousness of the righteous is to be overcome."[94] In other words, Niebuhr wondered whether history's fulfillment could consist of anything more than widespread condemnation.

---

[92] Niebuhr, *Human Destiny*, p. 5.
[93] Niebuhr grounded this belief in competing strands of Jewish Messianic thought: one stating that the fulfillment of history would be the triumph of Israel over unrighteous nations, while the other holding that no nations, including Israel, would be deemed righteous given the pride and injustice common to all, *Human Destiny*, pp. 19–25.
[94] Niebuhr, *Human Destiny*, p. 44.

Niebuhr went on to argue that it could on the basis that "the consummation of history can only be in a divine mercy which makes something more of history than recurring judgment."[95] Two critical elements of Niebuhr's thinking come into focus in this assertion. First, only God could resolve the problem of how the "unrighteous in the righteous" could be overcome given the culpability of all humanity. Gilkey correctly identifies this avowal by Niebuhr as a radical shift on his part in that "the resolution of the problem [of history] is immediately taken quite out of human hands."[96] This is a particularly significant change in Niebuhr's thinking, especially compared to the fraternal debate a decade prior in which he viewed God as playing no role in history. Second, Niebuhr explained that God's solution to the problem of history was an act of mercy rather than one of power. This revelation was the result of the life, death, and resurrection of Jesus Christ that formed the basis of Christian faith. These events taught that the divine powerlessness of God, represented by Christ's suffering on the cross, was the only way universal sin could be overcome. If God had acted vengefully to redeem one group at the expense of another, Niebuhr believed it would have only perpetuated, rather than overcome, human unrighteousness. Instead, God showed mercy as well as judgment by assuming the iniquity of humanity on and in Himself. The "paradoxical vulnerability" of the suffering servant, in Niebuhr's opinion, not only revealed the true nature of history's fulfillment but also served to clarify its meaning. He explained, "[F]or the judgment of God preserves the distinction of good and evil in history; and the mercy of God finally overcomes the sinful corruption in which man is involved."[97]

The way in which God's divine mercy manifests itself in our individual lives, according to Niebuhr, is through grace. Placed in juxtaposition against the doctrine of sin that he had advanced in *Human Nature*, Niebuhr explained that God's grace ultimately breaks the egoistic and self-centered forms of fulfillment that plagues humanity. The process by which this happens has three distinct steps: first, the sinful self is "shattered" into repentance; second, it undergoes a justifying experience as a result of divine forgiveness by which

---

[95] Niebuhr, *Human Destiny*, p. 30.
[96] Gilkey, *On Niebuhr*, p. 177.
[97] Niebuhr, *Human Destiny*, p. 71.

it becomes a new self; third, the new self is sanctified in that it is divinely empowered toward the realization of its salvation.[98] Despite the justifying forgiveness and sanctifying empowerment of grace, Niebuhr believed an aspect of an individual's self-centeredness to persist throughout. This led him to describe the doctrine of grace as representing "the conquest of sin in the heart of man, on one hand, and the merciful power of God over the sin which is never entirely overcome in any human heart, on the other."[99] In more basic terms, Niebuhr was conveying that through grace "sin is overcome in principle but not in fact."[100] The fact that the self could experience complete renewal while remaining in sin was the paradox of divine mercy, which, according to Niebuhr, helped explain "Jesus' insistence that the righteous are not righteous before the divine judgment."[101]

Niebuhr's interest in preserving this paradox was more than academic. He explained that if human perfection was a reality and not an intention, the "Christian faith would be forced to accept a doctrine of divine determinism which would seem to imperil every sense of human responsibility."[102] Indeed, Niebuhr seemed generally aware that his "radical shift" in *Human Destiny* to asserting the complete dependence of humanity on God would raise questions about what responsibilities individuals then held in the temporal world. Perhaps with this in mind, he asserted emphatically that his conception of grace did not "destroy moral endeavor or responsibility," rather it "prevented the premature completion of life" and diffused the "intolerable pretensions of saints who have forgotten they are sinners."[103] In short, Niebuhr thought that only by eliminating self-centered pursuits of fulfillment and preventing against any pretense of perfectionism could one act responsibly. He reinforced this point in his discussion of how the failures to correctly understand the doctrine of grace were at the heart of the failure of contemporary understandings of history to account for the current global challenges. Returning to a point he made first in "A Faith for History's Crisis," Niebuhr explained that his interpretation enabled

---

[98] Niebuhr developed this formulation through what Brown calls an "existential explication" of Paul's Letter to the Galatians 2:20, "I am crucified with Christ: nevertheless I live; yet not I, but Christ liveth in me," as found in *Human Destiny*, p. 111.

[99] Niebuhr, *Human Destiny*, p. 104.

[100] Niebuhr, *Human Destiny*, p. 51.

[101] Niebuhr, *Human Destiny*, p. 131.

[102] Niebuhr, *Human Destiny*, p. 120.

[103] Niebuhr, *Human Destiny*, p. 130.

individuals to act because it appreciated both the possibilities of human creativity and limits of human possibility in history where alternative viewpoints could only accommodate one or the other.

Niebuhr attributed the view of history as uninterrupted progress that he perceived was held by many, including Dewey and other "secular moralists," to what he called the Renaissance intellectual tradition. Originating in the fourteenth century, this tradition adopted a sanctifying view of grace in its belief that humanity could approach its potential in history. Ultimately, the Renaissance denied the involvement of God in this process, choosing instead to place its trust in mankind's own creative abilities to realize greater and greater possibilities in history.[104] It was in response to this optimistic attitude, according to Niebuhr, that the Reformation's intellectual tradition arose to which Barth belonged. The tradition restored belief in human sinfulness and embraced a justifying view of grace that focused on God's forgiveness but did not account for his sanctifying empowerment of mankind. Niebuhr explained that while this approach assured individual salvation, it relaxed moral imperatives and resulted in a negative view of historical achievement.[105] Niebuhr believed

---

[104] As Niebuhr had in his writings prior to the war, he grouped some Protestants within this category because he believed them to share the Renaissance belief in the unlimited capacity of mankind. To the extent that such groups held a doctrine of grace it was one only of the empowering kind given their disregard for human sinfulness and, as a result, the need for divine forgiveness. Niebuhr explained that a "typical modern statement of this belief and hope" could be found in Dewey's writings, *Human Destiny*, p. 246, n. 1. Although Niebuhr did not elaborate on how Dewey's beliefs left him unable to cope with the events of World War II, he would likely have been aware of the practical difficulties the philosopher experienced. On the evening of the attack on Pearl Harbor, Dewey had been scheduled to give a talk on the implications of World War I. Before an audience eager to learn his impressions of America's imminent engagement in the current world conflict, Dewey was left to acknowledge to the disappointment of those in attendance, "I have nothing, had nothing, and have nothing now, to say directly about the war," as found in Diggins, *The Promise of Pragmatism*, p. 1.

[105] Despite Barth's forceful response to Nazi aggression, Niebuhr did not alter his belief that Barth's theology resulted in a "general indifference to problems of political justice," *Human Destiny*, p. 288. Indeed Niebuhr continued, "His strong emotional reaction to Nazi tyranny has, however, persuaded him to change his emphasis. He now criticizes the Reformation for having regarded government as an ordinance of divine providence without at the same time setting it under the judgment of God. Nevertheless the influence of the Reformation perspectives is so powerful in his thought that his doctrinal justification for his opposition to Nazi tyranny is hardly sufficient to explain that opposition," *Human Destiny*, pp. 288–9.

there were merits to the interpretations put forth by both traditions and sought to correct the "the one-sided blindness" of each by forming a synthesis founded on a justifying and sanctifying view of grace. He explained, "On one hand life in history must be recognized as filled with indeterminate possibilities . . . and the obligation to realize them. It means on the other hand that every effort and pretension to complete life . . . or to eliminate the final corruption of history, must be disallowed."[106]

Although Niebuhr did not specifically mention his "in the battle and above it" formulation, he did explain that this synthesis reinforced his appreciation of "the two-fold character of all historic political tasks and achievements."[107] On the one hand, Niebuhr explained the Renaissance tradition had strengthened his commitment to the pursuit of proximate solutions and instilled in him greater confidence that partial successes could be achieved. Perhaps nowhere was Niebuhr's newfound optimism more apparent than in his discussion of the democratic system in *Human Destiny*. In a significant departure from his previous writings, Niebuhr asserted that the system actually promoted community instead of pitting interested parties within it against each other and offered unique protections to the lower classes in society. Indeed, the task for the United States following the current crisis, according to Niebuhr, would be to expand the democratic "principles of order and justice to transcend nationalistic parochialism sufficiently to fashion a world community."[108] On the other hand, Niebuhr credited his realization

---

[106] Niebuhr, *Human Destiny*, p. 244. Niebuhr's synthesis of the Reformation and Renaissance in *Human Destiny* bears some resemblance to his efforts in the 1930s to find in Christian socialism or prophetic radicalism a compromise between more optimistic and pessimistic theological and political elements. But Niebuhr's discussion of both the creative and destructive elements in history in *Human Destiny* revealed a level of nuance lacking in his previous works. This can be attributed to Niebuhr's greater understanding of the creative and destructive elements in human nature perhaps resulting from his engagement with Kierkegaard's understanding of sin and his notion of anxiety in particular. Niebuhr took from Kierkegaard that "the same action may reveal a creative effort to transcend natural limitations, and a sinful effort to give unconditioned value to contingent and limited factors in human existence," *Human Nature*, p. 196. This may have clarified in Niebuhr's mind how humanity's most creative effort to transcend its natural limitations could stem from the same source as its "sinful effort to give unconditioned value to contingent and limited factors in human existence," p. 196.

[107] Niebuhr, *Human Destiny*, pp. 294–5.

[108] Niebuhr, *Human Destiny*, p. 318, n. 1.

that such efforts could only succeed if American leaders avoided the human tendency to attempt to fulfill history on its own as told by the Reformation tradition. Niebuhr explained that his synthesis taught him that while "history may move toward the realization of the Kingdom, the judgment of God is upon every new realization" with the final one occurring at history's culmination.[109] With a view informed by his understanding of the cross, Niebuhr held the Bible's foretelling of the Second Coming of Christ and a Last Judgment did confirm the distinction between good and evil in history; however, the continued ubiquity of mankind's sinfulness ultimately revealed that God's completion of history could only be through another act of divine mercy.[110]

Reviews of *Human Destiny* lauded its "concern for due qualification and balance," especially compared to the more adversarial *Human Nature.*[111] What such observations seemed to confirm was Niebuhr's shift of emphasis in the second volume of his Gifford Lectures from a position more in the battle to one above the fray.[112] The shift, while noticeable, was by no means complete, as was also revealed by the work's reception. While many critics were complimentary of Niebuhr's "complex and subtle" discussion of grace, William Wolf, for one, expressed concern with the observation in *Human Destiny* that "sin is overcome in principle but not in fact."[113] Specifically, Wolf wondered whether such a formulation diminished the significant victory over sin brought about by Christ's suffering on the

[109]   Niebuhr, *Human Destiny*, p. 296.

[110]   See, on this point, Douglas John Hall, "'The Logic of the Cross': Niebuhr's Foundational Theology," in Rice, ed., *Reinhold Niebuhr Revisited*, pp. 62–74. Hall portrays Niebuhr's theology as primarily focused on the cross and goes further to argue that Niebuhr's "theology of the cross" is evidence of Luther's influence on his thought.

[111]   Robert Calhoun, "Review of *Human Destiny*," *Union Seminary Journal of Religion*, 24 (January 1944), p. 59; Joseph Haroutunian, "Review of *Human Destiny*," *Christianity and Society*, 8 (Spring 1943), pp. 36–9; John C. Bennett, "Human Destiny—Reinhold Niebuhr", *The Union Review*, 6:2 (March 1943), pp. 24–6.

[112]   Fox takes a different view in asserting, "The detached tone may have been an effort to accommodate the academic reviewers who had disparaged the aggressiveness of *Human Nature*. Perhaps too it was the product of repetition: Niebuhr had been restating these ideas for many years and may have had trouble mustering the dynamism of first discovery," *Reinhold Niebuhr*, p. 213. These explanations seem unsatisfactory, especially the second, given Fox's own assertion of the significant amount of new material that Niebuhr did cover in *Human Destiny*.

[113]   William J. Wolf, "Reinhold Niebuhr's Doctrine of Man," in Kegley and Bretall, eds, *Reinhold Niebuhr*, pp. 244–5.

cross. Niebuhr acknowledged this criticism and later agreed that the formulation did not do justice to "the fact there is sin in the life of the redeemed."[114] He attributed this mistake, as with his formulation of the equality of sin and the inequality of guilt in *Human Nature*, to an overarching effort to preserve the need for Christians to make responsible choices in history.[115] If this effort appears to be less central to *Human Destiny* than in *Human Nature*, a desire to preserve humanity's position "in the battle" deeply influenced the direction of Niebuhr's theological beliefs in both works.

Niebuhr's confidence in his country to be a responsible actor on the world stage increased significantly on the basis of what he perceived to be its successful mobilization to stem the Nazi tide. As a result, he took the opportunity in *Human Destiny* to outline the singular role the United States should assume following the cessation of hostilities. Subsequent events in 1943, such as the success of the Anglo-American forces in driving Germany out of North Africa and Sicily, only confirmed Niebuhr's impression that the first test of America's "coming of age," would be its treatment of its soon-to-be vanquished foe. If Niebuhr had previously called upon his fellow countrymen to treat Germany with magnanimity, his advocacy on this front toward the end of the war reflected his greater optimism toward America. Niebuhr asserted that the country's moral and political ideals were far more virtuous than any country, Germany especially, but any efforts to exact justice from its defeated foe following the cessation of hostilities would only obscure the divine judgment to be rendered on both the vanquished and the victor.[116] In this vein, Niebuhr encouraged the United States to acknowledge its own iniquities and recognize that its present prosperity was more the result of God's grace than any virtue on its part. Only by adopting an attitude of contrition could the United States' unparalleled global position following the war be one that "ceases to be a vehicle of pride and becomes the occasion for a new sense of responsibility."[117] A failure to adopt such a viewpoint, in

---

[114] Niebuhr, "Reply to Interpretation and Criticism," p. 437.

[115] Niebuhr, "Reply to Interpretation and Criticism," p. 437.

[116] See Niebuhr, "The German Problem," *Christianity and Crisis*, January 10, 1944, pp. 2–4; Niebuhr, "Soberness in Victory," *Christianity and Crisis*, May 28, 1945, pp. 1–2; and Niebuhr, "The Vengeance of Victors," *Christianity and Crisis*, November 26, 1945, pp. 1–2.

[117] Niebuhr, "Anglo-Saxon Destiny and Responsibility," *Christianity and Crisis*, October 4, 1943, p. 3.

Niebuhr's estimation, would only "bring judgment upon both us and the world."[118]

Niebuhr would build upon his reflections in *Human Destiny* on America's newfound responsibilities in a series of lectures at Stanford University in January 1944, which he published later that year under the title of *The Children of Light and the Children of Darkness*. The short book is primarily remembered today as the clearest expression of Niebuhr's political theory and for the oft-quoted aphorism, "Man's capacity for justice makes democracy possible; but man's inclination for injustice makes democracy necessary."[119] For the purposes of this work, however, its importance rests in Niebuhr's willingness to explicitly connect the theological arguments he advanced in *Human Nature* and *Human Destiny* to the looming challenge of how the United States should approach its mission of organizing the world for peace. Given the enormity of this commitment, Niebuhr made clear that the only prospect for success was if the country's leaders undertook this effort armed with the "indispensable resources" of the faith. What made the Christian standpoint unique, according to Niebuhr, was that it "understands the fragmentary and broken character of all historic achievements and yet has confidence in their meaning, because it knows their completion to be in the hands of a Divine power . . . whose suffering love can overcome the corruptions of man's achievements without negating the significance of our striving."[120] Without such a basis, Niebuhr was clear that the advancements and frustrations that would inevitably accompany such an effort would lead individuals into "alternate moods of sentimentality and despair."[121] As will become clear in the next two chapters, Niebuhr cast the results of adopting his ironic viewpoint without accepting his Christian presuppositions in remarkably similar terms.

The extent to which the United States was capable of "bringing ruin upon itself and the world" was made clear at the close of World War II with its August 1945 atomic bombing of Hiroshima and Nagasaki. Niebuhr could only surmise, "If ever a nation needed to be reminded of the perils of vainglory, we are that nation in the pride of our power

---

[118] Niebuhr, "Anglo-Saxon Destiny and Responsibility," p. 3.
[119] Niebuhr, *Children of Light and Darkness*, p. vi.
[120] Niebuhr, *Children of Light and Darkness*, p. 128.
[121] Niebuhr, *Children of Light and Darkness*, p. 128.

and of our victory."[122] Nevertheless, Niebuhr supported President Truman's decision, and the reasons he did so, in particular, highlighted a tension that was evident in his writings on the Allied effort throughout the war. Niebuhr may have continuously issued warnings from "above the battle" of the moral degradations associated with "the perils of vainglory," but, in practical terms, he sanctioned degrading acts throughout the war, such as the firebombing of the German towns of Dresden and Hamburg that killed an estimated 100,000 civilians. Niebuhr clearly struggled with these policies and made a strong case that the targeting of civilian households be minimized. Ultimately, however, he largely supported such bombing campaigns for two main considerations. The first was "in order to hasten [the war's] end" while the second was that "once bombing has been developed as an instrument of warfare it is not possible to disavow its use without capitulating to the foe who refuses to disavow it."[123] Whether Niebuhr's support of these policies was justified is open to debate, but his reasons for doing so seemed uncharacteristically weak. By citing the duration and means of enemy resistance as main considerations in determining the morality of Allied policies, Niebuhr seemed dangerously close to absolving Allied leaders of the very moral accountability he claimed to value in wartime leaders.

Niebuhr's struggles to respond effectively to the Allied bombing campaigns run parallel to those he experienced in determining the extent of American military involvement prior to Pearl Harbor, in that each situation represents the challenges he faced in translating his overall outlook into specific policy advice.[124] That he had

---

[122] Niebuhr, "Our Relations to Japan," *Christianity and Crisis*, September 17, 1945, p. 7.

[123] Niebuhr, "Our Relations to Japan," p. 5; "The Bombing of Germany," *Christianity and Society*, 3 (Summer 1943), pp. 3–4. Although "The Bombing of Germany" article is an unsigned editorial piece, its tone and content indicate that Niebuhr was the likely author. See Hulsether, *Building a Protestant Left*, p. 28 for more discussion of Niebuhr's largely unflinching support for U.S. military tactics.

[124] See, on this point, Haas, "Reinhold Niebuhr's 'Christian Pragmatism'," p. 625. Haas explains, "[W]hile to Niebuhr the regulative principles of justice were to be applied pragmatically . . . , they were to be derived deontologically. Though pragmatic concerns would necessarily limit the application of these principles, one's ultimate goals and means were to be guided by a transcendent standard. The qualitative difference between a strategy that attempts to apply deontologically derived principles in a pragmatic fashion and a strategy in which actions are determined solely with regard to ends should be clear. In the former, a transcendent standard of morality is believed to be normative, in the latter, prudence is elevated to the normative level,"

difficulties should not detract from that uniquely profound outlook, namely, that of remaining in and above the battle—with emphasis on the former before America's involvement, and on the latter thereafter. The contextualized analysis of *Human Nature* and *Human Destiny* alongside his journalistic writings of the period reveals just how effective Niebuhr was at both developing theologically and asserting politically his belief in the need to make partial judgments in history while remembering humanity's universal sinfulness before God. Nevertheless, when Niebuhr was most assertive in the need for the United States to make a partial judgment and protect the future of Western civilization from Hitler's advances, his specific suggestion was a half measure. Likewise, when Niebuhr was most decided of the common sinfulness shared between the United States and all combatants, he appeared willing to countenance dubious actions on the part of his own country. Such criticisms may be unfair given the extent to which Niebuhr was immersed in the conflict. Nevertheless, they are important, as the next chapter will reveal Niebuhr growing less interested in the theological foundations of his beliefs and more interested in their practical application.

p. 625. This was true of Niebuhr in most cases but fails to account for some of Niebuhr's actions during World War II when it appears he was swayed by events, not his "in the battle and above it" disposition. I agree with Haas's point that Niebuhr was not a consequentialist. Nevertheless, Haas fails to acknowledge the degree to which Niebuhr failed to live up to his own principles, whether in the case of U.S. entry into the war or in his response to the Allied bombing campaigns.

3

Discerning the Signs of the Times:
The Relevance of Niebuhr's Theological
Vision to the Cold War

In the last chapter we observed Niebuhr, in *Human Nature* and *Human Destiny*, developing his Christian understanding of history and then, most notably in his journalistic writings, using that understanding to interpret the events of World War II. The specific way that Niebuhr connected his theological beliefs to the contemporary problems facing humanity was through his "in the battle and above it" viewpoint. This chapter details the five years following the war, during which Niebuhr, with his theological foundation largely in place, almost exclusively focused on conveying the relevance of his Christian viewpoint to contemporary challenges, in particular the rise of the Soviet Union. This shift of emphasis is best seen in Niebuhr's *Discerning the Signs of the Times*, a collection of sermonic essays published in 1946 that has been largely overlooked by the majority of commentators.[1] Whereas Niebuhr acknowledged that his priority since the 1930s had been to develop a Christian interpretation of the meaning of history, his attention in *Discerning* was now on "the judgments we make" on the basis of "our interpretation of the meaning of history."[2] In the words of theologian Robert Fitch,

---

[1] Similar in format to *Beyond Tragedy*, *Discerning* has been largely ignored in Niebuhr scholarship, receiving scant attention in the three most prominent full-length works on Niebuhr's life. Fox and Stone fail to mention *Discerning*, while Brown only dedicates half a page to the work, *Niebuhr and his Age*, p. 132. *Discerning* was certainly noticed in Niebuhr's own time, as it was reviewed in *Time* magazine, "Religion: Niebuhr v. Sin," *Time*, April 29, 1946. As we shall see in the next chapter, *Discerning* plays a key role in revealing how Niebuhr's theological vision underpinned *Irony*.

[2] Niebuhr, *Discerning*, p. 10.

Niebuhr believed his mission during this period was no longer to be a "thinker who is speculating about history" but increasingly to be "the man of action operating in and upon history."[3] A key element of Niebuhr's efforts to operate in and upon history was to reach as broad an audience as possible. He explained as much in an article published in *Crisis* at the end of the war that set out to redefine the mission of the journal. Niebuhr acknowledged that, in the past, the inter-religious disputes which had "prompted the founding of [*Crisis*] . . . may have occasionally engrossed us too much."[4] Going forward, his focus would also be on communicating the unique insights of the faith to "Christians and non-Christians" alike. Numerous commentators have documented Niebuhr's efforts to engage with more secular audiences in the 1940s and 1950s, the most perceptive being Rasmussen, who notes Niebuhr increasingly wrote for non-theological journals and built strong relationships with policy-makers during this time.[5] This concerted effort on Niebuhr's part led to a significant increase in his popular notoriety, best evidenced by *Time* magazine's designating him "the No. 1 theologian of U.S. Protestantism."[6] During this period of growing tensions in American relations with Communist Russia, Niebuhr communicated to the political establishment a series of views that he explained could only be derived from an appreciation of the sinfulness of human beings and, in particular, how that sinfulness biased all historical judgments. It is no coincidence that Niebuhr became increasingly concerned with questions of his own objectivity as he became involved in the formulation of national policy as a result of his increased public stature and involvement with important officials at the U.S. State Department.

Niebuhr also established during this period that his writings on contemporary events were useful beyond their policy prescriptions. They also had an important apologetic purpose. Showing how Christianity was capable of revealing "unique insights . . . to the enlightenment of our generation" was precisely the "reaffirmation of the faith . . . that could regain the loyalty of the

---

[3] Robert Fitch, "Reinhold Niebuhr's Philosophy of History," in Kegley and Bretall, eds, *Reinhold Niebuhr*, p. 293.

[4] Niebuhr, "The Christian Perspective on the World Crisis," *Christianity and Crisis*, May 1, 1944, p. 2.

[5] See Rasumssen, *Reinhold Niebuhr*, p. 3.

[6] "Religion: Niebuhr v. Sin."

multitudes."[7] This shift in focus was clear in *Faith and History*, published in 1949.[8] In the work's preface he explained his goal was to reach those for whom the recent global turmoil had "refuted the modern faith in the redemptive character of history itself."[9] A failure to realize the increased priority Niebuhr placed on this segment of the population has led many commentators to dismiss *Faith and History* as merely a reiteration of Niebuhr's previous work. Fox goes so far as to interpret its unoriginality as a sign of Niebuhr's "physical fatigue and intellectual stagnation."[10] While Niebuhr's description of his Christian interpretation of history in *Faith and History* was virtually identical to that which he had established in *Human Destiny*, he did place a far greater emphasis on those aspects that might have the greatest appeal to non-believers. Moreover, Niebuhr's increased popular standing since the publication of his Gifford Lectures meant while much of the material in *Faith and History* may have appeared banal to his loyal readership, it was new to many.[11] If Niebuhr's effort to relate the Christian faith to the problems of the age increased his stature among the political elites, it raised suspicions among Niebuhr's theological peers. At the center of their critique over whether Niebuhr's approach was too accommodating was his continued inability to offer an adequate description of biblical symbols

[7] Niebuhr, "The Religious Level of the World Crisis," *Christianity and Crisis*, January 21, 1946, p. 5. See also Niebuhr, "Which Question Comes First for the Church?" as found in *Essays in Applied Christianity: The Church and the New World*, ed. D. B. Robertson (New York: Meridian, 1959), p. 88.

[8] Reinhold Niebuhr, *Faith and History: A Comparison of the Christian and Modern Views of History* (London: Nisbet, 1949).

[9] Niebuhr, *Faith and History*, p. v.

[10] Fox, *Reinhold Niebuhr*, p. 237. For contemporary criticism in this vein see Daniel Jenkins, "Review of *Faith and History*," *Union Seminary Quarterly Review*, 4 (May 1949), pp. 51–2. Niebuhr did not deny the similarities between *Faith and History* and *Human Destiny*, explaining that the former was "but an elaboration of the second part of my Gifford Lectures." Niebuhr, "Intellectual Autobiography," p. 9. Nevertheless he was clear that his audience for the message was changing.

[11] Stone, in particular, argues that the work was intended for a "theologically educated readership," thus failing to account for the number of more secular individuals that were starting to read Niebuhr's work for the first time. *Professor Reinhold Niebuhr*, p. 189. One of his more prominent new readers was historian Arthur Schlesinger, Jr., who explained in a review, "The distinction of [Niebuhr's] analysis is his success in restating Christian insights with such irresistible relevance to contemporary experience that even those who have no decisive faith in the supernatural find their own reading of experience and history given new and significant dimensions," "Review of *Faith and History*," *Christianity and Society* (Summer 1949), p. 27.

such as the crucifixion and resurrection. While he held them central to his Christian interpretation of history, he nevertheless refused to address them in detail out of concern over alienating the very audience most in need of this interpretation. As we will see in the next chapter, this dilemma looms over *Irony*, as it did in Niebuhr's writings immediately prior to its publication.

ILLUSIONS OF HISTORY AND THE SIGNS OF THE TIMES

The first significant evidence of Niebuhr's shifting focus following World War II can be seen in the publication of *Discerning the Signs of the Times*, a collection of sermons and talks he had delivered throughout 1945. Niebuhr's explanation of the title—"to discern the signs of the times means to interpret historical events"—revealed the work to be a practical application of his Christian interpretation of history.[12] This much was also made clear in the opening page of the work in which Niebuhr explained its theme to be the "special relevance" of the Christian faith to an "age confronted with so many possibilities ... but also confronting so many frustrations."[13] Niebuhr began his inquiry by explaining that the most useful contribution of Christianity was the understanding that human sin undermined every historical judgment. He believed this was "due not to a defect of the mind in calculating the course of history; but to a corruption of the heart, which introduced the confusion of selfish pride."[14] This understanding, according to Niebuhr, stood in stark contrast to the prevailing view of modern culture that the pursuit of objectivity was a fundamentally intellectual endeavor that could be readily achieved. Niebuhr placed the blame for this viewpoint squarely on the shoulders of his old nemesis, John Dewey, and his naturalist beliefs that the "objectivity of which the natural sciences boasts may be transferred

[12] Niebuhr took the title of the work from Matthew 16:1–3, a passage in which the Pharisees and Sadducees came to Jesus determined to test his messianic claims by demanding he perform a miracle. Jesus condemned them for the faithlessness that such a request revealed and questioned, "O ye hypocrites ... can ye not discern the sign of the times?" *Discerning*, p. 9.
[13] Niebuhr, *Discerning*, p. 8.   [14] Niebuhr, *Discerning*, p. 11.

to all historical, political and social judgments."[15] In contrast to this view, Niebuhr explained that the first step in developing a useful vantage point to understand history was acknowledging the impossibility of becoming completely detached. It was for this reason that Niebuhr believed the struggle was fundamentally one of faith. As he concluded, "The highest degree of objectivity and impartiality in the assessment of historical values is achieved by a quality of religious humility, which gains awareness of the unconscious dishonesty of judgment and seeks to correct it."[16] Such correction could only come with the acceptance that all humanity stood under a more ultimate judgment and was equally in need of God's divine mercy.

The ties between Niebuhr's discussion of objectivity in *Discerning* and his elaboration of the "above the battle" perspective he had developed in the past is clear. As we discussed in the last chapter, Niebuhr described the viewpoint as recognizing "the common humanity which binds us to even the most terrible of foes, and that we know also of our common need of grace and forgiveness."[17] The parallels become even more evident when Niebuhr turned his attention in *Discerning* to present affairs and, specifically, the challenges the United States faced in the post-war era. Niebuhr argued that the ever-increasing power of his country as a result of its nuclear capabilities made it even more critical that all its citizens realize the prejudices inherent in historical judgments. This resulted from the fact that "[a] nation which has the power to annihilate other nations does not achieve, as a concomitant of that power, the transcendent wisdom which would make it the safe custodian of such power."[18] In keeping with the theme of the work, Niebuhr argued that the proper management of such apocalyptic weaponry would not come down to "shrewd political intelligence," but rather was ultimately dependent upon the ability of America's political leaders to develop an outlook informed by religious humility.[19] Central to achieving this perspective, according to Niebuhr, was the realization that "it is not so much an

---

[15] Niebuhr, *Discerning*, p. 12. The main difference between assessments of nature and history, in Niebuhr's estimation, was the degree to which mankind was inextricably intertwined in the latter. He explained, "When we behold not a flower or star...but the course of human history, we are part of the drama we seek to comprehend," Niebuhr, *Discerning*, p. 14.

[16] Niebuhr, *Discerning*, p. 12.

[17] Niebuhr, "In the Battle and Above It," p. 3.

[18] Niebuhr, *Discerning*, p. 65.   [19] Niebuhr, *Discerning*, p. 66.

achievement as it is a gift of grace, a by-product of the faith which discerns life in its total dimension and senses the divine judgment which stands above and against all human judgments."[20]

Discerning certainly represented Niebuhr's clearest explanation of how his Christian interpretation of history could be made directly relevant to the contemporary age. That said, given the content of the work was extracted from writings during the war, it did not address the issue quickly emerging at its conclusion, namely, how to respond to the growing belligerency of the Soviet Union.[21] Niebuhr's journalistic writings during this period did, however, and reveal him struggling once more with how to remain above the battle. Niebuhr certainly noted Russian attempts to disrupt Europe's post-war reorganization by maintaining its sphere of influence in the East and expanding its reach into the war-ravaged countries of the West. He found particularly disconcerting Stalin's efforts to impose Communist regimes in Romania and Poland despite his agreements to the contrary with Britain and the United States.[22] Nevertheless, Niebuhr attempted to be as impartial as possible in his assessment of Soviet aggression by encouraging his readers to appreciate that just as America feared Russia was trying to dominate Europe, Russia likely feared the potential of American dominance on the continent. Indeed, Niebuhr continued to remind his readership of "the Russian fear that we intend to dominate Europe" and, above all, cautioned, "However

---

[20]   Niebuhr, *Discerning*, p. 67.

[21]   The literature on the origins of the Cold War is vast; nevertheless, there are select works that I relied upon in my analysis of the period: John Lewis Gaddis, *Strategies of Containment: A Critical Appraisal of American National Security Policy During the Cold War* (Oxford: Oxford University Press, 2005); John Lewis Gaddis, *The Long Peace: Inquiries into the History of the Cold War* (Oxford: Oxford University Press, 1987); Melvin P. Leffler, *The Specter of Communism: The United States and the Origins of the Cold War, 1917–1953* (New York: Hill & Wang, 2002); and Walter LeFeber, *America, Russia and the Cold War, 1945–2006*, 10th edn. (New York: McGraw-Hill, 2008).

[22]   While the United States had pushed for free elections in Poland, Stalin would allow no more than three pro-Western representatives in the eighteen-member provisional government, LaFeber, *America, Russia and the Cold War*, p. 17. After learning of Soviet intransigence with regard to elections and, moreover, its intention to sign a treaty of mutual assistance with its hand-picked Polish provisional government in April 1945, President Harry S. Truman admonished Russian Foreign Minister Vyacheslav Molotov, thereby providing, in Gaddis's estimation, an early signal of a "Getting tough with Russia" policy that would underscore future interactions with the country, *The United States and the Origins of the Cold War, 1941–1947* (New York: Columbia University Press, 1972), p. 206.

vexatious [Russia's] dictatorship,...we are not dealing with the moral cynicism of Nazism nor with conscious design of aggression."[23] Niebuhr's conciliatory views were challenged by Stalin's increasingly aggressive rhetoric in the opening months of 1946. The dictator warned in a fiery election speech of the splitting of the world into "hostile camps" and the likelihood of war.[24] A month later Winston Churchill gave his famous "Iron Curtain" address on the campus of Westminster College in Fulton, Missouri. While stopping short of predicting that war between the Soviets and the West was near, he argued that the former desired "all the fruits of war and the indefinite expansion of their powers and doctrines."[25] If Churchill's speech alerted the American public to the potential of future conflict with the Soviet Union, it was a cable from George Kennan, then deputy head of the U.S. mission on Moscow, a few weeks later that had a more chilling effect on government officials. In what Henry Kissinger described as "one of those rare embassy reports that would by itself reshape Washington's view of the word," Kennan's "Long Telegram" argued that the post-war U.S. policy of accommodation toward the Soviet Union was misguided because it was predicated on the incorrect notion that the Soviet Union, like other nations, was responsive to external influences.[26] Going against the prevailing wisdom, Kennan explained that the Soviet leaders would not "yield entirely to any form of rational persuasion or assurance" on the part of the United States and actually had an interest in maintaining the perception of an external threat to maintain internal legitimacy.[27] While the

[23] Niebuhr, "Russia and the Peace," *Christianity and Crisis*, November 13, 1944, pp. 8–9.
[24] Joseph Stalin, *Speech Delivered by Joseph Stalin at a Meeting of Voters of the Stalin Electoral Area of Moscow, 9 February 1946*, as found in LaFeber, *America, Russia and the Cold War*, p. 44.
[25] Winston Churchill, "Mr. Churchill's Address Calling for United Effort for World Peace: TRUMAN AND CHURCHILL IN MISSOURI," *The New York Times*, March 6, 1946, p. 4.
[26] Henry Kissinger, *Diplomacy* (New York: Simon & Schuster, 1995), p. 447. Gaddis describes the approach of the United States toward the Soviet Union immediately following World War II as one of "quid pro quo." In exchange for economic aid and political concessions, such as with Poland, policy-makers in the United States had expected concessions from the Soviets in return. Kennan's telegram, according to Gaddis, explains in plain terms why the "quid pro quo strategy had not worked," *Strategies of Containment*, pp. 18–21.
[27] Kennan to the State Department, February 22, 1946, U.S. Department of State, *Foreign Relations of the United States: Eastern Europe, the Soviet Union, 1946*, Vol. VI (Washington, D.C.: U.S. Department of State, 1969), p. 723.

"Long Telegram" did not offer conclusive suggestions as to what actions the United States should take, it laid the foundation for the policy of containment that Kennan would help develop and that would define the U.S. approach toward the Soviet Union for the next thirty years.[28]

As tensions between America and the Soviet Union continued to increase over the summer months, Niebuhr came to terms with the growing rift between the two countries and adopted a harder line. The extreme rhetoric of Soviet leaders and the country's continued aggression in Eastern Europe led him to make the very connection between Communist Russia and Nazi Germany he had previously taken pains to avoid. The United States, in Niebuhr's opinion, was once more in a "conflict between justice and injustice, or at least between freedom and totalitarianism."[29] He continued, "I do not see how it can be denied that the distinctions between Russian morality and our own are valid."[30] It should not come as a surprise that viewing the current conflict through the lens of the one recently completed led Niebuhr to resurrect the "in the battle and above it" formulation that had defined his thinking during World War II. With reference to the emerging Cold War, Niebuhr observed, "The Bible never denies that there are significant conflicts between good and evil forces in history between just and unjust nations" but he also acknowledged, "these distinctions did not prevent the prophets from understanding that there was a profounder conflict between all nations and God."[31] Given the official irreligiosity of the Soviet Union, however, Niebuhr argued that the American people had the greater capability and, thus, greater responsibility to mitigate their sinful tendencies. It was up to Christians such as himself to "insinuate

---

[28] George F. Kennan, "The Sources of Soviet Conduct," *Foreign Affairs*, 25:4 (July 1947), pp. 566–82. Kennan introduced the public to the need for "a long-term, patient but firm and vigilant" policy of containment to halt the spread of Soviet Communism. He explained, "Soviet pressure against the free institutions of the western world is something that can be contained by the adroit and vigilant application of counter-force at series of constantly shifting geographical and political points . . . ," p. 576.

[29] Niebuhr, "The Conflict Between Nations and Nations and Between Nations and God," *Christianity and Crisis*, August 5, 1946, p. 3.

[30] Niebuhr, "The Conflict Between Nations and Nations and Between Nations and God," p. 3.

[31] Niebuhr, "The Conflict Between Nations and Nations and Between Nations and God," p. 2.

something of this ultimate perspective into the competing and contradictory judgements of men and nations."[32]

Niebuhr's own efforts at this were tested by a five-week trip he took to Germany in 1946 as a part of a U.S. State Department delegation to examine the educational system being developed in the American zone of occupation.[33] In travels that took him to universities throughout Bavaria and ultimately to Berlin, Niebuhr came to realize the extent to which the Soviets were attempting to impose Communist rule not only in their area of occupation but throughout all of Germany. He was dismayed to discover, for instance, that the Russians had removed the railroad tracks connecting the American zone of occupation with the section of Berlin under its control to limit the transport of supplies and people to and from the capital city. The widespread suffering of the German population, moreover, which Niebuhr attributed to the inability of American authorities to restore economic health to the areas under their control, was only increasing the likelihood that Communism would overrun the country.[34] In a dispatch from Berlin published in the middle of his trip, Niebuhr warned, "As a divided Germany sinks into economic misery, Russia hopes to conquer her ideologically by attributing this misery to capitalistic exploitation."[35] Niebuhr's experience on the front lines did much to solidify in his mind the extent of Soviet ambitions in Europe and marked the official repudiation of his former belief that the U.S. had a minimal role to play in curbing them.

If Niebuhr had previously been preoccupied with preventing the United States from rushing headlong into another conflict in Europe, he became more concerned that his country was not prepared to do enough on the continent during his time in Germany. Specifically, Niebuhr was influenced by a highly publicized speech made by Henry Wallace, a high-level official in the Truman administration. In

---

[32] Niebuhr, "The Conflict Between Nations and Nations and Between Nations and God," p. 4.

[33] Niebuhr, in a posthumously published 1973 article reflecting on his time in Germany, explained the purpose of the mission: "We tried unsuccessfully to democratize the German universities and to persuade the German educational authorities to make less rigorous distinctions as early as the twelfth year of a child's life between those who would prepare for university in a 'gymnasium' and those who were fated to be the hewers of wood and the drawers of water," "Germany," *Worldview*, 16:6 (June 1973), p. 18, as found in Niebuhr Papers, Box 16.

[34] Niebuhr, "Will Germany Go Communist?," *The Nation*, October 5, 1946, p. 372.

[35] Niebuhr, "The Fight for Germany," *Life*, October 21, 1946, p. 67.

response to the increased hostility he perceived between the United States and Russia, Wallace set forth a vision for how the two countries could coexist peacefully. One condition he suggested was that the United States should not interfere with Soviet involvement in Eastern Europe. With regard to Germany he advocated a quick reunification of the country but failed to address how this could be accomplished in a way agreeable to the occupying powers. Overall, rather than categorizing the Soviet Union as a threat to the United States, Wallace explained that the two could live under "peaceful competition" and hoped the two would even "gradually become more alike."[36] Although this position was not much different from that which Niebuhr had expressed a mere three years prior, he now reacted quite harshly.[37] This was in part because Niebuhr was still in Berlin when news of the address reached Germany. He had the opportunity to observe how it was used for the purposes of propaganda by the Soviet authorities as well as the "disappointment and dismay" it caused amongst democratic forces in the country.[38]

Niebuhr, upon his return to the United States, offered a more comprehensive account of his new views in an article published in *Life* magazine, "The Fight for Germany." In his harshest language yet toward the Russians, Niebuhr argued that its leadership would not be content until it had brought the entirety of Europe under its control. Discussing the similarities with Nazism, Niebuhr explained, "The actual tyranny which has emerged and the fanatic fury which has been generated by [Soviet] illusions are unfortunately not distinguishable" from the previous scourge that had swept across Europe.[39]

---

[36] As quoted in Graham White and John Maze, *Henry A. Wallace: His Search for a New World Order* (Chapel Hill, NC: University of North Carolina Press, 1995), p. 228 and LeFeber, *America, Russia and the Cold War*, p. 50.

[37] As late as 1943 Niebuhr struck a conciliatory tone toward the Soviet Union not altogether different from Wallace's approach. Niebuhr observed, "Ideally a collaboration between the Communist and the democratic world might lead to a wholesome exchange of political experience . . . We have, on the whole, more liberty and less equality than Russia has. Russia has less liberty and more equality. Whether democracy should be defined primarily in terms of liberty or equality is a source of unending debate." Niebuhr, "Russia and the West," *The Nation*, January 23, 1943, p. 83. The uproar with which Wallace's speech was met by political and journalistic classes in America and his subsequent forced resignation shortly thereafter revealed, according to Walter LaFeber, "the distance American policy had moved since the close of World War II." LaFeber, *America, Russia and the Cold War*, p. 51.

[38] Niebuhr, "The Fight for Germany," p. 65.

[39] Niebuhr, "The Fight for Germany," p. 72.

Echoing his critique from the late 1930s of the inability of "moral illusionists" to appreciate the Nazi threat, Niebuhr categorized the notion of peaceful coexistence offered by Wallace as "refusing to contemplate the tragic aspects of human existence honestly."[40] Niebuhr went so far as to argue that Communist Russia now posed a greater threat to the West than Nazi Germany for the very reason that had led him to believe the opposite only a short while ago. That Russian ideology was less heinous than Hitler's creation was certain; nevertheless, the fact that well-intentioned individuals such as Wallace held a rose-tinted view of Moscow's intentions proved that "this new tyranny is not only unscrupulous but possesses the guile to exploit our moral and political weaknesses."[41] In what appeared an afterthought to his dire warning about the extent of the Soviet threat, Niebuhr attempted to inject a small dose of the "ultimate perspective" that had previously dominated his thinking. He urged his fellow countrymen "to avoid hysteria even while we abjure sentimental illusions" in the midst of this complicated international picture.[42]

Niebuhr's forceful words had a resounding effect on the American public. Perhaps the main reason for this was the fact that so many of them read his article, or at least a portion of it. As opposed to *Crisis* with its circulation of a few thousand, *Life* magazine was the most popular weekly magazine in America with around four million copies sold each week.[43] Moreover, Niebuhr's message was a perfect fit for the magazine given the strong anti-Communist views of its editor-in-chief, Henry Luce. Not content to let Niebuhr's words speak for themselves, Luce and his editorial team added the provocative subtitle to his piece: "A distinguished theologian declares America must prevent the conquest of Germany and Western Europe by the unscrupulous Soviet tyranny."[44] Luce saw so much potential in Niebuhr's article to advance his political views that he decided to run the most confrontational excerpts from Niebuhr's article in another major magazine under his editorial control, *Time*. As a result, five million more Americans were exposed to "The Fight for Germany" without the concluding paragraph where Niebuhr had urged his

---

[40] Niebuhr, "The Fight for Germany," p. 72.
[41] Niebuhr, "The Fight for Germany," p. 72.
[42] Niebuhr, "The Fight for Germany," p. 72.
[43] Loudon Wainwright, *The Great American Magazine: An Insider History of Life* (New York: Knopf, 1986), p. 141.
[44] Niebuhr, "The Fight for Germany," p. 65.

fellow countrymen to "avoid hysteria."[45] This abridged version was then condensed further for publication in *Reader's Digest*, a widely popular bi-weekly magazine with a similar ideological stance to *Time* and *Life*, which held the distinction of being the highest circulation general interest magazine in the United States.[46] With one article, Niebuhr had launched himself to national prominence as an even more powerful critic of the Soviet Union than he had perhaps intended.[47]

Niebuhr likely realized that his writings had actually contributed to the very "hysteria" he had warned against, and, as a result, tried to restore balance in his subsequent writings.[48] In an editorial in *Crisis* appearing less than a week after the *Life* piece, Niebuhr dismissed what he called the "hysterical talk about the inevitability of a third world war" and stressed that a successful counter to the Soviet threat involved not just firmness but also patience.[49] In an article in the next edition of *Crisis*, Niebuhr began to climb back up to his lofty perch above the fray by reminding the readership of "the ambiguous and tragic character of the struggle" between the United States and the Soviet Union and the need to "call upon the mercy of God to redeem us."[50] In another article he even offered kind words for Wallace and his followers, acknowledging that their beliefs likely sprung from "a Christian spirit of self-examination, which recognizes how quickly and how easily nations become self-righteous in dealing with competitor or foe and how necessary it is to remind them of the beam that is in their own eye."[51] He stopped short of commending their actual views on the current situation, however, arguing that religious self-examination had to be supplemented by proximate historical

---

[45] Niebuhr, "Europe's Hope: (Dr. Niebuhr's Report)," *Time*, October 21, 1946, p. 31.

[46] Joanne Sharp, *Condensing the Cold War: Reader's Digest and American Identity* (Minneapolis, MN: University of Minnesota Press, 2000), p. xiv.

[47] Niebuhr, "The Fight for Germany," *Reader's Digest*, 50 (January 1947), pp. 69–72. For more information on the republication of Niebuhr's article in *Reader's Digest*, see John Fousek, *To Lead the Free World: American Nationalism and the Cultural Roots of the Cold War* (Chapel Hill, NC: University of North Carolina Press, 2000), p. 216, n. 68.

[48] Fox, *Reinhold Niebuhr*, p. 229.

[49] Niebuhr, "American Power and European Health," *Christianity and Crisis*, June 9, 1947, p. 1.

[50] Niebuhr, "Democracy as a Religion," *Christianity and Crisis*, August 4, 1947, pp. 1–2.

[51] Niebuhr, "Our Chances for Peace," *Christianity and Crisis*, February 17, 1947, p. 1.

judgments required of any Christian or nation for that matter. Niebuhr argued that, as with the case of the Nazi threat, the country now faced the "same problem of the relation between religious self-criticism and political judgments."[52] Referencing Chamberlain's appeasement of Hitler at Munich, Niebuhr argued that firmness on the part of the United States would not only restrict Soviet advances, but, ultimately, offer a better chance of preserving the peace.[53]

Niebuhr may have satisfied his own conscience and reassured the readers of *Crisis* that he was not the strident anti-Communist he had appeared in *Life*, *Time*, and *Reader's Digest*. However, given the aforementioned variances in subscription size, the majority of Americans still only knew Niebuhr for his hard-line writings in the wake of his trip to Germany. Although certainly a victim of editorial discretion, Niebuhr, in keeping with the direction he had outlined at the end of World War II, had been eagerly seeking out journalistic forums in which his views could reach a broader audience. He increasingly contributed to such popular outlets as the *New Republic*. Even those articles that Niebuhr continued to write in *Crisis* were more overtly political in nature and, according to Hulsether, contained fewer explicit references to Christian themes.[54] Moreover, Niebuhr's determination to influence public debate beyond the pews was not limited to the printed page but also extended into politics. Niebuhr had long been active in public affairs, as we recall from his failed efforts to secure elected office earlier in his career. He revealed a renewed commitment in 1946, however, by founding the political organization, Americans for Democratic Action (ADA), as a vehicle for sensible policy discussions and to bring about a world where the "fear of Communism did not drive some people into the arms of reaction, while the fear of reaction did not drive others into the arms of Communism."[55] In his capacity on the national board of the ADA, Niebuhr was involved in tasks ranging from growing the organization to just under 20,000 members in the United States

---

[52] Niebuhr, "Our Chances for Peace," p. 1.

[53] Niebuhr, "Our Chances for Peace," p. 2.

[54] Hulsether notes, "By the end of the war, [*Christianity and Crisis*] was more likely to project itself into the role of international policy planner than chaplain," *Building a Protestant Left*, p. 29.

[55] Niebuhr, "The Organization of the Liberal Movement," *Christianity and Society* (Spring 1947), p. 10.

to assisting in the development of policy papers and the endorsement of political candidates in state and national races.

Niebuhr's participation in the ADA is useful not just for showing where his interests resided but also in revealing the increased prestige of the company he was keeping. The fellow founders of the organization included historian Arthur Schlesinger, Jr., former first lady Eleanor Roosevelt, and future vice-president Hubert Humphrey. That same year Niebuhr also joined the Council on Foreign Relations, an exclusive membership organization based in New York that counted on its rolls influential figures ranging from cabinet officials to leaders of industry. While the common narrative today is that it was Niebuhr who was bringing his fresh perspective to these power-brokers, it is also certain he learned a great deal from them.[56] In particular, his writings during this period reveal a better grasp of the specific policy considerations and an increased competency in speaking to these issues in his own right. We recall, for instance, that in Niebuhr's fraternal debate his advice to American officials on the appropriate response to the Manchurian Crisis was virtually unintelligible. Moving forward fifteen years, Niebuhr's policy suggestions in "The Fight for Germany," although overlooked in his discussion of the Soviet threat and actually omitted from the abridged version in *Reader's Digest*, were quite coherent. Specifically he argued that the United States could best stem the growing Communist threat through generous loans to all of Europe and a specific focus on "the reconstruction of German industry" given its importance to the overall economic health of the continent.[57] When Secretary of State George Marshall announced in June 1947 the creation of a long-term

---

[56] See, on this point, Kenneth W. Thompson, "Niebuhr and the Foreign Policy Realists," in Rice, ed., *Reinhold Niebuhr Revisited*, p. 150. Thompson observes, "[Niebuhr] often remarked on the advantages for him of this relationship. Through the Council, he felt he was able to hear first hand from diplomats and policymakers who were close to the scene of action. When conversations turned to specific topics in foreign policy, he could draw on information from such sources," p. 150. Niebuhr's letter of invitation to join the Council on Foreign Relations captures the dual nature of his involvement in the foreign policy establishment. On the one hand it stressed the "important Americans and foreign guests" that Niebuhr would now be exposed to, while, on the other hand, it discussed the opportunity he would have to increase his own knowledge: "The object of the Council is to study the international aspects of America's political, economic and financial policy." Letter from Elihu Root to Niebuhr, November 20, 1946, Niebuhr Papers, Box 3. For more information on Niebuhr and the Council on Foreign Relations, see Brown, *Niebuhr and His Age*, pp. 129–30.

[57] Niebuhr, "The Fight for Germany," p. 70.

program of economic aid to Europe that contained these elements among its objectives, Niebuhr reacted positively to the policy.[58] Niebuhr's public stature only grew in March 1948 when he was featured on the cover of a special edition of *Time* magazine that celebrated the twenty-fifth anniversary of its founding. Although Luce had been referring to Niebuhr as "America's most influential Protestant theologian" in his magazines since the publication of "The Fight for Germany," he now deemed the theologian deserving of a cover story of his own. In a flattering article written by Whittaker Chambers, Niebuhr was identified as "the greatest Protestant theologian born in America since Jonathan Edwards."[59] Although there was no indication in the article, Niebuhr's political writings certainly influenced Luce's decision to honor the theologian.[60] In any event, the designation from *Time* served to "seal [Niebuhr's] reputation as the nation's leading theologian" according to his contemporaries, and Fox as well.[61] Niebuhr, given his concerns over impartiality expressed in *Discerning* and elsewhere during this period, must have reflected on being indebted to the figure that unabashedly described the contemporary age as "The American Century."[62] Indeed, less than a year after the *Time* cover story, problems arose as Luce rejected an article

[58] Niebuhr, in an editorial a week following the announcement, applauded the American effort to restore the economic health of Europe. He singled out for praise the Marshall Plan's focus on reviving German production, or, more specifically, production in Allied zones of occupation that happened to contain the majority of German industry. Niebuhr was supportive of the Marshall Plan not only because he thought it was good policy, but, on a deeper level, because he also viewed it as an act of magnanimity from a victorious nation to a defeated one, Niebuhr "The Marshall Plan," *Christianity and Crisis*, October 13, 1947, p. 3. As we observed in the last chapter, much of Niebuhr's writings during the war, as well as in its immediate aftermath, warned that the "vindictive passions of the nations" that had suffered losses at the hands of the Nazis could cloud their judgment with regard to the reconstruction of Germany, "The Vengeance of Victors," p. 1.

[59] Whitaker Chambers, "Faith for a Lenten Age," *Time*, March 8, 1948, pp. 70–2, 74–6, 79.

[60] It may or may not be coincidental that Chambers, the most anti-Communist writer for *Time*, was assigned to cover Niebuhr's story. Chambers, in his autobiography, relates that when writing the Niebuhr article he had in mind his upcoming testimony in court against Alger Hiss, a State Department official accused of being a Communist spy, *Witness* (New York: Random House, 1952), pp. 505–7.

[61] Fox, *Reinhold Niebuhr*, p. 233.

[62] Henry Luce, "The American Century," *Life*, February 17, 1941, pp. 61–5.

on American self-righteousness submitted by Niebuhr. His reasoning was that Niebuhr's concern may have been appropriate for a confident nation on the offensive, but, America, in Luce's estimation, was "actually very uncertain of itself" and "on the defensive."[63] As a result he concluded that Niebuhr's "words of prophecy" were not "relevant" in the contemporary age.[64] These words would likely have hurt Niebuhr even more so because he must have realized it was patronage of Luce's magazines that had made his viewpoint available to many throughout the nation.

CHRISTIAN HOPE AND THE PINNACLE OF THE FAITH

Niebuhr may have been experiencing unease over his own efforts to bring his theological beliefs to bear on the issues of the day, but he remained resolute in his belief that doing so was the duty of all Christians. The circles in which he advocated this view most strongly were not the political ones in which he was now traveling but among his fellow clergymen, who were deeply divided over the appropriate role of the church in addressing the contemporary challenges facing society. In fact, this was the subject of discussion at the First Assembly of the World Council of Churches in Amsterdam in 1948. The prevailing, though by no means unanimous, assumption of the seven hundred religious leaders in attendance was, in the words of ecclesiastical historian, Edward Duff, that the church had "a corporate responsibility and specific function in the field of economic activity and political life."[65] To reinforce this point, Niebuhr, in the three years prior to the gathering, had been part of a committee charged with drafting a comprehensive report on the specific steps the church could take in addressing the ongoing social crisis following World War II.[66] Determined to achieve more than the vague and non-binding statements that often resulted from these gatherings,

---

[63] Letter from Henry Luce to Niebuhr, January 8, 1949, Niebuhr Papers, Box 8.
[64] Letter from Henry Luce to Niebuhr, January 8, 1949, Niebuhr Papers, Box 8.
[65] Edward Duff, *The Social Thought of the World Council of Churches* (London: Longmans, Green 1956), p. 163.
[66] Duff, *The Social Thought of the World Council of Churches*, pp. 164–5.

Niebuhr argued emphatically for the Amsterdam Assembly to take a hard line toward the Soviet Union in his presentation before the body. Despite being aware of the Marxist sympathies held by a number of the African and Asian Christians that would be attending, he advocated, "The self-righteous fury of a consistent Marxism may be as dangerous to the establishment of a community as the cynicism of consistent facism."[67]

With a rousing address at the opening session of the assembly, however, Karl Barth threw the entire gathering into chaos by calling into question its fundamental premise.[68] Deliberately intending to provoke those in attendance, he urged, "We ought to give up, even on this first day of our deliberations, every thought that the care of the church, the care of the world, is our care."[69] While Barth had clearly found the threat of Nazi Germany sufficient to engage the concerns of the community of believers, he made clear that the current social and political ills afflicting the world did not merit such action.[70] Barth was adamant that the church should not get involved in such affairs and criticized those who thought otherwise for being flawed messengers

---

[67] Niebuhr, "God's Order and the Present Disorder of Civilization," October 1947, as found in Will Inboden, *Religion and American Foreign Policy, 1945–1960: The Soul of Containment* (Cambridge: Cambridge University Press, 2008), p. 42.

[68] Barth, as one contemporary theologian later recalled, played a "decisive, if negative, part in the outlook of the World Council . . . on social questions," as found in Duff, *The Social Thought of the World Council of Churches*, p. 152. Duff offers a more charitable account of Barth's role in the ecumenical assembly, commenting, "His theological emphasis and not least the appeal and force of his character have been a constant reminder that political preoccupations have their place, but a subordinate place, in the Christian vision of the world," p. 152.

[69] Karl Barth, "No Christian Marshall Plan," *The Christian Century*, December 8, 1948, p. 1331.

[70] For a discussion of Barth's refusal to condemn Soviet Communism as he had Nazism see Charles C. West, *Communism and the Theologians: Study of an Encounter* (Philadelphia: Westminster Press, 1958), pp. 290–325; Matthew Hockenos, "The German Protestant Debate on Politics and Theology after the Second World War," in Dianne Kirby, ed., *Religion and the Cold War* (Basingstoke: Palgrave Macmillan, 2003), pp. 37–49; and Rudy Koshar, "Where is Karl Barth in Modern European History?" *Modern Intellectual History*, 5:2 (2008), pp. 333–62. Koshar most succinctly explains how Barth thought that the totalitarian threat emanating from Russia did not need to be combated like the one that developed in Germany because "Communism had never been guilty of the outright sacrilege of National Socialism, the displacement of the real Christ with a national Jesus, or of anti-Semitism," p. 360. Regardless of the merits of this claim, Barth's contingent calculations seem to go against his seemingly absolute language during this time period urging the Christian church not to involve itself in contemporary affairs.

of the Gospel. What the faithful should be focused on, rather than the outlines of a "Christian Marshall Plan," such as the one prepared by the Assembly, was a complete paradigm shift as to the perceived function of the church.[71] He explained that Christians should be asking, "How can we free ourselves from all quantitative thinking, all statistics, all calculations of observable consequences, all efforts to achieve a Christian world order, and then shape our witness into a witness to the sovereignty of God's mercy, by which alone we can live."[72]

Niebuhr was visibly agitated by Barth's address according to those in attendance. The source of his frustration was not only the arguments Barth had enlisted but the fact they went completely counter to the moral stand that the Swiss theologian had taken in the recent world conflict. Setting aside what he believed to be Barth's personal hypocrisy, Niebuhr attempted to offer a rebuttal to the Swiss theologian's general viewpoint toward the end of the gathering. In an animated address that, in the words of one delegate, appeared more "spontaneous outburst" than reading of a prepared text, Niebuhr acknowledged there was some merit to Barth's belief that "repentance is always required even as evil always flourishes."[73] He continued, however, by arguing that it "was wrong to preach this gospel *sub specie aeternitatis* as if there were no history with its time and seasons."[74] Niebuhr concluded his address, as one might expect, by urging the Assembly to play an active role in the rehabilitation of Europe while retaining the appropriate perspective as to the extent of their ability to achieve the desired ends. Niebuhr explained, "The final victory over mankind's disorder is God's and not ours; but we do have responsibility for the proximate victories. Christian life without a high sense of responsibility for the health of our communities, our nations and our cultures degenerates into an intolerable other-worldliness."[75]

Niebuhr's ire toward Barth only increased at the conclusion of the proceedings, as he blamed the Swiss theologian for the Amsterdam Assembly's ultimate decision to condemn capitalism and Communism

[71] Barth, "No Christian Marshall Plan," p. 1330.
[72] Barth, "No Christian Marshall Plan," p. 1332.
[73] Niebuhr, "The Christian Witness in a Social and National Order," in *Christian Realism and Political Problems* (New York: Charles Scribner's Sons, 1954), p. 108.
[74] Niebuhr, "The Christian Witness in a Social and National Order," p. 108.
[75] Niebuhr, "The Christian Witness in a Social and National Order," pp. 111–12.

equally in its published reports.[76] In his first article published in *Century* since the founding of *Crisis*, Niebuhr went so far as to accuse Barth of being "obliquely pro-Communist" on account of his unwillingness to distinguish between the Western and Soviet models.[77] Niebuhr elaborated on this critique in terms that confirmed the "in the battle and above it" lens through which he was viewing the conflict: "Barth seems inclined today to regard the differences between Communism and the so-called democratic world as insignificant when viewed from the ultimate Christian standpoint. But we are men and not God, and the destiny of civilizations depends upon our decisions."[78] The fact that Barth was unwilling to make a similar decision with regard to the dangers of Communism as he had with Nazism was a matter of failed political judgment in Niebuhr's estimation, and, more seriously, resulted from a fundamental flaw with Barth's theology. Slightly qualifying his well-worn quietist critique, Niebuhr observed, "[I]t fails to provide sufficient criteria of judgment and impulses to decisive action in moments of life when a historic evil, not yet full blown and not yet requiring some heroic witness, sneaks into the world . . ."[79] This was tragic in Niebuhr's mind because such judgments were not only necessary in the predicament posed by Soviet aggression but also in the vast majority of the problems Christians faced in their daily lives.[80]

[76] See, on the decision of the Assembly to equally reject Communism and capitalism, Fox, *Niebuhr*, p. 236 and Inboden, *Religion and American Foreign Policy*, p. 48.

[77] Niebuhr, "Protestantism in a Disordered World," *The Nation*, September 18, 1948, p. 312.

[78] Niebuhr did credit the Swiss theologian for puncturing the simple moralism he observed among many of his fellow Americans: "One cannot deny that much of what passes for Christianity in the Western world is no more than a simple confidence that God is our ally in our fight with Communism even as he was our ally in our fight with nazism. And isn't it nice that God is always on our side! Let us not forget to pay tribute to Barth's influence in the Anglo-Saxon world in extricating the Christian faith from the idolatries of our day." "An Answer to Karl Barth," *The Christian Century*, February 23, 1949, p. 234.

[79] Niebuhr, "An Answer to Karl Barth," p. 236. Niebuhr had touched on this point in a previous article, explaining that Barth's theology "seems to have no guidance for a Christian statesman for our day. It can fight the devil if he shows both horns and both cloven feet. But it refuses to make discriminating judgments about good and evil if the evil shows only one horn or the half of a cloven foot," "We are Men not God," *The Christian Century*, October 27, 1948, p. 1139.

[80] The greater force of Niebuhr's response in this instance, as compared to past exchanges with the Swiss theologian, is instructive in that it reveals just how

Lost in Niebuhr's vociferous criticisms of Barth was a grudging recognition that the Swiss theologian "outlined the final pinnacle of the Christian faith and hope with fidelity to the Scriptures."[81] He appeared more willing than he had in the past to acknowledge the power of Barth's writings on the revelatory and redemptive power of Jesus Christ. Of course he qualified this admiration with the belief that Barth's thought "requires correction, because it has obscured the foothills where human life must be lived."[82] Nevertheless, Niebuhr's greater receptivity to Barth's eschatological focus following Amsterdam may have resulted from the fact he was concurrently completing his next work, *Faith and History*, in which he was exploring the relationship between the pinnacle and those foothills. Building directly on the themes he had explored in *Human Destiny*, Niebuhr set out to argue that the Christian interpretation of history was better able to explain the complexities of human existence than the modern alternatives. The similarities between *Faith and History* and *Human Destiny* were so striking, as we discussed in the introduction to this chapter, that a number of commentators in Niebuhr's time as well as today have criticized the work for saying nothing new.[83] There is merit to such charges, but, ultimately, they fail to recognize how *Faith and History* represents a greater focus on the relevance as opposed to the explication of his Christian understanding of history.

Niebuhr's central thesis was one that had dominated the majority of his writings over the decade. He argued that the modern view of history as a redemptive process was ill-equipped to address the present challenges facing humanity, as it had been in the past. As he explained on the opening page, "The history of mankind exhibits no more of an ironic experience than the contrast between the sanguine hopes of recent centuries and the bitter experiences of contemporary man."[84] Rather than focusing primarily on the philosophical critique of the modern belief in progress as he had in *Human Destiny*, Niebuhr was preoccupied in *Faith and History* with examining the practical issues and specifically the misguided perspective that arose from such an understanding of history. As he had in *Discerning*,

committed he had become to proving the immediate relevance of the Christian faith to the present perplexities facing mankind.

[81] Niebuhr, "We are Men not God," p. 1140.

[82] Niebuhr, "We are Men not God," p. 1140.

[83] Fox, *Reinhold Niebuhr*, p. 237.　　[84] Niebuhr, *Faith and History*, p. 1.

Niebuhr explained that perspective was based on the belief that humanity was capable of gaining an objective viewpoint from which to evaluate the historical process.[85] Where Niebuhr broke from his previous writing was in the detail with which he attempted to disprove the notion that mankind could be a disinterested spectator.

Niebuhr began with the basic argument he had outlined in *Discerning*, namely, an individual could not achieve objectivity in examining history because he was an observer as well as an agent in the historical process. However, he quickly moved into a discussion of the conceptions of causation and prediction, which he found infinitely more complex in the social realm than in the natural one. Among many factors, Niebuhr singled out the challenges posed by the sheer contingency of historical events resulting from the uniqueness of that human agency. Given the "multifarious vitalities and configurations of history," Niebuhr believed it impossible to identify—much less forecast—recurrences and cycles in the realm of human affairs.[86] Furthermore, this meant that individuals were unable to establish simple analogies in history as could be done in examinations of the natural world. Amidst this discussion of the complex patterns of history, however, the practical question arises of what to make of Niebuhr's own use of analogy, particularly between Communist Russia and Nazi Germany. While he had certainly made overtures regarding the uniqueness of the two situations, the basic message propelling his writings over the past year had been that Europe was again in danger of being overrun by a totalitarian menace. Nonetheless, Niebuhr, in *Faith and History*, appeared to slide over this practical inconsistency in the interest of making his argument.

The most novel aspect of the work was Niebuhr's effort to prove how the human situation could be made more intelligible from a viewpoint informed by the Christian understanding of history. While

---

[85] Niebuhr, as he had in the past, explained underlying both was the modern belief that the scientific method could be applied to the realm of history as represented in Dewey's writings. Other commentators on Dewey have credited him with a more nuanced understanding of the challenges the historian faces in achieving objectivity with regard to past events. For an account of Dewey's philosophy of history that, interestingly enough, portrays him with views similar to Niebuhr, see Burleigh Taylor Wilkins, "Pragmatism as a Theory of Historical Knowledge: John Dewey on the Nature of Historical Inquiry," *The American Historical Review*, 64:4 (July 1959), pp. 878–90.

[86] Niebuhr, *Faith and History*, p. 65.

Niebuhr's description of this understanding was virtually identical with previous writings, as we have established, the fact that he was now writing to a broader audience led to a change in how he went about substantiating this viewpoint. Although maintaining that the Christian faith was not proven true by rational analysis, Niebuhr argued, "A limited rational validation of the truth of the Gospel was possible."[87] Expanding on this statement, Niebuhr asserted that such validation could occur when the "the truth of faith is correlated with all truths which may be known by scientific and philosophical disciplines and proves itself a resource for co-ordinating them into a deeper and wider system of coherence."[88] Rather than explaining how this correlation was supposed to occur, however, Niebuhr merely identified the errors that Christians often committed in pursuing this task.[89] On the one hand, he criticized those who drew simple parallels between their faith and systems of rational coherence, while, on the other hand, in a thinly veiled critique of Barth, he warned against those who seemed to guard Christian truth against other forms of knowledge and experience.[90] The best that Niebuhr could offer as to his own view was that there should be a "constant commerce" between specific truths, revealed by the various scientific and historical disciplines, and the final truth, known from the standpoint of the Christian faith.[91] In practical terms Niebuhr appeared to be now explaining how his historical analogy between the threat of Soviet Communism and German Nazism worked within his overall Christian understanding of history. Rather unsatisfactorily, however, Niebuhr did not explain how this commerce between truths was supposed to work for anyone else.

[87] Niebuhr, *Faith and History*, p. 172. In the English edition of *Faith and History*, the sentence has been printed to state, "A limited rational validation of the truth of the Gospel was impossible." Given what we will see to be Niebuhr's inability to prove the possibility of this fact, this misprint is telling. See, on the subject of Niebuhr's understanding of limited rational validation, Robin Lovin, "Reinhold Niebuhr in Contemporary Scholarship: A Review Essay," *Journal of Religious Ethics*, 31:3 (2003), pp. 498–500.

[88] Niebuhr, *Faith and History*, p. 172.

[89] This point appears to have first been made in Robert E. Fitch, "Reinhold Niebuhr's Philosophy of History," in Kegley and Bretall, eds, *Reinhold Niebuhr*, p. 295.

[90] Niebuhr, *Faith and History*, pp. 188–9.

[91] Niebuhr, *Faith and History*, p. 189.

If *Faith and History* marked Niebuhr's greatest effort to relate faith and reason, paradoxically, it also contained one of his strongest statements on the importance of its otherworldly elements. Niebuhr unequivocally asserted, "The eschatological expectations in the New Testament, however embarrassing when taken literally, are necessary for a Christian interpretation of history."[92] Although this fact had been understood in *Human Destiny*, Niebuhr perhaps felt the need to assert this explicitly following his efforts to validate Christianity rationally. To that end, Niebuhr explained that if the final judgment and resurrection "were sacrificed, the meaning of history is confused by the introduction of false centers of meaning taken from the contingent stuff of the historical process."[93] As we recall from the second chapter, Niebuhr's discussion of the "eschata" in *Human Destiny* had centered on the Last Judgment and how it would reaffirm the meaning of history established by the Atonement that the rebellion of sin is finally overcome while the distinction between good and evil is preserved. This focus on the Last Judgment had led him to call for "a decent measure of restraint in expressing the Christian hope."[94] In *Faith and History*, however, Niebuhr placed more emphasis on the resurrection and its role in the fulfillment of history and appeared more hopeful as a result. Niebuhr explained that it was the resurrection that allowed Christians to "look toward the end of history with faith and hope, rather than with fear, despite its anticipation of increased antinomies and contradictions between good and evil in history."[95] This was particularly important, according to Niebuhr, in light of the "sense of eschatological urgency" he detected throughout the world as a result of the advent of atomic weaponry.[96] The hope of the resurrection was an antidote to such fears according to Niebuhr, because it shattered feelings of despair that, while pronounced in the current age, invariably accompanied those who identified the end of the world with the end of history. Christians were able to distinguish between the two, or, as he put it, the *finis* and the *telos*, because the risen body of Jesus Christ pointed to "a final mystery of divine fulfillment beyond all provisional meanings."[97]

If Niebuhr's intention in *Faith and History* was to relate the pinnacles of the Christian faith to the foothills of society, his efforts

---

[92] Niebuhr, *Faith and History*, p. 243.
[93] Niebuhr, *Faith and History*, p. 243.
[94] Niebuhr, *Human Destiny*, p. 309.
[95] Niebuhr, *Faith and History*, p. 268.
[96] Niebuhr, *Faith and History*, p. 269.
[97] Niebuhr, *Faith and History*, p. 244.

were hampered by a problem that had been plaguing him since *Reflection*. Niebuhr's discussion of the "embarrassing" eschatological symbols led Arthur E. Murphy, among other reviewers, to ask how they were to apprehend "a meaning to which no positive content can be given."[98] Indeed, Niebuhr's evasion of the issue seemed even more irresponsible after he more clearly asserted in *Faith and History* than he had in the past that his interpretation of history was of little use without the "otherworldly elements." In Niebuhr's journalistic writings at the end of the 1940s, he did address this tension between his efforts to broaden the appeal of his Christian message and his desire to stress its otherworldly elements. For instance, Niebuhr observed, "The more Christians seek to commend their faith as the source of the qualities and disciplines required to save the world from disaster, the less does that kind of faith prove to have the necessary resources."[99] In one article, Niebuhr went so far as to call for what he termed "a less relevant faith," along the lines of Barth but, in the same article, criticized the Swiss theologian for his unwillingness to engage with the issues of the day.[100] In any event, Niebuhr seemed to be placing himself in a bind by asserting that the relevance of the Christian view of history was derived from its "otherworldly elements," while simultaneously holding that those "otherworldly elements" had to remain irrelevant in order to relate to the contemporary world.

One factor that may have contributed to the quandary in which Niebuhr found himself was the seemingly solitary nature of his quest toward the end of the 1940s. While still readily willing to identify those individuals he opposed, Dewey and Barth for instance, Niebuhr rarely acknowledged Christian thinkers with whom his views aligned. Northrop Frye touched on this point in his review of *Faith and History*, observing, "The people [Niebuhr] disagrees with make up

---

[98] Arthur E. Murphy, "Niebuhr's Answer to a Loss of Faith," *The Christian Register*, November 1949, p. 2 as found in Niebuhr Papers, Box 20. Despite his criticisms, Murphy seemed to understand Niebuhr's increased emphasis on the foothills. He explained that although Niebuhr "tells us little of the transcendent truth beyond history," he "does give a remarkably vivid and penetrating expression to a present human predicament within it," p. 3.

[99] Niebuhr, "Utilitarian Christianity and the World Crisis," *Christianity and Crisis*, May 29, 1950, p. 66.

[100] Niebuhr explained that "[n]eutrality between justice and injustice . . . derived from . . . a too sophisticated Barthian theology, is untrue to our gospel," "Utilitarian Christianity and the World Crisis," p. 68.

quite a large company . . . one begins to reflect rather irritatedly that everyone seems to be out of step but our Reinhold."[101] This was not because Niebuhr was the only theologian thinking about how to apply Christian views of history to the pressing questions of the day. On the contrary, as C. T. McIntire observes in *God, History, and Historians*, there were many theologians and historians throughout America and Europe wrestling with the very same questions as Niebuhr at the midpoint of the twentieth century.[102] Moreover, we know that Niebuhr was in frequent contact with many of these figures given his involvement at ecumenical gatherings such as the WCC assemblies. The most obvious candidates for Niebuhr to enlist, however, would have been his closest confidants in the past, Union Theological Seminary colleague, Tillich, and his brother, Richard. Both theologians were seriously exploring issues directly related to a Christian understanding of history during this period. In the case of Tillich, the first volume of his *Systematic Theology* was dedicated, in part, to this very subject. Niebuhr was certainly aware of this, as he authored a revealing article on Tillich's understanding of history in 1951.

---

[101] Northrop Frye, "The Rhythm of Growth and Decay," in Robert D. Denham, ed., *Northrop Frye on Culture and Literature* (Chicago: University of Chicago Press, 1978), p. 145.

[102] McIntire, *God, History and Historians*, pp. 15–17. The one figure identified by McIntire with whom Niebuhr did engage in a substantive way in *Faith and History* was naturally one he disagreed with, Arnold Toynbee. Niebuhr roundly criticized the historian for applying cyclical patterns to the enterprises of civilizations throughout history, *Faith and History*, pp. 123–5. For a less systematic treatment, Niebuhr could have turned to Cambridge historian Herbert Butterfield, a contemporary whose writings on the Christian interpretation of history were remarkably similar to his own. Butterfield gained renown throughout the United Kingdom during World War II, as Niebuhr had in the United States, for providing a religious perspective on the tragic struggle. He then continued to parallel Niebuhr by giving a series of lectures shortly following the war on his philosophy of history that ultimately was published as *Christianity and History* (London: Bell, 1949) in the same year as *Faith and History*. The only mention of Butterfield by Niebuhr during this period, however, can be found in an exchange between him and his British publisher blaming the poor sales of *Faith and History* in the United Kingdom on competition from *Christianity and History*. In an attempt to show sympathy toward Niebuhr, the publisher claims, "It was most unfortunate that [*Faith and History*] should have come right up against Butterfield's much less important but more popular and somewhat cheaper book . . ." Letter from Bertram Christian to Niebuhr, May 25, 1951, Niebuhr's Papers, Box 7. One reason for Niebuhr's coolness toward Butterfield could have been the historian's tendency to critique equally Western capitalism and Communism. Kenneth W. Thompson observes that Butterfield is often overlooked in discussions of Niebuhr's thought in "Niebuhr and the Foreign Policy Realists," in Rice, ed., *Reinhold Niebuhr Revisited*, pp. 142–4.

If Niebuhr had looked to Tillich for theological guidance in the 1930s, he was clear this was no longer the case at the midpoint of the century. The reason for this was that Tillich had increasingly become distracted with what Niebuhr dismissively referred to as "ontological speculation."[103] Rather than analyzing the structure of being to understand the relationship between humanity and the divine, as Tillich had done in *Systematic Theology*, Niebuhr held that "specific historical events" could tell us more about its nature. He explained it was precisely the latter approach that enabled him to understand history "primarily in terms of the contest of all men and nations with God, and secondarily in terms of a conquest between good and evil in history."[104] Another problem that Niebuhr had with Tillich's metaphysics was how it affected his understanding of biblical symbols. In looking at the Fall, Niebuhr believed that an ontological approach resulted in too great an emphasis being placed on "the fatefulness of sin rather than upon our responsibility."[105] As we know from Chapter 2, this was a serious charge coming from Niebuhr, given the lengths to which he went in his writings to affirm moral accountability. It was also an ironic one given the target was the individual whom Niebuhr had previously relied on to counter Barth's determinism.[106]

Humility aside, the main reason why Niebuhr did not feel a greater need to walk this tightrope at this time was that it was of little importance to the broader audience with which he was increasingly most concerned. This fact was not lost on Richard, who, in a paper prepared in response to *Faith and History*, once again proved himself to be his brother's most insightful critic.[107] Richard, unsurprisingly,

[103] Niebuhr, "Biblical Thought and Ontological Speculation," in Kegley and Bretall, eds, *The Theology of Paul Tillich*, p. 216.
[104] Niebuhr, "Biblical Thought and Ontological Speculation," p. 216.
[105] Niebuhr, "Biblical Thought and Ontological Speculation," p. 219.
[106] As Stenger and Stone explain, this reversal may have had much to do with the growing political differences between the Union Theological Seminary colleagues. If Niebuhr had renounced much of the political platform they had held in common prior to World War II, Tillich carried the banner for religious socialism well into the 1950s, *Dialogues of Paul Tillich*, p. 47.
[107] The paper, entitled "Reinhold Niebuhr's Interpretation of History," was given before a collection of twenty-five academics (including Reinhold) named the "Theological Discussion Group" that gathered regularly. For more information on this group, see Richard R. Niebuhr's introduction to William Stacey Johnson, ed., *H. Richard Niebuhr, Theology, History and Culture: Major Unpublished Writings* (New Haven, CT: Yale University Press, 1998), pp. xxvi–xxvii.

questioned Reinhold's use of symbols in the work and singled out his portrayal of the resurrection as the primary impediment to appropriating Reinhold's view as his own. Nevertheless, Richard stopped short of condemning his brother as others had and, instead, generously observed, "Reinie's thought appears to me to be like a great iceberg of which three-fourths or more is beneath the surface and in which what is explicitly said depends on something that is not made explicit."[108] Richard explained that his brother's unwillingness to explain the substantive reality behind his use of symbols did not mean that no substance existed but rather was a product of the audience he was trying to reach.[109] He explained, "It is evident for me that for Reinie himself Christ's resurrection is a fact in his own history . . . Yet he speaks to men who do not know that they live between the resurrection of Jesus Christ and their own resurrection . . . And in speaking to them he takes their ground and does not make explicit the whole content of his interpretation of history."[110]

KOREA, NUCLEAR ARMS, AND DELUSIONS
OF VAINGLORY

Niebuhr, throughout 1949, not only continued his effort to shape public opinion on U.S.–Soviet relations but, in June, was also given the opportunity to exert influence directly on American officials responsible for that policy. Thoughts of theological precision likely were the furthest thing from his mind as he spent three days at the U.S. Department of State at the invitation of Kennan, now the Director of Policy Planning, to discuss how America could facilitate greater

---

[108] Richard Niebuhr, "Reinhold Niebuhr's Interpretation of History," p. 97.

[109] Some of Niebuhr's harshest critics, such as Hauerwas, have proven largely unwilling to make such a distinction given the belief that the "truth of Christian conviction requires a . . . confident use of Christian speech about God," *With the Grain of the Universe*, p. 140.

[110] Richard Niebuhr, "Reinhold Niebuhr's Interpretation of History," pp. 98–9. Reinhold acknowledged in 1953 that "the Christological center of my thought has become more explicit and more important" than it had been in the past, but, equally acknowledged that "[he had] elaborated the Christological theme only in the context of inquiries about human nature and human history," "Reply to Interpretation and Criticism," in Kegley and Bretall, eds, *Reinhold Niebuhr*, p. 439.

European integration.[111] What advice Niebuhr actually contributed to these discussions is unknown, as is the extent to which it had any tangible influence on the formation of U.S. foreign policy. The reasons behind Kennan's interest in Niebuhr's thoughts are clear, however, as he also viewed the conflict with the Soviet Union from a religious perspective.[112] This much was evident by the fact that he compared his "Long Telegram" to "an eighteenth century sermon" and concluded his famous "X-article" on containment by expressing "gratitude to a Providence" for "providing the American people this implacable challenge."[113] Moreover, Kennan's religious perspective had similarities to the "in the battle and above it" one held by Niebuhr.[114] This is most recognizable in a 1954 article Kennan published in *Crisis*, of all outlets. On one hand, the diplomat unequivocally criticized Communism as an example of "totalitarian outlooks that go the whole hog on the path of Godlessness."[115] On the other hand, he firmly established

[111] See, for the best description of the meeting, David Mayers, *George Kennan and the Dilemmas of US Foreign Policy* (Oxford: Oxford University Press, 1988), p. 149. Additional information can be found in Wilson Miscamble, *George F. Kennan and the Making of American Foreign Policy, 1947–1950* (Princeton, NJ: Princeton University Press, 1992), p. 283.

[112] Many commentators have underestimated the degree to which Kennan was religious and the extent that his beliefs played a role in his policy writings. Fox exemplifies this failure in his observation that "Kennan . . . typified the growing band of secular liberals" to whom Niebuhr was appealing during this period, *Reinhold Niebuhr*, p. 246. That Kennan was receptive to Niebuhr's theological, as well as political, writings is evident in a 1966 letter to Niebuhr in which he explained, "I don't think I ever learned from anyone things more important to the understanding of our predicament, as individuals and as a society, than those I have learned, so to speak, at your feet," Letter from Kennan to Niebuhr, April 12, 1966, Niebuhr Papers, Box 49. For the best discussion of the role Kennan's faith played in his policy formulation, see Inboden, *Religion and American Foreign Policy*, pp. 17–18. For the best discussion of Niebuhr's relationship with Kennan, see Halliwell, *The Constant Dialogue*, pp. 194–215.

[113] George Kennan, *Memoirs, Volume I: 1925–1950* (Boston: Little, Brown, 1967), p. 293; Kennan "The Sources of Soviet Conduct," as found in Inboden, *American Religion and Foreign Policy*, p. 18.

[114] This was evident in a private letter Kennan authored to Dean Acheson explaining the beliefs that underlay his policy advice. He explained in strikingly Niebuhrian terms, "It is simply not given to human beings to know the totality of the truth . . . no one can see in its totality anything so fundamental and so unlimited in all its implications as the development of our people in relation to their world environment," as found in Gaddis, *Strategies of Containment*, p. 52. This concern was not a peripheral matter but rather the "central dilemma" for Kennan, according Gaddis, the foremost student of Kennan's thought, p. 52.

[115] George Kennan, "To Be or Not to Be a Christian," *Christianity and Crisis*, October 18, 1953, p. 51.

that "whatever the effective response to Communism may be . . . it does not lie in smug temporizing or opportunism with respect to the overriding moral issues" and went on to conclude that "we are not to be spared the fire of conscience and decision in which our fathers' faith was forged."[116] Readers of *Crisis* could have mistaken Niebuhr to be the author of the article.

It should come as no surprise then that Niebuhr's approval of American foreign policy was at its peak during the period when Kennan was seen to have maximum influence over its formulation. In a 1949 article, "Streaks of Dawn in the Night," written shortly after another consultation with Kennan and the policy planning staff, Niebuhr offered his most positive assessment of the world situation during the entire Cold War era. He highlighted the success of the Marshall Plan in restoring economic stability to large parts of Europe. He went so far as to suggest that America had the "right to congratulate ourselves" for this strategic and magnanimous act—although in typical fashion, stressed twice "not for more than a moment."[117] Niebuhr was also quite pleased by the cooperation he observed between the United States, Britain, and France during the Berlin Airlift, which overcame Soviet road and rail blockades by flying over two million tons of supplies into West Berlin. This was only one part of the ongoing success he observed in "coordinating Western Germany, both politically and economically, into the European world."[118] Finally, Niebuhr's observation of how nationalist movements in the Eastern European countries of Yugoslavia and Hungary were threatening Soviet interests in the region led him to believe that time was on the side of the West. He explained that the United States could "afford to continue a policy of firmness without provocation" and argued the "chances of avoiding conflict are brighter than they have been for a long time."[119]

---

[116] Kennan, "To Be or Not to Be a Christian," p. 53.

[117] Niebuhr, "Streaks of Dawn in the Night," *Christianity and Crisis*, December 12, 1949, p. 162.

[118] Niebuhr, "Streaks of Dawn in the Night," p. 163.

[119] Niebuhr, "Streaks of Dawn in the Night," pp. 163–4. Niebuhr, while acknowledging the deterrent power of U.S. military might, gave credit for these positive developments to Kennan and his colleagues observing, the "State Department is much more in charge of foreign affairs, and less under the pressure of the defense departments, than at any time since the close of the war," Niebuhr, "Streaks of Dawn in the Night," p. 164.

The unexpected detonation of an atomic bomb by the Russians in August 1949 led Washington to reassess the appropriate balance between diplomacy and defense in combating a greater Soviet threat. The immediate question debated was whether the United States should respond by building a more powerful thermonuclear weapon, otherwise known as the hydrogen bomb. Kennan advocated against its development on the basis that the eradication of, as opposed to any increased reliance on, such weapons was in the national interest. Niebuhr shared this overarching belief, but, nevertheless, argued in favor of constructing the bomb since Russia would inevitably acquire the technology and "no responsible statesman [could] risk putting his nation in that position of defenselessness."[120] What Niebuhr could not anticipate is that Truman's ultimate decision to pursue the weapon against Kennan's advice would weaken the bureaucrat's position within the administration and precipitate his departure from government.[121] The repercussions of this personnel move were significant, not only because it brought an end to Niebuhr's visits to Foggy Bottom. The national security review conducted by Kennan's eventual successor, Paul Nitze, institutionalized an important shift in American strategy vis-à-vis the Soviet Union. Rather than prioritizing the political and economic instruments of containment as it had in the past, the Truman administration's overriding concern became obtaining "the military power to deter, if possible, Soviet expansion and to defeat, if necessary, aggressive Soviet or Soviet-directed actions of a limited or total character."[122] Niebuhr now found himself once

---

[120] "The Hydrogen Bomb," *Christianity and Society* (Spring 1950), p. 6. Although the article is an unsigned editorial piece, its tone and content indicate that Niebuhr is the likely author.

[121] For a more detailed description of Kennan's last months as Policy Planning Staff director, see Gaddis, *George F. Kennan: An American Life* (New York: Penguin, 2011), 337–70.

[122] NSC-68, April 14, 1950, U.S. Department of State, *Foreign Relations of the United States, National Security Affairs: Foreign Economic Policy* (Washington, D.C.: U.S. Department of State, 1950), p. 282. This shift in priority was evidenced in the money distributed by the United States to Europe. For the fiscal year 1951, U.S. congressional appropriations to Europe almost doubled. That said the funding for the Marshall Plan was cut in half. The vast majority of U.S. money was going to military expenditures and even those that were going to support economic and political activities were brought under the control of the defense establishment per the Mutual Security Act, which President Truman signed into law in October 1951. For this information, I am indebted to Nita Colaco, "The Anglo-American Council on

again on the sidelines of the policy debate and more concerned than ever that conflict between the United States and Soviet Union was inevitable.

Niebuhr's fears were realized in June 1950 when the Communist regime in North Korea, with support from the Soviet Union, crossed the 38th parallel to invade South Korea, a country that had been under American occupation since the conclusion of World War II. Niebuhr had previously advocated a policy of non-intervention in Asia, even following the Communist takeover of China in 1949, such was his concern that the full resources of the United States be focused on countering Soviet aggression in Europe. Nevertheless, he supported the Truman administration's mobilization of forces to South Korea, but only for the limited purpose of restoring the 38th parallel and, even then, only to the extent that it did not distract the country from the fight against Communism in Europe.[123] Predictably, Niebuhr reacted angrily when General Douglas MacArthur led the multinational force under his command deep into North Korean territory, thereby inciting the Chinese, previously bystanders to the conflict, to commence combat operations against the United States. As the United States became bogged down in Korea throughout 1951, Niebuhr came to view the war as more than just a distraction. He expressed "the uneasy feeling" that it represented the larger temptation of national pride to which the country was prone. It was for this reason that Niebuhr stressed in a February 1951 article in *Crisis*, "the necessity of humility for the defenders of even a just cause."[124]

If Niebuhr's message in *Crisis* on the tenth anniversary of its founding was an effort to temper the self-righteousness he was detecting among his fellow citizens, it also appeared an effort to come to terms with his own struggles of the past few years. As we discussed at the beginning of the chapter, Niebuhr began the post-war era convinced that it was the responsibility of Christians to contribute their unique insights to the contemporary problems facing the country. With that end in mind, Niebuhr had spent the past five years publishing hundreds of articles, lecturing across the United States and occupied Germany, and meeting with officials in the American

---

Productivity: A Study of Industry, Labour Relations, and the Drivers of Productivity, 1948–1952," MPhil Thesis, University of Oxford, 2010.

[123] Niebuhr, "Editorial Notes," *Christianity and Crisis*, December 25, 1950, p. 170.

[124] Niebuhr, "Ten Fateful Years," *Christianity and Crisis*, February 5, 1951, p. 3.

government. Rather than leaving Niebuhr more confident in the mission to assert the relevance of the Christian faith, however, these efforts appeared to have had the opposite effect. Discussing the role of Christians in ensuring "survival of a free society" in 1951, Niebuhr answered, "Perhaps they had better not try to make too many direct contributions."[125] One could interpret Niebuhr's statement as a warning of the dangers of associating the Christian faith too closely with politics. His uncomfortable experiences with Luce and even the realization that his advice to the State Department was now falling on deaf ears must have led to some disillusionment. The conclusion of the article, however, revealed that not to be the case. Niebuhr explained his pessimism stemmed from the simple fact that he believed Christians had not been effective enough in influencing the debate. Despite his own efforts to bring his theological message to millions of Americans, the country was as ill equipped to meet the challenges of current events as it was ten years ago at the birth of *Crisis*.[126]

---

[125] Niebuhr, "Ten Fateful Years," p. 3.
[126] Niebuhr, "Ten Fateful Years," p. 4.

4

The Irony of *The Irony of American History*

This chapter will address Niebuhr's *The Irony of American History* and, more importantly, argue that it is inextricably tied to his theological vision that we have traced over the course of this book. As we discussed in the introduction, *Irony* is primarily read today as a work of history or international relations, with little regard paid to its theological foundation. The most compelling evidence against such an interpretation, as this chapter will demonstrate, is the continuity between Niebuhr's views in *Irony* and those in the past that were explicitly derived from his Christian interpretation of history. A close examination of the work reveals that Niebuhr writes little on the perplexing situation in which the United States now found itself that he had not previously stated in explicitly theological works, such as *Faith and History*, or articles from religious journals such as *Crisis*. Just as the content of *Irony* was largely unoriginal, Niebuhr's reliance on the category of irony to describe the incongruities of history was also an approach found in his previous theological works, *Discerning* in particular. In fact, the most novel aspect of *Irony* was the length to which Niebuhr went to avoid explicit references to the Christian faith throughout the work. To the degree that commentators have discussed the theological aspect of *Irony*, they have simply argued that Niebuhr submerged it beneath the surface in order to broaden the work's appeal. Indeed, even the most perceptive students of Niebuhr's thought argue that an understanding of Niebuhr's theology is unnecessary to appreciate his commentary in *Irony*. This perspective fails to take into account the fundamental point that Niebuhr saw his discussion of the current ironies in history as a stalking horse for his theological beliefs.

As we saw in the third chapter, Niebuhr became increasingly concerned with exposing more secular audiences to his theological vision in the years immediately following World War II. This trend continued throughout the 1950s, as he explained his interests were in "practical or 'apologetic'" pursuits as opposed to engaging in academic debates with "stricter sets of theologians."[1] Niebuhr's focus, therefore, was to attract a population to his Christian message that he believed would recoil at a symbolic, much less literal, interpretation of biblical events. In *Irony* he tried to circumvent this perceived barrier by continuing the argument he made in *Faith and History* with regard to the "limited rational validity" of the Christian faith. Specifically, he hoped that by using the category of irony to highlight the incongruities of history it would lead unbelievers to the very Christian presuppositions that allowed him to identify those incongruities in the first place. Niebuhr's failure to explain adequately how this process occurred, however, rendered it as ineffective as it had been in *Faith and History*, and only added to the confusion over the relationship between his Christian views and ironic interpretation of history. Niebuhr also turned to a familiar historical figure, Abraham Lincoln, in the concluding pages of the work to convey his theological vision. His reference to Lincoln in *Irony* was distinct from previous mentions, however, in that the president became the primary, as opposed to complementary, way by which he communicated his "in the battle and above it" viewpoint. Niebuhr would continue this approach in dozens of letters and articles written after *Irony* by portraying Lincoln as incarnating "the two dimensions of discriminate judgment about good and evil, and the ultimate judgment which calls our immediate judgments into question."[2]

The fact that Niebuhr appeared to place more emphasis on Lincoln than Jesus Christ in *Irony* is but one reason why theologians have largely ignored this work. This is a mistake, however, as *Irony* sheds light on the productive tension that had been at the heart of Niebuhr's previous writings. On the one hand, Niebuhr had maintained a strong belief in his duty to communicate the relevance of his theological perspective to the ongoing current events. On the other hand, Niebuhr was aware that those aspects of his Christian interpretation of history that made his theological viewpoint insightful—the eschatological expectations of the New

---

[1] Niebuhr, "Intellectual Autobiography," in Kegley and Bretall, eds, *Reinhold Niebuhr*, p. 3.

[2] Letter from Niebuhr to June Bingham, Niebuhr Papers, October 24, 1955, Box 26.

Testament—were actually less so when called upon for solely practical means. He explained, "It is significant that a purely utilitarian justification of Christianity . . . is more likely to become a source of confusion to the conscience of the nation than a spiritual resource."[3] In *Irony*, Niebuhr seemingly chose to dissolve this paradox by largely abstaining from mentioning biblical events in order to maximize the book's contemporary relevance. This was problematic whether the decision was made with an apologetic purpose in mind or purely out of a desire to share with the broader public his concern over the nuclear arms race with the Soviet Union and the present catastrophe in Asia. *Irony* marked a noticeable shift in Niebuhr's theological approach in that over the subsequent decades he would not only hide central elements of his Christian message, but increasingly criticize them and, in the case of some, even discard them to appeal to more secular audiences. With this overarching trend in mind, it is to the development of *Irony* that we now turn.

NIEBUHR AND BARTH: THE "SUPER-THEOLOGIANS" MEET

If Niebuhr, in his article commemorating the decennial anniversary of *Crisis*'s founding, had questioned the role of the Christian church in addressing contemporary social and political problems, he reaffirmed his steadfast support for greater engagement on its part that July. The specific occasion was another clash with Barth at a World Council of Churches gathering, this time in Geneva. A group of twenty-five theologians had been summoned to a lakeside resort for the first of three yearly meetings, the purpose of which was to prepare a preliminary study on the subject of Christian hope for deliberation at the WCC's Second Assembly to be held in Evanston, Illinois in 1954.[4] Despite the change of scenery, Niebuhr and Barth picked up right where they had left off three years earlier in Amsterdam. Barth, predictably, argued that the discussion should avoid worldly concerns and instead focus exclusively on the subject of

---

[3] Niebuhr, "Utilitarian Christianity and the World Crisis," p. 66.
[4] Henry Pitney Van Dusen, "The 'Super-Theologians' Meet," *Union Seminary Quarterly Review*, 7 (January 1952), p. 25.

"Jesus Christ, the Crucified Lord, the Only Hope for the World."[5] Niebuhr's response, as to be expected, was that responsible Christians "had no right to express their faith in such purely eschatological terms, that is, in terms which minimize the conquest of evil in particular instances and which place the whole emphasis upon God's final triumph over evil."[6] Despite the aim, according to one attendee, that "unhurried annual meetings . . . might produce a mutual understanding, respect and trust," the informal setting seemed only to inflame the personal animus between the two men.[7] Barth, during the conference, spoke disdainfully of the "Americans (Niebuhr at their head!) with bright, healthy teeth, great determination and few problems."[8] Indeed, at one point, he became so angry with Niebuhr that he threatened to leave the gathering early.[9] Niebuhr attempted to remain professional in his dealing with the Swiss theologian, but referred to Barth in letters to Ursula written during the conference as "a man of unbelievable self-confidence" and as "much more irresponsible personally and theologically than he had imagined."[10]

Fox holds that Niebuhr's time in Geneva had important implications for the subsequent development of *Irony* because his "argument with Barth made him freshly aware of the complexity of American reality."[11] This unsubstantiated observation is dubious, as Niebuhr did not have enough respect for Barth's views on political affairs to change his own as a result of a debate with the Swiss theologian,

---

[5] As found in Eberhard Busch, *Karl Barth: His Life from Letters and Autobiographical Text*, trans. John Bowden (London: SCM Press, 1976), p. 396. Moreover, Barth dismissed any discussion of worldly concerns, bemoaning those who advocated such topics for forcing the group to "tear our hair so much over Christian hope, of all things, instead of rejoicing at it," as found in Busch, *Karl Barth*, p. 396.

[6] Niebuhr, "The 'Super-Theologians' Meet," *Union Seminary Quarterly Review*, 7 (January 1952), pp. 27–8.

[7] Barth spoke of approaching a private meeting with Niebuhr prior to the Geneva gathering with some concern over whether "we would sniff at each other cautiously like two bull mastiffs, or rush barking at each other, or lie stretched out peacefully in the sun side by side." After the meeting, he reported they had "a good conversation," as found in Busch, *Karl Barth*, p. 342.

[8] As found in Busch, *Karl Barth*, p. 395.

[9] As Barth reported in a letter to his wife, Nelly, a Japanese delegate had to intervene and arrange a private meeting between Niebuhr and Barth in order to restore order, as found in Busch, *Karl Barth*, p. 396.

[10] Letter from Niebuhr to Ursula Niebuhr, July 24, 1951, Niebuhr Papers, Box 59; Letter from Niebuhr to Ursula Niebuhr, July 27, 1951, Niebuhr Papers, Box 59.

[11] Fox, *Reinhold Niebuhr*, p. 244.

especially on the subject of America. That said, what Niebuhr's frustrating experience in Geneva may have done, especially given his view that any ecclesial action to address the issues of the day was "hopeless" if Barth was involved, was further confirm his shift toward focusing on more secular audiences that, if not initially receptive to his theological views, at least agreed with his action-oriented focus.[12] Niebuhr's daughter, Elisabeth, reflecting on this period in her father's life, notes that, on a personal level, he increasingly found the company of his colleagues at the ADA "a welcome relief from the sometimes inane, always piously cautious, and frequently self-congratulatory churchmen among whom he might otherwise have had to spend his time."[13] It apparently was with one of them in mind that he wrote a journal article that very summer, "Coherence, Incoherence, and the Christian Faith."[14] At least part of Niebuhr's purpose with the article seemed to be to build on his largely unsubstantiated assertion in *Faith and History* of the "limited rational validation of the truth of the Gospel." At the outset Niebuhr seemed to pull back from his previous claim by stating that, "faith in the sovereignty of a divine creator, judge, and redeemer is not subject to rational proof."[15] Nevertheless, Niebuhr's subsequent arguments revealed that he was dedicated, as in *Faith and History*, to offering a negative and positive approach to relating the truth of the Gospel to that of this world.

Niebuhr's focus was on reiterating the negative argument he had been offering in one form or another since prior to *Human Destiny*, namely, that such was the complexity of history, any rational scheme to comprehend it would actually "point to the limits of rational coherence in understanding contradictory aspects of reality."[16] Niebuhr explained while such a fact would be obvious to Christians, absent religious beliefs, it could only be understood by examining "every cultural discipline . . . seriously up to the point where it becomes conscious of its own limits."[17] As in *Faith and History*,

---

[12] Letter from Niebuhr to Ursula Niebuhr, July 24, 1951, Niebuhr Papers, Box 59.

[13] Elisabeth Sifton, *The Serenity Prayer: Faith and Politics in Times of Peace and War* (New York: Norton, 2003), p. 321. See, on this point, Gary Dorrien, "Christian Realism: Reinhold Niebuhr's Theology, Ethics, and Politics," in Rice, ed., *Reinhold Niebuhr Revisited*, p. 22.

[14] Niebuhr, "Coherence, Incoherence and the Christian Faith," *Union Seminary Quarterly Review*, 7 (January 1952), 11–24.

[15] Niebuhr, "Coherence, Incoherence and the Christian Faith," p. 24.

[16] Niebuhr, "Coherence, Incoherence and the Christian Faith," p. 23.

[17] Niebuhr, "Coherence, Incoherence and the Christian Faith," p. 21.

however, Niebuhr argued that there was also a positive aspect to
pointing out the incongruities of history. Going further than he had
in the past, Niebuhr explained that "highly sophisticated" analyses
were not only capable of proving a discipline's limits but also capable
of pointing to central presuppositions of Christianity that "all judgments passed upon [humans] by history are subject to a more ultimate judgment" and that all humans are "abortively involved in
overcoming the incongruity of [their] existence...by denying
[their] finiteness."[18] While Niebuhr may have provided additional
details on the outlines of his positive apologetic, however, he did not
answer the most fundamental question: how could an analysis of the
incongruities of history point directly to the very theological presuppositions that were at the heart of his Christian interpretation of
history? Or to turn Niebuhr's own words against him, what exactly
was this "proof of the Christian faith, which the unbelievers may
see"?[19]

In fairness to Niebuhr, it should be said that he was well aware of
his failure to provide a compelling answer to this question. He said as
much by explaining that whatever traction he had gained with unbelievers was exclusively a result of the "negative proofs of the
Christian faith" in his writings.[20] Niebuhr explained that these had
"not [been] lost on the most sophisticated moderns who have recognized the inadequacy of the smooth pictures of man and history in
modern culture."[21] As evidence for this claim, Niebuhr pointed to an
unnamed Harvard historian, who could have been none other than
his friend, Arthur Schlesinger, Jr. As we discussed in the last chapter,
the two were actively involved in the ADA and, in the early 1950s,
began to spend time together on a personal basis. It was thus with
great pride and satisfaction that Niebuhr quoted the Harvard historian as observing, "It cannot be denied...that Christian analyses of
human conduct and of human history are truer to the facts of experience than alternative analyses."[22] Further confirming the work that
remained on a meaningful positive approach, Niebuhr included
Schlesinger's additional observation, "Whether the truth of these

---

[18] Niebuhr, "Coherence, Incoherence and the Christian Faith," pp. 23–4.
[19] Niebuhr, "Coherence, Incoherence and the Christian Faith," p. 24.
[20] Niebuhr, "Coherence, Incoherence and the Christian Faith," p. 24.
[21] Niebuhr, "Coherence, Incoherence and the Christian Faith," p. 24.
[22] Niebuhr, "Coherence, Incoherence and the Christian Faith," p. 24.

analyses can be derived only from presuppositions of the Christian faith remains to be determined."[23] Niebuhr's reference to Schlesinger in the context of a discussion on apologetics sheds light on his motivations in writing *Irony*, a process that was ongoing at the time.

Irony, initially titled *This Nation Under God*, was primarily based on two series of lectures that Niebuhr delivered at Westminster College in Fulton, Missouri and Northwestern University in 1949 and 1951, respectively. Both series, according to Niebuhr, were primarily concerned with "the position of our nation in the present world situation, as interpreted from the standpoint of the Christian faith." Reading the available transcripts of these addresses confirms this fact and, further, reveals the analysis of the world situation to be virtually identical in substance and style to Niebuhr's contemporary writings on this very subject we discussed in the last chapter.[24] For instance, Niebuhr's "in the battle and above it" viewpoint can be seen in his observations that Americans "must strive within their powers to do the duty God gives us to do. We must also recognize the limit of our power, the limit of our comprehension of the future."[25] The only significant difference appeared in Niebuhr's lectures at Westminster College in which he traced in greater detail the origins of American self-righteousness to the country's founding. As Niebuhr prepared the work for publication, it was its historical focus that ostensibly motivated Niebuhr to send a manuscript to Schlesinger for his professional opinion.[26] Given that the historical section was merely a

---

[23] Niebuhr, "Coherence, Incoherence and the Christian Faith," p. 24.

[24] Niebuhr, "Love and Justice in the Realm of Politics," First Centennial Conference on International Understanding, Northwestern University. Cahn Auditorium, Evanston, IL. January 28, 1951; Niebuhr "The Christian Faith and the International Community," First Centennial Conference on International Understanding, Northwestern University. Cahn Auditorium, Evanston, IL. January 29, 1951; Niebuhr "Christian Insights on America's Position in the World Today," First Centennial Conference on International Understanding, Northwestern University. Cahn Auditorium, Evanston, IL. January 30, 1951. Little is known about the Northwestern Conference or its participants with the exception that Niebuhr identified George Kennan as being in attendance, "The Christian Faith and the International Community," pp. 10, 16. With regard to Niebuhr's remarks at Westminster, it is quite unfortunate that no transcript appears to exist.

[25] Niebuhr, "The Christian Faith and the International Community," p. 35.

[26] Niebuhr explained in his letter to Schlesinger, "Since I am treading on ground which you know so much better than I, I am almost tempted to send you the manuscript if you have any time to read it, in the hope that you will save me from some bad errors," as found in Ursula M. Niebuhr, ed., *Remembering Reinhold Niebuhr*, pp. 370–1. Niebuhr seemed keen to reiterate his ignorance in the preface

small fraction of the overall work, however, Niebuhr may have had additional reasons for sending the draft to Schlesinger for review. *Irony* was, in part, an effort to show even "the most sophisticated of the moderns" how his analysis of history pointed in the direction of the Christian faith.[27]

This fact is seen in the most significant change that Niebuhr made to the initial text of his lectures—his decision to make irony the work's interpretive framework. Niebuhr first discussed this development, along with his decision to change the title from *This Nation Under God* to *The Irony of American History*, in a letter to Schlesinger in November, a mere two months before the work's publication.[28] Given that the majority of the book had been written before this major development, Niebuhr went through the entire work to "make explicit, what was only implicit in his original lectures."[29] Evidently concerned that even this was not enough, Niebuhr included a preface in *Irony* detailing his use of the concept. Niebuhr made no specific Christian references in his definition of the irony, rather explaining it to be "apparently fortuitous incongruities in life which are discovered, upon closer examination, to be not merely fortuitous."[30] His characterization of what situations qualified for the category of irony, however, revealed its close relationship with his theological beliefs: "If virtue becomes vice through some hidden defect in the virtue; if strength becomes weakness because of the vanity to which the strength may prompt the . . . nation; if wisdom becomes folly because it does not know its own limits."[31] Niebuhr, at the conclusion of the preface, wrote that the

to *Irony*, acknowledging, "I must add that I have no expert competence in the fields of American history; and I apologize in advance to the specialists in the field for what are undoubtedly many errors of fact and judgment," *The Irony of American History* (New York: Charles Scribner's Sons, 1951), pp. viii–ix.

[27] This is supported by the fact that despite soliciting Schlesinger's professional opinion on *Irony*, Niebuhr appeared to adopt very few of the historian's suggestions. For instance, a major one that Niebuhr ignored was Schlesinger's suggestion that "one irony deserving comment is the relationship between [America's] democratic and egalitarian pretensions and our treatment of the Negro," as found in Ursula Niebuhr, ed., *Remembering Reinhold Niebuhr*, p. 371. There were a number of stylistic and language suggestions from the historian that Niebuhr appeared to dismiss as well.

[28] As found in Ursula Niebuhr, ed., *Remembering Reinhold Niebuhr*, p. 372.

[29] Niebuhr, *Irony*, p. vii.

[30] Niebuhr, *Irony*, p. viii.

[31] Niebuhr, *Irony*, p. viii. Further confirming the religious nature of this concept, Niebuhr explained that the only way to resolve an ironic situation was through

concept was merely "a fruitful principle for the interpretation of current history."[32] His previous uses of irony confirm that he also saw it as just the "highly sophisticated" analysis that might serve as "a proof of the Christian faith, which the unbelievers may see."[33] Although *Irony* would be the first time that Niebuhr would formally introduce irony as a central element of his thought, he had used the concept in the past as a bridge to communicate his theological views. His first significant use of the concept can be found in *Discerning* where Niebuhr highlighted the importance of "ironic humor," as he would six years later in *Irony*, in acknowledging the "incongruities of our existence."[34] Niebuhr explained that the concept represented a "higher form of wisdom" than any system of philosophy, first and foremost, because it helped avoid the mistake of reducing the surrounding world into an easily explainable model.[35] More importantly, however, Niebuhr not only highlighted the benefits of recognizing the ironic humor of external situations but also of one's own actions. As he wrote, "If men do not take themselves too seriously, if they have some sense of the precarious nature of human enterprise, they prove they are looking at the whole drama of human life, not merely from the circumscribed point of their own interests, but from some farther and higher vantage point."[36] Given this description, it should be clear why Niebuhr believed that ironic humor and faith were closely related. He explained in *Discerning*, as he would in *Irony*, that ironic humor was the "prelude" to faith.[37]

recognition of the pretension involved and a subsequent act of humble contrition. Indeed a failure to do so, in Niebuhr's opinion, would lead "to a point where irony turns into pure evil," *Irony*, p. viii.

[32] Niebuhr, *Irony*, p. viii.

[33] Niebuhr, "Coherence, Incoherence and Christian Faith," pp. 23–4.

[34] Niebuhr, *Discerning*, p. 99. It is surprising that the vast majority of commentators have not made the connection between Niebuhr's discussion of ironic humor in *Discerning* and his use of irony in *Irony*. An exception is Robert E. Fitch, a contemporary of Niebuhr's, who acknowledged that a reading of *Discerning* was necessary to "get the full development of Niebuhr's thought [on the concept of irony], Fitch, "The Irony of American History," *Religion in Life* Autumn 1952, p. 613. This critical oversight in Niebuhr scholarship may be attributed to the fact that *Discerning* has been widely ignored or because in the specific essay, "Humor and Faith," in which Niebuhr made reference to irony, he used the term interchangeably with humor, thereby creating some confusion, pp. 99–115. It is clear, however, that the concept Niebuhr was referring to in *Discerning* and *Irony*, whether "ironic humor" or "irony," is one and the same given his descriptions are virtually identical. See, for instance, Niebuhr's discussion of irony and the powerful or prideful person, *Irony*, p. 154 and Niebuhr, *Discerning*, p. 100.

[35] Niebuhr, *Discerning*, pp. 110–11.

[36] Niebuhr, *Discerning*, p. 111.   [37] Niebuhr, *Discerning*, p. 111.

In *Faith and History*, Niebuhr also utilized irony as a part of his efforts to relate his theological message to a broader audience.[38] We recall from the last chapter that Niebuhr observed on the first page of the text: "The history of mankind exhibits no more ironic experience than the contrast between the sanguine hopes of recent centuries and the bitter experiences of contemporary man."[39] The specific ironic experience Niebuhr pointed to with greatest frequency in *Faith and History* was the great peril brought on by the development of atomic weaponry. Niebuhr observed wryly that "the same technical instruments by which men have gained a comparative security against the perils and caprices of nature...have created a technical civilization in which men are in greater peril of each other than in simple communities."[40] Niebuhr continued to rely on the concept throughout the work, such as when he noted the irony that not only was the United States presently less safe as a result of its desire to master historical destiny, but its enemy, the Soviet Union, was also engaged in efforts to bring history under control through Communist ideology. Moreover, in between *Faith and History* and *Irony*, Niebuhr turned to the concept of irony to highlight the pretensions he viewed behind America's decision to engage in operations north of the 38th parallel. As the military campaign bore little fruit throughout 1951, Niebuhr increasingly saw the situation through the same lens as the atomic one in that both quandaries were initiated and resulted, in his opinion, from the country's efforts to control history.

The gradual and unsystematic way in which the concept of irony gained currency in Niebuhr's thought over time appears to undercut the efforts of some commentators to identify a specific source.[41]

---

[38] The words, "irony" or "ironic," appear multiple times throughout *Faith and History*, e.g. pp. 1, 8, 9, 88.

[39] Niebuhr, *Faith and History*, p. 1.

[40] Niebuhr, *Faith and History*, p. 88.

[41] Richard Reinitz, rather unsatisfactorily, explains that it was "Niebuhr's neo-orthodox Christianity that led him to the idea of ironic history" without taking the time to explain exactly what those neo-orthodox views were or how they informed his view of irony, *Irony and Consciousness: American Historiography and Reinhold Niebuhr's Vision* (Lewisburg, PA: Bucknell University Press, 1980), p. 34. More perceptive is Larry Rasmussen, who observes that "a more extensive introduction to Niebuhr's thought would necessarily include his study of irony" which he attributed to the "influence of Kierkegaard upon Niebuhr," *Reinhold Niebuhr*, p. 290, n. 61.

Niebuhr's wife, Ursula, in response to one such attempt following his death, rejected it with the observation, "I find always a little difficulty with those who analyze and interpret Reinhold's thought systematically, without always knowing the historical context that produced that particular theme in his thought."[42] Two scholars, Robert Fitch and Ronald Stone, follow this model and attempt to trace the historical development of Niebuhr's understanding of the ironic. Fitch, for instance, argues that the concept, if not in so many words, had been a central element of the theologian's thought since his publication of *Reflections* in 1934.[43] Stone, in an effort to counter this claim, adopts a more literal approach in tracing its origins to Niebuhr's writings following World War II.[44] Rather than seeing these two views in opposition, this chapter claims that both have merit. On one hand, Fitch is correct in that Niebuhr's concept of irony finds its origins in his Christian interpretation of history, which, in the first chapter, we explained began to take form in *Reflections*. On the other hand, Stone is right, as we saw in the third chapter, in that Niebuhr only began to explicitly rely on the category of irony to communicate his Christian interpretation of history beginning with *Discerning* in 1946. In any event, it is clear that the major themes in *Irony*, to which we now turn, had been previously presented in Niebuhr's more explicitly theological writings.

[42] Rasmussen was unaware that Larry L. Adams had explored the subject of Niebuhr's indebtedness to Kierekgaard in the late 1970s. Adams argues, without substantiating this point, that "Niebuhr was profoundly impressed by Kierkegaard, and by his understanding of irony, as a transitional moment for the listener, a moment of exchange of meanings, a moment in which the speaker using irony was inviting personal engagement and response from the listener," "Reinhold Niebuhr and the Critique of American Liberal Ideals," prepared for delivery before the Northeastern Political Science Association, November 10, 1978, as found in Niebuhr Papers, Box 54. Ursula responded directly to Adams's assertion in a letter to a friend by acknowledging that while Niebuhr had read Kierkegaard, "that [was] not the point." Moreover, she expressed the desire that in general, "people would stop analyzing Niebuhr's thought from a perspective that may not have been his at the time," Letter from Ursula Niebuhr to Hugh (unknown), Niebuhr Papers, January 31, 1980, Box 54. For an overview to Niebuhr's general aversion to literary motifs, see Halliwell, *The Constant Dialogue*, p. 160.
[43] Robert E. Fitch, "Reinhold Niebuhr's Philosophy of History," in Kegley and Bretall, eds, *Reinhold Niebuhr*, pp. 302–4.
[44] Stone, *Professor Reinhold Niebuhr*, pp. 192–5.

THE IRONY OF AMERICAN HISTORY

Irony begins in a similar fashion to *Faith and History* with the observation, "Our age is involved in irony... because our dreams of bringing the whole of human history under the control of human will are ironically refuted..."[45] Niebuhr also targeted a familiar foil for propagating this misplaced viewpoint—Dewey and those, like him, who assumed that human nature could be manipulated by methods similar to those used in physical nature. Such "philosopher-science-kings," in Niebuhr's opinion, failed to recognize the complexity of causation in history and the fact that humans were at the same time creatures and creators in their own drama.[46] Echoing his previous writings, Niebuhr explained the fact that Americans were not masters of their historical destiny was most evident in the present atomic struggle with the Soviet Union. Despite remarkable technological advances in our "understand[ing] and control of the atom," there had not been accompanying progress in the understanding and control of human nature.[47] The current state of insecurity in which the country found itself revealed that, if anything, the exact opposite had occurred. The fact that America, at the peak of its global influence, was more vulnerable to outside threats than in its nascency led Niebuhr to conclude, "The pattern of the historical drama grows more quickly than the strength of even the most powerful man or nation."[48]

If much of Niebuhr's use of the ironic was merely a reiteration of his views over the previous decade, his explanation of what made the American situation "doubly ironic" built on arguments he had been making as early as the 1930s. Niebuhr explained that his use of this concept was appropriate because the country with which America was engaged in this nuclear showdown, the Soviet Union, was animated by a view of history as hubristic as its own. If many Americans were guilty of holding on to the belief that a complete social harmony was imminent, Communists argued that such a society was already in place in their country following the Russian Revolution. Niebuhr, with this argument, clearly was echoing the criticisms he leveled at the Soviet Union following his tour of the country in 1931. This fact was

[45] Niebuhr, *Irony*, pp. 2–3.   [46] Niebuhr, *Irony*, p. 4.
[47] Niebuhr, *Irony*, p. 80.   [48] Niebuhr, *Irony*, p. 3.

further confirmed when he explained throughout *Irony* that the sharpest critique of the Marxist historical narrative was the brutally coercive nature in which Moscow turned theory into practice. If Niebuhr had pointed to the Soviet Union's oppression of its own population twenty years prior, he now documented the brutal actions the government took to spread its Communist ideology throughout Eastern Europe. Given the severity of these actions, Niebuhr was willing to distinguish between what he called the "partially harmful illusions" of the United States and the "totally noxious one" of the Soviet Union.[49] Nevertheless, he was clearly more concerned with asserting that differences between the two countries were measurable only in degrees. He explained, "Communism changes only partly dangerous sentimentalities and inconsistencies in the [American democratic] ethos into consistent and totally harmful ones."[50]

Niebuhr was so intent on highlighting the similarities between the two nations precisely because many in the United States had been doing just the opposite by portraying the Cold War as a struggle between good and evil. Such an approach was to be expected, how-ever, given the fact that America, according to Niebuhr, believed itself to be "the most innocent nation on earth."[51] There was a cultural and historical reason behind this misguided belief in his estimation. The cultural was the rejection of the Christian doctrine of original sin by modern intellectuals. This misguided step led too many influential Americans to claim positions of complete objectivity when examining the problems encountering the world, even those directly influencing their own lives. In the case of Cold War, such convictions resulted in the willingness of those in the United States to draw "neat and sharp distinctions between justice and injustice" with regard to their country and the Soviet Union.[52] Niebuhr traced the historical source for this illusion of innocence to the nation's founding and the two dominant traditions of that era, the New England Puritans and Virginia-based Jeffersonians. Although the two traditions held vastly different views, both, according to Niebuhr, shared the belief that America "had been called out by God to create a new humanity."[53] The vast majority of the Founding Fathers, Niebuhr explained, viewed their nation as "God's American Israel" and

[49] Niebuhr, *Irony*, p. 14.   [50] Niebuhr, *Irony*, p. 15.
[51] Niebuhr, *Irony*, p. 23.   [52] Niebuhr, *Irony*, pp. 18–19.
[53] Niebuhr, *Irony*, p. 24.

that belief, according to Niebuhr, still remained almost two hundred years later.[54] While acknowledging that most nations took a similarly inflated view of their national destiny, Niebuhr held that what distinguished the United States was its historical and cultural pretension had the double effect of "heighten[ing] the whole concept of a virtuous humanity which characterizes the culture of our era."[55]

Niebuhr explained that the incongruity between America's illusions and the realities it faced only added to the irony of its present situation. For instance, the country, regardless of its pious preening, was now the custodian of a weapon that "perfectly embodies and symbolizes the moral ambiguity of physical warfare."[56] Even though dropping the atomic bomb might be required, as it had been at the conclusion of World War II, to preserve the lives of millions of Americans, its use, according to Niebuhr, would nevertheless "cover the [United States] with a terrible guilt."[57] It was for this reason, in particular, that Niebuhr observed, "The perennial moral predicaments of human history have caught up with a culture which knew nothing of sin or guilt, and with a nation which seemed to be the most perfect fruit of that culture."[58] Moreover, he stressed that America's unparalleled position of authority in the world, combined with this illusion of innocence, left the country exposed to the double pretension of power and virtue. Both, Niebuhr explained, were on full display in the ongoing stalemate in Korea. America had been blind to the fact that its noble effort to halt the advance of Communism would, on one hand, come up against such fierce resistance from a seemingly outmatched foe and, on the other, be viewed as a form of imperialism in its own right.[59] In order to find a precedent for the position in which the country now found itself, Niebuhr turned to the Bible. He observed, "One has the uneasy feeling that America as both a powerful nation and as a 'virtuous' one is involved in ironic perils which compound the experiences of Babylon and Israel."[60]

Niebuhr was clearly discouraged about America's prospects for successfully overcoming the ironic pretensions presently undermining its global engagements. He explained this pessimism was only compounded by the fact that America's "unenviable position [was]

---

[54] Niebuhr, *Irony*, p. 25.   [55] Niebuhr, *Irony*, p. 24.
[56] Niebuhr, *Irony*, p. 39.   [57] Niebuhr, *Irony*, p. 39.
[58] Niebuhr, *Irony*, p. 39.   [59] Niebuhr, *Irony*, p. 57.
[60] Niebuhr, *Irony*, p. 160.

made the more difficult because the heat of the battle gives us neither the leisure nor the inclination to detect the irony in our own history or to profit from the discovery of the double irony between ourselves and our foe."[61] What caused Niebuhr further angst was what he perceived to be the inadequacy of the responses provided by America's brightest foreign policy minds to these challenges. The one he decided to single out for closer scrutiny was his close friend, George Kennan.[62] Although complimentary of Kennan's ability to identify the problems facing the country, Niebuhr disputed the diplomat's suggestion from his memoirs that the solution was a return to an approach exclusively dedicated to advancing the national interest.[63] Niebuhr justified his opposition to this approach on what appeared to be theological beliefs. He explained, "The cure for a pretentious idealism, which claims to know more about the future and about other men than is given to moral man to know, is not egoism" but "a modest awareness of the limits of [one's] own knowledge and power."[64] Niebuhr acknowledged that the likelihood of the United States developing such awareness was small given the self-righteousness of all nations. As a result, the most encouragement he could offer was that it did make a "difference whether the culture in which the policies of nations are formed" was influenced by "the standpoint of which the element of vanity in all human ambitions and achievements is observed."[65]

WHERE IS THE THEOLOGY?

Niebuhr's observations of the contemporary situation in *Irony*, when analyzed closely, are revealed to be primarily reiterations of those he had previously offered. The most striking break with the past was that these observations were advanced without the underlying theological

[61] Niebuhr, *Irony*, p. 16. Although Niebuhr did not directly mention his own struggles with maintaining the perspective that was documented in the last chapter, his observations reflect a newfound appreciation for this difficulty.

[62] Niebuhr's critique was taken in full from a review he wrote in *Crisis* of Kennan's *American Diplomacy 1900–1950*, "Editorial Notes," *Christianity and Crisis*, October 28, 1951, pp. 138–9.

[63] Niebuhr, *Irony*, p. 148.

[64] Niebuhr, *Irony*, p. 148.   [65] Niebuhr, *Irony*, pp. 149–50.

vision on which they had previously been situated. Niebuhr was certainly aware of this issue but chose largely to ignore it until the concluding chapter of *Irony*. It was only then that he raised the question, "Is an ironic interpretation of current history generally plausible; or does its credibility depend upon a Christian view of history in which the ironic view seems to be particularly grounded?"[66] Even then, Niebuhr, as we have discussed, equivocated in his response. On the one hand, he pointed out that there were many aspects of contemporary history that were so obviously ironic that any observer could detect them.[67] On the other hand, Niebuhr held that the only consistent way to observe these ironic elements was through the adoption of the Christian faith, which embodied "[t]he combination of critical, but not hostile, detachment, which is required for their detection."[68] Niebuhr explained, as he had in the past, that what enabled Christians to develop a detachment of this type was "a basic faith" in the fact that the "whole drama of human history is under the scrutiny of a divine judge who laughs at human pretensions without being hostile to human aspirations."[69] This was the very presupposition on which Niebuhr's Christian interpretation of history had rested since the 1930s.

If Niebuhr believed that the Christian faith was necessary to sustain his ironic framework, why did he choose to make this fundamental point at the end, rather than the beginning, of *Irony*? Marty explains that Niebuhr wanted to establish his ironic interpretation of history "without making a demand for faith."[70] But, in light of the strategy Niebuhr outlined in "Coherence, Incoherence, and the Christian Faith," the more accurate interpretation may be that Niebuhr established his ironic interpretation of history precisely in order to make a demand for faith. The ironic, in his opinion, was just the "highly sophisticated" analysis of history's incongruity that could point unbelievers in the direction of

[66] Niebuhr, *Irony*, p. 152.
[67] The primary aspect of America's current situation that Niebuhr found ironic was the fact that the country, despite being at the height of its global influence following World War II, faced greater existential threats than ever before due to the extent of its foreign commitments and the advent of nuclear weaponry.
[68] Niebuhr, *Irony*, p. 155.
[69] Niebuhr, *Irony*, p. 155.
[70] The broader context for Marty's opinion is his observation that "Such few passages in the last chapter aside ... the rest of the book treats the Christian grounding as an element in American history. It was therefore 'reasonable' and not at all an evidence of ignorance in the face of a not always explicit Niebuhr ... to draw on this historical resource with its witness to paradoxes-without making a demand for faith": "Reinhold Niebuhr and *The Irony of American History*," p. 169.

Christianity.[71] In other words, Niebuhr revealed the Christian presuppositions on which the ironic viewpoint was based after demon-
strating its superiority in shedding light on the contemporary
situation in order to lead the reader to accept those very presuppositions. If this was his intention with *Irony*, then, unfortunately, what
hampered it was an inability to solve the issue that had plagued such
efforts since *Faith and History*. Niebuhr could not adequately explain why attempts to adopt his ironic perspective without accepting
the Christian presuppositions on which it was based would fail.
He attempted to address this point indirectly in *Irony* by suggesting
that the ironic and Christian viewpoints were more compatible than
one might expect: "The Biblical view of human nature and destiny
moves within the framework of irony with remarkable consist-
ency."[72] Instead of making unbelievers more amenable to the faith,
Niebuhr's argument that the main tenets of Christianity were compatible with the category of irony seemed to undermine the notion
that the faith offered something irony did not.

What makes Niebuhr's inability to justify this belief in *Irony* more
frustrating is that he had done just this in *Discerning*. Indeed, Niebuhr, in "Humor and Faith," had convincingly explained the inability
of ironic humor to address the more pressing challenges facing
humanity absent an underlying belief in Jesus Christ. Just as he did
in *Irony*, Niebuhr began by explaining that ironic humor was "a more
adequate resource for the incongruities of life than the spirit of
philosophy."[73] In *Discerning*, however, he went further to argue that
when "pressed to solve the ultimate issue, [it] turns into a vehicle of
bitterness."[74] This is because ironic laughter was unable to come to
grips with the universal sinfulness that was at the core of the incongruities of history. This core, in Niebuhr's estimation, could only be
"overcome by the power and the love of God and the love which
Christ revealed."[75] Furthermore, Niebuhr explained the difference
between Christian and ironic interpretations of history in stark
terms: "Either we have a faith from a standpoint of which we are
able to say, 'I am persuaded that neither death or life . . . shall be able
to separate us from the love of God which is in Christ Jesus our Lord'

[71] Niebuhr, "Coherence, Incoherence and the Christian Faith," p. 23.
[72] Niebuhr, *Irony*, p. 158.   [73] Niebuhr, *Discerning*, p. 110.
[74] Niebuhr, *Discerning*, p. 112.   [75] Niebuhr, *Discerning*, p. 114.

or we are overwhelmed by the incongruity."[76] Niebuhr left little room for doubt in *Discerning* as to why the ironic led an individual to the Christian faith: otherwise he would sink into despair. Conversely, in *Irony*, Niebuhr would only say an "ironic smile must turn into bitter laughter or into bitterness without laughter" absent a "religious sense."[77]

Niebuhr's decision to avoid any reference to Jesus Christ in *Irony* also distinguishes it from *Discerning*. His most explicit reference to the foundational narrative of Christianity was a general assertion that "life has a center and source of meaning beyond the natural and social consequences which may be rationally discerned."[78] Niebuhr clearly thought such benign language would make his religious viewpoint more palatable to those unbelievers who might be drawn in by his ironic framework. However, as he had shown in *Discerning*, the only way to justify a move beyond the ironic to a position of faith was through discussion of the crucifixion and resurrection. Niebuhr's decision to avoid any reference to the central events of the Bible not only undermined his ability to share his theological vision, it also undermined the vision itself. Regardless of the past difficulties Niebuhr had explaining the meaning of the "eschatological expectations in the New Testament," he nevertheless had left no doubt that they were "necessary for a Christian interpretation of history."[79] As Niebuhr explained on multiple occasions, it was only the resurrection, for instance, that allowed Christians to "look toward the end of history with faith and hope, rather than fear," especially given the growing uncertainties of the present age.[80] As a result of his decision to avoid explicitly theological language in *Irony*, Niebuhr painted an even bleaker picture of the present global situation than he had previously and had little positive to say with regard to the future. Instead, Niebuhr was left to submit that "evil and destructiveness [were] not regarded as the inevitable consequence" of the atomic age.[81]

A less obvious, but equally damaging, result of Niebuhr's decision to submerge the theological basis for *Irony* was that, by doing so, he

---

[76] Niebuhr, *Discerning*, p. 113. Niebuhr ended the essay with a poetic observation, "That is why there is laughter in the vestibule of the temple, the echo of laughter in the temple itself, but only faith and prayer, and no laughter, in the holy of the holies," *Discerning*, p. 115.

[77] Niebuhr, *Irony*, pp. 168–9.   [78] Niebuhr, *Irony*, p. 168.

[79] Niebuhr, *Faith and History*, p. 243.   [80] Niebuhr, *Faith and History*, p. 268.

[81] Niebuhr, *Irony*, p. 158.

obscured the means by which he made historical judgments. Niebuhr had been arguing explicitly since *Human Destiny* that an understanding of Christ was necessary to preserve "moral endeavor and responsibility" in history since it gave us a "faith by which we can seek to fulfill our historic tasks... without despair."[82] In *Discerning*, Niebuhr came at this point from the opposite direction by explaining how ironic humor, on its own, did not contain the necessary resources to foster decisive historical action. He went so far as to say that it could do little to help the victims of tyranny and actually "turned to bitterness when it faces serious evil, precisely because" it has not "power in it to deter the evil against which it is directed."[83] Not only did Niebuhr make historical judgments in *Irony*, in some cases, he appeared to make them more clearly than in the past. At the outset, he asserted, "We are defending freedom against tyranny and are trying to preserve justice against a system, which has, demonically, distilled injustice and cruelty out of its original promise of a higher justice."[84] Moreover, Niebuhr seemed to sanction harsh measures on the part of the United States to defend its freedom by famously observing, "We take, and must continue to take, morally hazardous actions to preserve our civilization."[85] Once Niebuhr introduced irony into the work as the paradigm though which to view current history, he stopped making such forceful statements. While he did criticize the Soviet Union in select places, it was largely to highlight the ironic relationship between its misbehavior and the illusions of the United States.[86] What appeared missing was the clear assertion in *Discerning*, namely, that discussing irony when engaged in conflict with the "most insufferable forms of tyranny" was the height of "irresponsibility."[87] In the majority of the text, Niebuhr offered a diluted version of his "in the battle and

---

[82] Niebuhr, "Christian Otherworldliness," *Christianity and Society* (Winter 1943), p. 12.

[83] Niebuhr, *Discerning*, 103. Niebuhr made explicit the fact that "there was no humor in the scene of Christ upon the Cross... save the ironic inscription on the Cross, ordered by Pilate: 'The King of the Jews'," *Discerning*, p. 105.

[84] Niebuhr, *Irony*, p. 1.

[85] Niebuhr, *Irony*, p. 5.

[86] Niebuhr repeatedly referred to the Soviet Union as "vexatious" and "tyrannical" throughout *Irony*, but it was largely against the backdrop of his larger efforts to reveal its similarities with the United States.

[87] Niebuhr, *Discerning*, pp. 103, 107.

above it" formulation primarily because he downplayed its theological core.

Niebuhr, in the final pages of *Irony*, did reassert the theological vision that had been lurking underneath the surface the work, as he explained that faith, not irony, was "the most significant frame of meaning for the interpretation of life as a whole."[88] Given his desire to avoid overtly Christian language, Niebuhr, rather than crowning this point by referring to Jesus Christ as he had in the past, looked to none other than Abraham Lincoln. This unlikely turn to Lincoln rather than to Christological faith can only be understood in the context of Niebuhr's past writings where he had done just this by channeling his "in the battle and above it" viewpoint through the president. Niebuhr entered into his discussion of Lincoln by observing that the detachment he was able to achieve during the Civil War was almost inconceivable given his position as the leader of the Union cause. For this reason Niebuhr held it must have been a "religious awareness of another dimension of meaning than that of the immediate political conflict" that allowed Lincoln, in his Second Inaugural Address, to acknowledge, "Both sides . . . read the same Bible and pray to the same God."[89] Niebuhr was clear, however, that this detachment was not the only quality of Lincoln's that impressed him. Echoing his analysis fifteen years earlier in *Beyond Tragedy*, Niebuhr observed that Lincoln's religious beliefs also led him to advocate against slavery and ultimately take the necessary steps for emancipation. He explained that this "combination of moral resoluteness about the immediate issues with a religious awareness of another dimension of meaning and judgment must be regarded as almost a perfect model of the difficult . . . task of remaining loyal and responsible toward the moral treasures of a free civilization while yet having some religious vantage point over the struggle."[90] In explaining how this applied to the present situation, Niebuhr adopted a formulation strikingly similar to his "in the battle and above it" approach. On the one hand, Lincoln's model revealed that "modern Communist tyranny is certainly as wrong as slavery" but, on the other had, it confirmed that America could not "establish the righteousness of our cause by a monotonous reiteration of the virtues of freedom compared with the evils of tyranny."[91]

---

[88] Niebuhr, *Irony*, p. 167.   [89] Niebuhr, *Irony*, p. 171.
[90] Niebuhr, *Irony*, p. 172.   [91] Niebuhr, *Irony*, pp. 172–3.

Contemporary reviews of *Irony* were mixed in that Niebuhr's use of irony was widely hailed and his references to faith, if acknowledged, were largely dismissed. A number of prominent historians such as Perry Miller and Henry F. May praised this ironic interpretation of history and C. Vann Woodward explicitly incorporated it into his own work.[92] Miller's response was perhaps most telling, however, as he claimed to be one of many who "copiously availed themselves of Niebuhr's conclusions without pretending to share his basic, and to him indispensable, premise."[93] If Miller at least acknowledged the theological premises of *Irony*, Schlesinger, with whom Niebuhr had been in direct communication prior to its publication, appeared to stress the exact opposite. Schlesinger, in his review, singled out for praise his friend's willingness to "draw a firm line ... designed to keep the absolute out of the relative."[94] The only individual to understand fully that Niebuhr's conclusions could not stand apart from their theological premises rejected both. Morton White, an acolyte of Dewey, saw *Irony* less as an analysis of the contemporary situation and more as "the work of a theologian defending religious views about the nature of man and history."[95] In his estimation, Niebuhr's ironic outlook was not merely intended to combat "simpleminded optimism" but actually designed as a gateway for such irrational principles as "the doctrine of original sin."[96] White also raised the

---

[92] For a detailed discussion of Niebuhr's influence on professional historians, see Marty, "Reinhold Niebuhr and *The Irony of American History*," pp. 162–5. With regard to Woodward, Marty notes that he "acknowledged Niebuhrian influence sufficiently to title an address and essay in 1952, 'The Irony of Southern History,'" p. 164. See, on this point, C. Vann Woodward, "The Irony of Southern History," *Journal of Southern History*, 19:1 (February 1953), pp. 3–19. In general, John E. Smith observes that "No work of Niebuhr's elicited a more spirited response from historians, theologians, and students of politics than *The Irony of American History*," "Niebuhr's Prophetic Voice," in Rice, ed., *Reinhold Niebuhr Revisited*, p. 50.

[93] As found in Marty, "Reinhold Niebuhr and *The Irony of American History*," p. 162.

[94] Arthur Schlesinger, Jr., "Niebuhr and Some Critics," *Christianity and Society* (Autumn 1952), p. 27.

[95] Morton White, "Of Moral Predicaments," *The New Republic*, May 5, 1952, p. 18.

[96] White, "Of Moral Predicaments," p. 18. To a lesser extent historian Crane Brinton seemed to have realized the significance of Niebuhr's theological presuppositions. He offered that *Irony* not only required an acceptance of political conclusions but "if not Dr Niebuhr's Christian theism ... then his pessimistic view of human nature, his concept of original sin," "The Problem of Evil in Human History," *New York Herald Tribune Book Review*, April 6, 1952, p. 5. White's opposition to Niebuhr's theology was shared by historian William Leuchtenburg, who, in his review of *Irony*,

central question of why an acknowledgment of history's "ironic failures" necessitated an acceptance of "obscure [Christian] dogmas about 'historical fate'."[97] Instead of a turn to faith, he suggested that individuals would be better off relying on their reason and "proceed by trial and error."[98] Importantly, not even White, in his otherwise penetrating critique, discerned the theological significance of Lincoln for Niebuhr.

LINCOLN AS "AMERICA'S GREATEST THEOLOGIAN"

Niebuhr's theological vision is present in *Irony*, but, rather than being readily apparent, it is more like a watermark beneath the text. His decision to avoid explicit references to the Christian faith in the work certainly enabled it to reach a broader audience than those he had authored in the past. What is less clear, however, is whether this increase in readership was worth the sacrifice to his core message. Such analysis has not been conducted since the few commentators that have explored the theological basis for *Irony* have not acknowledged the very trade-offs that Niebuhr highlighted in *Discerning*. Marty, in his discussion of the work, fails to find any problems with Niebuhr's approach, and, moreover, portrays it as a prime example of a modern theologian inhabiting multiple realities.[99] What he means by this is that Niebuhr had the ability to adopt a different "stance" when crafting insightful political analysis as compared to a more academic theological work.[100] In simple terms, Marty approves of Niebuhr de-emphasizing his theological presuppositions in *Irony* because, surely, when the theologian subsequently addressed "'God

criticized Niebuhr reliance on doctrines such as original sin and chided the theologian for positing "a mocking God who laughs at our 'exertions'," "Niebuhr: The Theologian and the Liberal," *New Leader*, November 24, 1952, pp. 23–4.

[97] White, "Of Moral Predicaments," p. 19.

[98] White, "Of Moral Predicaments," p. 18.

[99] Marty continued by explaining that those who inhabit multiple realities "express themselves through the language of various 'provinces of meaning.' Niebuhr the prophet witnessed in the pulpit; Niebuhr the philosopher wrote for the academics; Niebuhr the theologian influenced also those who could pick up on his motifs without believing in the God who 'sitteth in the heavens,' thence showing justice and mercy alike," "Reinhold Niebuhr and *The Irony of American History*," p. 172.

[100] Marty, "Reinhold Niebuhr and *The Irony of American History*," p. 167.

fearing' fellow-believers," he would restore those same presuppositions to a position of prominence.[101] There are two main problems
with Marty's interpretation. The first is that it fails to acknowledge the
possibility that Niebuhr's approach in *Irony* could influence the
direction of his more theological works given the remarkable continuity that did exist across the spectrum of Niebuhr's writings. This
continuity could be seen during World War II in the nuanced
relationship between Niebuhr's journalistic commentary and his
more academic *Nature and Destiny*. The second, and more important, is that Niebuhr's approach in *Irony* did influence the direction of
his future theological writings. Rather than restoring his Christian
presuppositions following *Irony*, Niebuhr continued to minimize
their importance in all of his writings. Moreover, he increasingly
became more dependent on Lincoln as the vehicle through which to
express his theological vision.

To be fair, Niebuhr may have had trouble retaining the balance in
his writings after *Irony* due to his failing health.[102] Throughout the
first half of 1952 Niebuhr experienced a series of small strokes that left
his speech impaired and the left side of his body partially paralyzed.
After months of convalescence, Niebuhr would regain the necessary
strength to resume his writing and teaching responsibilities but was
unable to continue the frenetic travel schedule that had served to keep
him closely engaged with influential figures across the fields of theology and politics. Niebuhr missed the remaining sessions in Geneva
at which his fellow theologians continued their discussions on Christian hope in preparation for the Evanston Assembly. It is unlikely that
Niebuhr and Barth would have come to a "mutual understanding" on
Christian hope in the full allotment of meetings as the organizing
body hoped, given their lifetime of divergent opinions and quite
serious personal differences. Nevertheless, Niebuhr would have

[101] Marty, "Reinhold Niebuhr and *The Irony of American History*," p. 174.
[102] There is significant debate among Niebuhr scholars over the influence of the
theologian's medical issues on his intellectual vitality. For instance, Fox categorizes
the period following the stroke as Niebuhr's "declining years," whereas Brown, in his
discussion of the affliction, counters that "[m]uch of [Niebuhr's] best work lay ahead,"
Reinhold Niebuhr, p. 273; *Niebuhr and His Age*, p. 164. The actual answer lies
somewhere between these views. Niebuhr continued to provide insightful analysis
on political and religious subjects in subsequent works, but the theological vision that
had animated his previous writings increasingly was lacking. For a useful discussion of
the scholarly debate over Niebuhr's later years, see Halliwell, *The Constant Dialogue*,
pp. 132–4.

benefited from additional interactions with Barth and the other attendees at these gatherings, given how important such events had been in the past to his intellectual development and, particularly, given the topic of debate was the one most noticeably absent from his analysis in *Irony*. Instead, Niebuhr's participation in the group was limited to journalistic commentary written from the confines of his apartment in New York.

A 1954 article in *Crisis* shows that Niebuhr's main criticism of the preparatory committee's final report remained largely unchanged from the one he had offered on the draft developed at the initial gathering at which he was present—it bore too much of Barth's influence.[103] His reasons for opposing what he believed to be its overly eschatological focus extended beyond the charge of political quietism he typically leveled at the Swiss theologian's work, however. Niebuhr expressed a broader concern that a topic of Christian hope was the wrong one for the church to be discussing if it wanted to address the contemporary needs of society. He explained, "The New Testament eschatology is at once too naive for a sophisticated world . . . [that] has become so accustomed to try to make sense out of life by measuring history in terms of some scheme of rational intelligibility."[104] This observation was clearly an argument in favor of the approach that Niebuhr had adopted in *Irony*. More than this, Niebuhr's subsequent discussion of Christian eschatology revealed a degree of skepticism that had not been evident previously in his writings. At one point, Niebuhr observed, "It is just as foolish to bear witness to our faith by insisting on what will seem to the world a fantastic hope as to bear witness to our faith by our personal hope of 'the resurrection.'"[105] Such words appear particularly jarring in *Crisis*, given he had called a decade earlier in its pages for a "reaffirmation of the Christian faith in terms which will gain the loyalty of the

---

[103] With regard to the last two preparatory meetings that Niebuhr had been unable to attend, Barth commented, "Perhaps it was because now we had got to know each other. And perhaps it was because in the meanwhile we had all thought more about the matter, read our Bibles and therefore had automatically been brought closer to each other . . . but it happened that we not only spoke of the Christian hope but also grew together in it," as found in Busch, *Karl Barth*, pp. 396–9. The dynamic and conclusions of the preparatory committee would likely have been far different had Niebuhr been able to remain actively involved.

[104] Niebuhr "The Theme of Evanston," *Christianity and Crisis*, August 9, 1954, p. 110.

[105] Niebuhr, "The Theme of Evanston," p. 110.

multitudes," which he explained to be a recognition that "there is no final fulfillment of life except in 'the forgiveness of sins, the resurrection of the body, and the life everlasting.'"[106] If Niebuhr had previously suppressed the importance of Christianity to his thought in order to attract a broad audience, he apparently now believed that doing so required expressing doubts about the faith as well.

Niebuhr's 1955 publication of *The Self and the Dramas of History* further confirmed the growing disconnection between his present and past writings on the Christian faith. Although Niebuhr explained *Self* was intended to build on the interpretation of history he previously developed in *Nature and Destiny* and *Faith and History*, it appeared to undermine the main themes of those two works.[107] Niebuhr began *Self* by reiterating the role that biblical insights could play in addressing the challenges of the age. True to form, he explained that only the Christian faith could "encourage the modesty and patience which will prevent tensions [between the United States and Soviet Union] from becoming catastrophic," given both countries were "trying to bring history to a premature conclusion."[108] In previous works, Niebuhr had explained the source of such modesty and patience was a faith in Jesus Christ. Rather than reasserting this claim in *Self*, however, Niebuhr repeated his uneasiness with any historical claims about the bodily resurrection of Christ. He explained it to not "be well attested as an historical event" and further "question[ed] whether the experience of the 'Living Lord' was not the private experience of his disciples and was later justified and made more vivid by the empty tomb."[109] Unsurprisingly Niebuhr did not end *Self*, as he had *Faith and History* and *Nature and Destiny*, with a testimony to the ultimate hope provided in the death and resurrection of Christ. The most he would offer was the observation that Christianity's "incredible hope for the end of history" had more to offer than "the alternative hopes which have beguiled, and then disappointed, past generations."[110] Given Niebuhr's skepticism about the physical resurrection, however, the basis of this incredible hope was unclear.

---

[106] Niebuhr, "The Religious Level of the World Crisis," p. 5.

[107] Letter from Niebuhr to June Bingham, Niebuhr Papers, December 1, 1953, Box 26.

[108] Niebuhr, *The Self and the Dramas of History* (New York: Charles Scribner's Sons, 1955), pp. 160–1.

[109] Niebuhr, *The Self and the Dramas of History*, p. 237.

[110] Niebuhr, *The Self and the Dramas of History*, p. 238.

While Niebuhr believed that his questioning of the literal truth of biblical events was intellectually honest and a useful tool in his outreach to unbelievers, he was also aware that it would raise questions among his fellow theologians. Although the majority had been critical of Niebuhr's mythological or symbolic interpretation of these events, many had appeared to table their objections on the basis that they were useless given Niebuhr's unwillingness to explain what he meant.[111] This became increasingly difficult for Niebuhr's colleagues to do over the course of the 1950s, however, as Niebuhr's view of resurrection appeared more incredulous than symbolic. This issue came to a head in 1956 when Niebuhr was the featured theologian of a "Library of Living Theology" volume. This entailed him writing an article on his intellectual development, serving as the subject of a series of articles by his colleagues, and then responding to those articles with one of his own. Niebuhr, in his intellectual biography, tried to preempt the coming criticisms by explaining, "I have been frequently challenged by the stricter sets of theologians ... to prove that my interests were theological rather than practical or 'apologetic,' but I have always refused to enter a defense, partly because I thought the point was well taken and partly because the distinction did not interest me."[112] As one would expect, Niebuhr's colleagues, although uniformly complimentary of Niebuhr's contributions, rigorously questioned Niebuhr's interpretation of biblical events. For instance, Alan Richardson, a British theologian, argued, regardless of Niebuhr's previous claims to the contrary, *Self* had exposed Niebuhr's symbolic interpretations as part and parcel with Bultmann's demythologizing efforts.[113] In the same vein, Emil Brunner expressed dismay at Niebuhr's portrayal of the resurrection. Specifically, he questioned what hope could be derived from a symbolic understanding of the event: "Is it an everlasting life, for which we should hope in the hour of death? Is it the fulfillment of the Biblical expectation of the kingdom

---

[111] This sentiment can certainly be found in Richard Niebuhr, "Reinhold Niebuhr's Interpretation of History," p. 101, as well as in Paul Tillich, "Reply to Criticism," in Kegley and Bretall, eds, *The Theology of Paul Tillich*, pp. 338–9.

[112] Niebuhr, "Intellectual Autobiography," in Kegley and Bretall, eds, *Reinhold Niebuhr*, p. 3.

[113] Richardson explained that Niebuhr's recent use of biblical symbols was, "after the manner of Bultmann, as a merely mythological means of bringing out the significance of the historical," "Reinhold Niebuhr as Apologist," in Kegley and Bretall, eds, *Reinhold Niebuhr*, p. 225.

of God?"[114] Moreover, Brunner argued that Niebuhr's claim not to be interested in such "theological" questions was not sufficient, as every Christian thinker had a responsibility to express "what he has to hope for in Christ."[115]

Niebuhr's reply, in spite of his colleagues' efforts to pin him down, was merely another exercise in artful evasion. In response to Richardson's accusations, rather than distinguishing his writings from those of Bultmann more clearly, Niebuhr returned to his previous discussion of permanent and primitive myth. The one concession he made was that his use of the word "myth" had created confusion given its "subjective and skeptical connotations," and as a result, he "was sorry [he] ever used it."[116] As to the criticism of his subjective and skeptical interpretation of the resurrection, however, Niebuhr would only concede that "a real issue" existed with his understanding of the "crucial" event.[117] Rather than explaining what hope he derived from the risen Christ, as Brunner had requested, Niebuhr chose to analyze the authenticity of the event. In light of "modern historical scholarship," he explained that, at most, it was accurate to say that disciples personally believed in the resurrection and the "Church was founded on the assurance that Christ was indeed risen."[118] Niebuhr may have justified his evasion of Brunner's question on the basis that such questions from "the stricter sets" had no "practical" importance. On the contrary, Niebuhr had previously held that the very survival of Western civilization was dependent on the ability of Christians to "look toward the end of history with faith and hope, rather than fear."[119] In this sense, Brunner's question had imminently practical implications—did Niebuhr's recent writings on biblical eschatology embody enough Christian hope to meet his own high standards?

If Niebuhr's discussion of the resurrection appeared to raise more issues than it solved, his explanation of the Fall was merely a

---

[114] Brunner, "Reinhold Niebuhr's Work as a Christian Thinker," in Kegley and Bretall, eds, *Reinhold Niebuhr*, p. 32. Richardson made the same point as Brunner in his article: "There is nothing in Niebuhr's own analysis . . . to account for the hesitation and (to speak plainly) the equivocation which appear in so much of his historicity of the Gospel," "Reinhold Niebuhr as Apologist," p. 227.

[115] Brunner, "Reinhold Niebuhr's Work as a Christian Thinker," p. 33.

[116] Niebuhr, "Reply to Interpretation and Criticism," in Kegley and Bretall, eds, *Reinhold Niebuhr*, p. 439.

[117] Niebuhr, "Reply to Interpretation and Criticism," p. 438.

[118] Niebuhr, "Reply to Interpretation and Criticism," p. 438.

[119] Niebuhr, *Faith and History*, p. 268.

restatement of the position he had been advocating since the 1930s: It
"is essential to the Christian message and to an understanding of the
human situation; but I do not think its validity depends on the idea of
the Fall as a historical event."[120] However, even this "essential"
symbol was not safe toward the end of Niebuhr's career. In a series
of writings, Niebuhr repudiated his use of original sin for the simple
reason that, although he thought he had "cleansed the doctrine for the
modern mind, as well as making it relevant," he had failed.[121] As to
the steps Niebuhr had previously taken to "cleanse" the doctrine,
Niebuhr explained, "I thought in my Gifford Lectures I had made
the doctrine of original sin acceptable both by disavowing the historicity of the Garden of Eden story and by disavowing Augustine's
rather horrible doctrine of the transmission of original sin through
the sexual lust in the act of procreation."[122] Rather than going to such
lengths, Niebuhr, upon reflection, held that the more effective strategy would have been to assert the "persistence and universality of
man's self-regard."[123] Niebuhr, in each of these articles, made clear he
was not disavowing his personal belief in these presuppositions but
rather only coming to terms with their limited applicability. He held,
"I was right . . . in my theology, but wrong in my pedagogy."[124]

Niebuhr's disavowal of the pedagogy by which he had previously
related his theological message to contemporary issues did not mean
that his efforts to this end would cease. On the contrary, he explained
throughout the 1950s that he remained committed to finding an
"adequate description of the situation which will allow for discriminate judgments between good and evil on one hand, and which will, on
the other, preserve the Biblical affirmation that all men fall short
before God's judgment."[125] With references to biblical symbols now
taboo, however, Niebuhr increasingly looked to Lincoln when
appealing not only to non-religious audiences but also to those
consisting primarily of churchmen. This much was clear from his
address at the 1954 Evanston Assembly, which he was forced to

[120] Niebuhr, "Reply to Interpretation and Criticism," p. 438.
[121] Ronald Stone, "An Interview with Reinhold Niebuhr," *Christianity and Crisis*,
March 17, 1969, p. 51.
[122] Stone, "An Interview with Reinhold Niebuhr," p. 51.
[123] John Cogley, "An Interview with Reinhold Niebuhr," *McCall's*, February 1966,
p. 166.
[124] Stone, "An Interview with Reinhold Niebuhr," p. 52.
[125] Niebuhr, "Reply to Interpretation and Criticism," p. 437.

submit in absentia due to lingering health problems. In explaining to this ecumenical gathering how to balance an appreciation of "overarching providence and grace" with the drive to "fight for our causes in history," he observed that it was Lincoln who had "solved this problem more satisfactorily than any statesman or theologian."[126] The extent to which Niebuhr actually believed this to be true can be seen, for instance, in his critique of how a statesman and theologian responded to the Soviet Union's brutal suppression of the Hungarian Revolution two years later.

As Niebuhr discovered the extent of the Russian aggressiveness in Budapest, he began to criticize President Eisenhower for failing to provide any support for the revolutionaries.[127] Although Niebuhr did not advocate for the U.S. military to intervene on behalf of the Hungarians, he believed the seeming indifference shown by the president was "a hell of a way to exercise responsible dominion in a troubled world."[128] It was against this backdrop that Niebuhr explained how much America's present-day leaders could "learn from Lincoln in the larger question of resisting Communist despotism on the one hand, and learning on the other that we must share the world with Communism for decades to come."[129] The crisis also led Niebuhr to engage Barth, as the Swiss theologian had a close relationship with the Hungarian Reformed Church and had advised the body earlier that decade to accept their incorporation into the Soviet bloc "without grumbling and resentment."[130] What infuriated Niebuhr more than this advice was the fact that Barth refused to speak out during the revolution. In a scathing series of articles in *Crisis*, Niebuhr once more criticized the Swiss theologian for his failure to resist

---

[126] Niebuhr, "Our Dependence is on God," *The Christian Century*, September 1, 1954, p. 1037.
[127] Niebuhr, "The Eisenhower Doctrine," *The New Leader*, November 15, 1956, pp. 8–10.
[128] Niebuhr, "The Eisenhower Doctrine," p. 10.
[129] Niebuhr, "The Image of America," *The New Leader*, February 23, 1959, p. 10.
[130] For additional information on Barth's dialogue with the Hungarian Reformed Church, as well as his most complete explanation of the distinction between National Socialism and Communism, see Karl Barth, *Against the Stream: Shorter Post-War Writings, 1946–1952*, trans. E. M. Delacour (London: SCM Press, 1954). Niebuhr was exceedingly critical in his review of the work: "In short these essays reveal political naiveté, posing in the guise of theological sophistication, together with a consequent incapacity to make any prudent or sensible moral judgments," "The Peril of Sophistication," *Christianity and Society* (Autumn 1954), p. 29.

Soviet Communism as he had Nazism in the previous decade.[131] In a statement that was revealing of his own decision to rely less on his theological beliefs in his writings on current events, Niebuhr explained, "The whole performance prompts revulsion against every pretension to derive detailed political judgments from ultimate theological positions."[132] In the transcript of a public address written during this period, Niebuhr compared Barth unfavorably to Lincoln. He insinuated that the president, although lacking theological sophistication, had greater "religious depth" than the Swiss theologian. Lincoln, unlike Barth, provided a model for how individuals could "stand for the values of Western Civilization, and yet be so steady so as not to bring all of civilization to an end via nuclear warfare."[133]

Niebuhr's reliance on Lincoln in the context of his writings on Barth is especially helpful in revealing the degree to which Niebuhr used the president to state his own views. For instance, just as Niebuhr looked to Lincoln as a contrast to Barth's inactivity with regard to Soviet action in Hungary, we recall from the second chapter that Niebuhr had looked to Lincoln as a contrast to Barth's call for the West to use military force against the Nazis. This shows that Lincoln, in addition to being a model for Niebuhr, was a mirror. The theologian invariably found his own political and theological beliefs reflected back at him when looking at the president.[134] Niebuhr's

---

[131] Niebuhr, "Why is Barth Silent on Hungary?," *The Christian Century*, January 23, 1957, pp. 108–10; Niebuhr, "Barth on Hungary: An Exchange," *The Christian Century*, April 10, 1957, pp. 453–5. Niebuhr went so far as to attribute Barth's political neutrality to an anti-American bias and used stronger language than normal in portraying the distinctions between American democracy and Soviet totalitarianism. Unsurprisingly, this appeal resonated with the anti-Communist editors at *Time* magazine, who, as with "The Fight for Germany," a decade prior, published the most anti-Communist excerpts for its readership, "Battle of the Theologians," *Time*, April 22, 1957, p. 72. The battle the article referred to was between Niebuhr and a group of Barth's American students who wrote an article in their mentor's defense, "Barth on Hungary: An Exchange," *The Christian Century*, April 10, 1957, 453–4. More interesting than their defense is the fact that John H. Yoder was amongst their ranks. Niebuhr's reply to the group was largely dismissive, "Barth on Hungary, An Exchange" pp. 453–5.

[132] Niebuhr, "The Peril of Sophistication," p. 29.

[133] Niebuhr "International Banquet Address," Niebuhr Papers, n.d., Box 41. That the speech was given in late 1957 can be discerned from Niebuhr's mention that the world stood on the cusp of West India's Federation, which occurred on January 3, 1958.

[134] Niebuhr was not unique in this regard. See Schwartz, *Abraham Lincoln and the Forge of National Memory*, pp. 5–7 and Merrill Peterson *Abraham Lincoln in American Memory* (Oxford: Oxford University Press, 1995), pp. 33–6.

mention of Lincoln in a sermon during his early ministry only confirms this point. He observed, "We venerate [Lincoln] partly because of a shrewd suspicion that [it] is ourselves glorified."[135] It was thus natural for Niebuhr to see Lincoln as the "most vivid symbol of the meaning of our national existence" in the 1950s, given he saw the president playing that role in his own life.[136]

Niebuhr's description of Lincoln as a most "vivid symbol" shows the depth of his admiration for Lincoln, but hints at its shallowness as well. In the vein of his symbolic understanding of biblical events, Niebuhr took limited interest in the actual life and character of Lincoln. In his dozens of references to the president, Niebuhr relied almost exclusively on one speech, the Second Inaugural Address, and provided biographical analysis more suitable for a schoolboy than the highly sophisticated audiences to which Niebuhr was writing. As we observed earlier in this chapter, if the theological viewpoint that Niebuhr read into Lincoln had developed significantly from *Beyond Tragedy* to *Irony*, his general characterization of the president was largely the same. This changed slightly toward the end of Niebuhr's life, as he learned more about Lincoln's life in order to contribute an article, "The Religion of Abraham Lincoln" to a collection commemorating the centennial anniversary of his Address.[137] Rather than being deterred by questions surrounding Lincoln's

---

[135] Niebuhr, "Ask and It Shall Be Given Unto You," Niebuhr Papers, n.d., Box 14.
[136] Niebuhr, "The Image of America," p. 8.
[137] Niebuhr, "The Religion of Abraham Lincoln," in Alan Nevins, ed., *Lincoln and the Gettysburg Address* (Urbana, IL: University of Illinois Press, 1964), pp. 72–87. Niebuhr documented the development of Lincoln's political thought beginning with his time as a young Whig in the Illinois State Legislature and discussed surrounding influences precipitating the national crisis over slavery that ultimately called Lincoln to center stage in the Lincoln–Douglas Debates. Niebuhr's treatment of Lincoln's presidency against the backdrop of the Civil War is equally comprehensive with detailed analysis ranging from the politics of his cabinet officials to many of his wartime decisions in addition to references from a number of his lesser-known speeches. An unpublished essay on Lincoln's life written in the 1960s has an added advantage of containing footnotes, thus providing a glimpse of the secondary sources Niebuhr utilized in developing his understanding of Lincoln, Niebuhr, "Abraham Lincoln, The Hero of National Unity," Niebuhr Papers, n.d., Box 38. Niebuhr frequently referenced influential scholars of the period such as Richard Hofstadter, Nathaniel Wright Stevenson, and Sydney Mead. Niebuhr attributed the quotations of Lincoln he used to Mead, who, coincidentally, also identified Lincoln as the most profound theologian of the American experience. For Mead's most comprehensive interpretation of Lincoln's faith, see *The Lively Experiment: The Shaping of Christianity in America* (New York: HarperCollins, 1963), pp. 72–89.

personal faith that arose in his additional study, Niebuhr explained
that he only had greater admiration for Lincoln's "heterodox but
profound religious ideas."[138] Niebuhr argued in the article, "It was
Lincoln's achievement to embrace a paradox which lies at the
center of the spirituality of all Western culture with: namely, the
affirmation of a meaningful history and the religious reservation
about the partiality and bias which the human actors and agents
betray in the definition of meaning."[139] Given this was the very
paradox Niebuhr, in one form or another, had been struggling with
in his writings on the Christian interpretation since the 1930s, it is
understandable that he held the president in such high esteem.

What is certain from Niebuhr's many references to Lincoln over
the course of his life is that he attributed great religious significance to
the historical figure. The fact that Lincoln was the "almost perfect
model" on which Niebuhr relied in *Irony* should only further confirm
the extent to which the work was an expression of the latter's theological vision. Given this fact, the more interesting question to ask is
whether the shift in Niebuhr's approach represented by his increased
reliance on Lincoln was a positive one. More specifically, if Niebuhr's
interest was to communicate his theological vision to a broader
audience, was it wise to rely more on the symbol of America's greatest
president than on symbols of biblical events such as the crucifixion
and resurrection? The reason Niebuhr gave for doing this was that he
increasingly found it fruitless to engage with "secular friends and
opponents about the problem of whether God exists or whether the
biblical accounts are credible and in what sense credible."[140] The role
of the Christian, therefore, according to Niebuhr, was "not to prove
anything but to 'bear witness' to the revelation of God in Christ."
And an effective way of "bearing witness" was to convey the importance and relevance of the Christian faith through a figure such
as Lincoln that was almost universally admired by the American
population.[141] While Niebuhr's decision to submerge any theological
references may have allowed his political views to reach an audience

---

[138] Letter from Niebuhr to Will Scarlet, Niebuhr Papers, July 9, Box 33.
[139] Niebuhr, "The Religion of Abraham Lincoln," p. 77.
[140] Niebuhr, "Not Argument but Witness is Required," *Messenger*, March 6,
1956, p. 7.
[141] Niebuhr, "Not Argument but Witness is Required," p. 7.

it otherwise would not have, it also served to obfuscate his central vision. As we mentioned in the introduction, Viereck was prescient in acknowledging that *Irony* would ultimately be threatening to Niebuhr's "noble and beautiful religious message." What he failed to understand, however, was that Niebuhr was not an innocent bystander but rather a knowing agent in this attenuation of Christian witness.

Conclusion

This book has endeavored to identify and describe Niebuhr's theological vision and show how it shaped his understanding of the world. Such a study is necessary because many of Niebuhr's readers today appear unaware or purposely ignore the Christian presuppositions that underlie and animate his writings. This inability to engage with Niebuhr's primary motivations and intellectual underpinnings has been partially responsible for the superficial reception of Niebuhr's thought today. In particular many readers fail to appreciate the central theological vision uniting Niebuhr's writings, namely, the "combination of moral resoluteness about the immediate issues with a religious awareness of another dimension of meaning and judgment" or, as we have described it in shorthand throughout this work, being "in the battle and above it."[1] As we have seen in successive chapters across this book, Niebuhr's theological vision first emerged in the 1930s through his Christian interpretation of history that came into focus during this period. This theological vision played an important role in the context of World War II, as it undergirded both Niebuhr's more academic writings in *Human Nature* and *Human Destiny* as well as his journalistic endeavors during this period. At the outset of the Cold War, Niebuhr applied his theological vision to the relationship between the United States and the Soviet Union and became increasingly committed to sharing his views with as influential and broad an audience as possible. *Irony* represents the apex of this effort in that the work was clearly derived from previous theological writings but was presented in a decidedly non-theological way. Indeed, one of the most surprising findings

---

[1] Niebuhr, *Irony*, p. 172.

from this work is that Niebuhr's efforts to share his theological vision with a non-theological audience in *Irony* and subsequent writings are partially responsible for the misinterpretation of his thought today. The first step we have taken to recover Niebuhr's theological vision is to detail his own Christian beliefs. This is more challenging than it might seem given the muted way in which he often chose to express his commitments. Indeed, Richard Niebuhr's well-known comparison of his brother's thought to a "great iceberg of which three-fourths or more is beneath the surface" is worth revisiting, especially in light of recent reception.[2] For instance, in the 2011 *Why Niebuhr Now*, the late John Patrick Diggins argued, "Whether a supreme being exists was of less importance to Reinhold Niebuhr than the message Christianity holds out to humankind."[3] As this book has endeavored to show, this is a fundamentally misguided reading of Niebuhr's beliefs. First, he clearly believed that the message Christianity held out for humanity was predicated on the *existence* of a supreme being. As Niebuhr explained in *Human Destiny*, what distinguished the Christian view of history from secular alternatives was the fact that it derived its meaning from a source outside of history as opposed to the progression of events themselves. The second and more important issue, however, is that Niebuhr found significance not only in the existence of a supreme being but, moreover, in His divine, redemptive action in history. Specifically, it was the life and death of Jesus Christ that solved the contradiction at the center of human existence: the need to distinguish between good and evil while acknowledging the universal corruption of humanity. For Niebuhr, despite his struggle to formulate this witness in a way he found appropriate to his age, the death and resurrection of the suffering servant reveals how to maintain moral responsibility in a fallen world, giving humanity the hope to live this out on a day-to-day basis.

While Diggins's interpretation bears little resemblance to Niebuhr's actual beliefs, it does come closer than many to approximating how Niebuhr communicated his Christian message to more secular colleagues. That Niebuhr tailored his theological vision for his secular audience may be surprising to some, but is entirely in keeping with his view of himself as less a systematic theologian and more a

---

[2] Richard Niebuhr, "Reinhold Niebuhr's Interpretation of History," p. 97.
[3] John Patrick Diggins, *Why Niebuhr Now?* (Chicago: University of Chicago Press, 2011), p. 110.

Christian apologist.[4] When Niebuhr perceived resistance to his religious appeals from the high-level government officials and academics he increasingly encountered as his public profile rose, his response was not to unapologetically assert the truth of the Christian message. Rather, he discerned that the best way to make inroads with "the most sophisticated of moderns" was to appeal to the unique historical insights Christianity offered to help navigate the tumultuous mid-twentieth century.[5] Once he established this foothold, he would then work backwards to a discussion of the first principles on which those insights were based. The power of Niebuhr's approach can be seen in his influence on precisely that "most sophisticated of moderns" he no doubt had in mind, Harvard historian Arthur Schlesinger. As we discussed in Chapter 4, Schlesinger credited Niebuhr with convincing him that the Christian faith offered a compelling framework to understand the contemporary age. More broadly, Schlesinger acknowledged that "Christian analyses of human conduct and of human history are truer to the facts of experience than alternative analyses."[6]

Niebuhr's ability to convince a largely secular figure such as Schlesinger to take another look at the Christian faith is worthy of admiration. The challenge, however, is that he seemed unable to convince such skeptics to do much more. Niebuhr could never fully explain how an appreciation of the relevance of the Christian faith necessarily required the acceptance of its central beliefs. We recall that Niebuhr toyed in *Faith and History* with developing what he called a "limited rational validation of the truth of the Gospel" that would serve this very purpose; however, he never followed through and ultimately acknowledged the difficulty in coming up with a "proof of the Christian faith, which the unbelievers may see."[7] The result of Niebuhr's inability to make this connection was fairly predictable—unbelievers such as Schlesinger were quite happy to have their proverbial cake and eat it as well or, in the historian's words, to derive "rewarding insights from the Christian conception of man without accepting the Christian drama of sin and salvation

---

[4] Niebuhr, "Intellectual Autobiography," in Kegley and Bretall, eds, *Reinhold Niebuhr*, p. 3.

[5] Niebuhr, "Coherence, Incoherence and the Christian Faith," p. 24.

[6] Niebuhr, "Coherence, Incoherence and the Christian Faith," p. 24.

[7] Niebuhr, *Faith and History*, p. 172; Niebuhr, "Coherence, Incoherence and the Christian Faith," p. 24.

as true . . ."[8] Niebuhr's relevance-based approach may have allowed him to make inroads with skeptical agnostics; however, if his aim was also to induce these same readers to accept the fundamental beliefs of Christianity, then he clearly fell short.

How are we then to understand a theologian who, on one hand, could speak so movingly about the sacrifice of the suffering servant on the Cross but could, on the other hand, dismiss public discussion of the event as the height of foolishness? The unsatisfactory answer is that we must understand him as someone who was fundamentally conflicted over this very issue. His unwillingness to explain the reality that existed behind his symbolic interpretation of the crucifixion and resurrection was not merely an academic problem, as Emil Brunner correctly observed. Rather, it was one that prevented him from being able to answer a question that was at the center of his theological vision: what exactly did he have to hope for in Christ? After all, this hope, as Niebuhr explained in *Discerning*, was the only means by which humanity could face the "ultimate issues" of its existence. But with such a claim, however, he appeared to place more of a burden on his symbolic interpretation than it could bear. At best, we can take the word of Niebuhr's brother, who explained that Reinhold personally accepted the historicity of these central biblical events, but did not make this belief explicit due to the widespread skepticism he perceived among contemporaries to such views.[9] Should this be the case—and the poignancy of Niebuhr's sermonic essays, in particular, suggests that it very well may be—one still must question his willingness to submerge his private beliefs to advance what he perceived to be a more palatable public message.

Niebuhr accurately captured the tension at the center of his writings when he once described his theological project as the "defense and justification of the Christian faith in a secular age."[10] And it is his tendency to elevate the justification of the Christian faith over its defense that leads more orthodox commentators to fault his project today. Indeed, Stanley Hauerwas used the occasion of his own Gifford Lectures—given 60 years after Niebuhr's—to criticize Niebuhr for his focus on the practical applications of Christianity and

[8] As found in Crouter, *Richard Niebuhr: On Politics, Religion, and Christian Faith*, p. 96.
[9] Richard Niebuhr, "Reinhold Niebuhr's Interpretation of History," pp. 98–9.
[10] Niebuhr, "Intellectual Autobiography," in Kegley and Bretall, eds, *Reinhold Niebuhr*, p. 3.

his tendency to sidestep dogmatic elements that might limit its appeal. Both characteristics of Niebuhr's apologetic approach represent to Hauerwas troubling compromises of "truthful Christian speech."[11] In his lectures, the Duke theologian juxtaposes Niebuhr's writings against those of his one-time rival, Karl Barth, whose writings he lauds for "assert[ing] dogmatically the total truth of the Biblical myth with no effort to validate Christianity in experience."[12] In particular, Barth's central focus on the revelation—rather than the relevance—of God is said to offer the type of unapologetic witness required to nourish Christian belief in the modern social order. Rather than tailoring the Christian message to the prevailing currents of contemporary thought, Barth is applauded for his "refusal to submit theological claims to non-theological standards."[13] Hauerwas's appraisal of the two mid-twentieth century contemporaries can be summarized as follows: while Barth led "a frontal attack on some of the most cherished conceits of modernity," Niebuhr operated firmly within its parameters.[14]

Such criticisms of Niebuhr's Christian witness are not without merit. They do, however, appear to overlook the examples of Niebuhr's "truthful" Christian witness that can be found in his writings such as *Beyond Tragedy* and *Discerning*, which he published at the height of his career. The fundamental issue for Hauerwas, however, is that Niebuhr was willing to engage contemporary society on its own terms. Rather than see in this trait unqualified weakness, this book has portrayed it more positively. Contrary to Hauerwas's critique, Niebuhr did not use his familiarity with the landscape of modern secular thought merely to confine Christianity to its contours. Rather Niebuhr, at his best, engaged directly with the twin illusions of the secular age—the perfectibility of human nature and the inevitability of historical progress—to disprove them and offer a more compelling Christian alternative. Put another way, unlike Barth's "frontal attack," Niebuhr's was an inside job in that he used his position within the edifice of contemporary society to expose the flawed foundations on which it rested. Niebuhr's gift lay clearly in compelling those of his generation to give Christianity another look;

---

[11] Hauerwas, *With the Grain of the Universe*, p. 140.
[12] Hauerwas, *With the Grain of the Universe*, p. 110.
[13] Hauerwas, *With the Grain of the Universe*, p. 206.
[14] Hauerwas, *With the Grain of the Universe*, p. 145.

unlike Barth's, his gift did not lie in nurturing germinating faith into flowering and mature belief.

***

Coming to terms with Niebuhr's theological beliefs and approach to Christian witness has been a primary aim, but not the sole objective of this work. Armed with a better understanding of Niebuhr's theological vision, this book also set out to understand what exactly Niebuhr was trying to communicate in his writings on current affairs. The reason this is necessary is that much of what gets called "Niebuhrian" today amounts to little more than a diluted form of his actual message at best. One example of this can be found in Andrew Bacevich's introduction to the re-released 2008 edition of *The Irony of American History*. As I noted in the introduction, Bacevich did not reference the theological basis for Niebuhr's writings, much less how that basis might have influenced *Irony*. Revealingly, Bacevich's account is one almost exclusively focuses on pessimism and despair. This is partially because Bacevich is explicitly using the work to critique what he sees as the "disastrous consequences" of American overreach following the attacks of September 11th.[15] Even if America's leaders were to begin to take to heart the "the truths Niebuhr describes," Bacevich holds that the best we can hope for is a "ratcheting down [of] our expectations" and that the country might avoid "even greater catastrophes."[16] Rather than viewing the American situation through an ironic lens—with a degree of detachment to see the current situation as the unintended consequence of potentially noble aims—Bacevich appears to see contemporary affairs in purely tragic terms. This is clear from the lessons that he derives from Niebuhr's interpretation of history. He explains that *Irony* teaches us that "it is time for Americans to give up their Messianic dreams and cease their efforts to coerce history in a particular direction."[17]

The most remarkable aspect of Bacevich's pessimistic interpretation is that it is precisely the outcome Niebuhr (writing in *Discerning*) predicted would arise if an individual tried to adopt his ironic viewpoint without explicitly accepting the underlying Christian

---

[15] Andrew Bacevich "Introduction," in Niebuhr, *Irony of American History* (Chicago: University of Chicago Press, 2006), p. xx.
[16] Andrew Bacevich "Introduction," p. xvi, xx.
[17] Andrew Bacevich "Introduction," p. xvi.

presuppositions.[18] Niebuhr explained that an ironic viewpoint devoid of faith must inevitably "sink into despair" in the face of the "irrational and unpredictable fortunes which invade the order and purpose of our life."[19] As we discussed in the last chapter, Niebuhr marshaled remarkably stark terms to make this point. He observed, "Either we have a faith from a standpoint of which we are able to say, 'I am persuaded that neither death nor life . . . shall be able to separate us from the love of God which is in Christ Jesus our Lord' or we are overwhelmed by the incongruity."[20] Niebuhr was acutely aware of the centrality of faith in propelling one's view of history beyond tragedy, because this was the realization he had come to himself at the end of the 1930s. As we recall, Niebuhr observed in *Beyond Tragedy* that "the Christian view of history passes through the sense of the tragic to a hope and assurance which is 'beyond tragedy.'"[21] Niebuhr may not have expressed this point as clearly in *Irony*, but one of his most beautiful and oft-cited eschatological reflections can be found within its pages: "Nothing worth doing is completed in our lifetime; therefore, we are saved by hope. Nothing true or beautiful or good makes complete sense in any immediate context of history; therefore, we are saved by faith."[22] While Bacevich views *Irony* as a call for Americans to "ratchet down their expectations," a theological reading of the work reveals Niebuhr's eternal optimism for what can be accomplished in and beyond history when individuals place their abiding faith in God.[23]

To be clear, it is perfectly reasonable to appreciate the theological basis for *Irony* and still interpret the work as a prescient critique of American hubris. As Bacevich suggests, Niebuhr warned against the pretensions of the United States' project to "coerce" history in a

---

[18] Bacevich, by all accounts, takes his Catholic faith quite seriously which is why it is surprising that he does not appear to take Niebuhr's seriously, especially in the context of *Irony*. For more information on the personal faith of Bacevich, see Wendy Murray, "U.S. Delusions: An Army Man Changes his Mind," *The Christian Century*, August 11, 2009, pp. 26–29.

[19] Niebuhr, *Discerning*, pp. 115, 112.

[20] Niebuhr, *Discerning*, p. 113.

[21] Niebuhr, *Beyond Tragedy*, p. x.

[22] Niebuhr, *Irony*, p. 63.

[23] Andrew Bacevich "Introduction," p. xvi. Richard Crouter comes to this very conclusion in his discussion of *Irony*, ultimately concluding "it's important to see that irony, for all its critical posture, is something more than just negative judgment," *Reinhold Niebuhr*, p. 94.

particular direction. Contrary to Bacevich's implication, however, Niebuhr most certainly did not call for the country to "cease its efforts" to be a dynamic actor in the drama of world affairs. As Niebuhr explained in *Irony*, the challenge facing America in coming to terms with the frustrations of history was symbolic of humanity's efforts to deal with the same perplexity. Given his belief that there was "no limit of achievement in any sphere of activity in which human history can rest with equanimity," Niebuhr believed a need to venture was inherent in the country's character and consistently led it to push the boundaries of history.[24] At its best this inherent trait led America to take upon itself responsibility for "the preservation of the sacred fire of liberty and the destiny of the republican model of government," as George Washington prophesized in his First Inaugural Address. At its worst, this trait led the country to commit acts that served to threaten the very flame it was trying to protect. But above all else, Niebuhr was clear that "the recognition of historical limits must not, however, lead to a betrayal of cherished values and historical obtainments."[25] It is for this reason that Niebuhr consistently reserved his harshest judgment over the course of his career for those he considered to be abdicating moral responsibility. Fittingly, Niebuhr hailed in *Irony* those American statesmen "who know from experience that the mastery of historical destiny is a tortuous process," and not those who chose not to try in the first place.[26]

Foremost among such statesmen, and the one to whom Niebuhr turned time and time again over the course of his career was, of course, Abraham Lincoln. This, as we have made clear, was largely because Lincoln came to embody Niebuhr's "in the battle and above it" perspective. As we have seen in this work, Niebuhr may have placed greater emphasis on one side or the other depending on the historical circumstance; nevertheless, his advocacy was almost always presented in the context of this formulation. This recognition, with Lincoln as its paradigm, was clearly the animating belief not only behind Niebuhr's way of thinking but also his way of living. At the height of his influence during World War II and at the outset of the Cold War, Niebuhr authored an article a week on current affairs,

[24] Niebuhr, *Human Nature*, 196.   [25] Niebuhr, *Irony*, p. 143.
[26] Niebuhr, *Irony*, p. 143.

published multiple books of theological significance, founded his own journal, assisted in the organization of numerous political organizations of national scope, contributed to numerous ecumenical conferences, and advised the U.S. government on matters of grand strategy, all the while maintaining a full-time teaching position at Union Theological Seminary.

Interested individuals today will not have to rely solely on Lincoln for an "almost perfect model" for being in and above the battle because Niebuhr, himself, also provides a vivid example. The fact that there has been no one like Niebuhr since his death is a testament to his unique ability not only to develop a theological vision suited to the age in which he lived, but also to employ it in order to shape the trajectory of current events. Indeed, this book argues that Niebuhr offers would-be acolytes something far more valuable than commentary on U.S. foreign policy that can be recycled for contemporary debates; rather, as Robin Lovin suggests, we should understand how Niebuhr's "way of thinking" can "give us the capacity to respond theologically to present-day events."[27] This is precisely what Niebuhr provides through his "in the battle and above it" perspective. In other words, rather than asking what Niebuhr would say, we should be trying to learn from what he did, in particular, how he exercised responsibility and distinguished between immediate and ultimate judgments in history. Niebuhr did not always succeed. In the case of his policy guidance during World War II, Niebuhr's emphasis on being in the battle prior to Pearl Harbor did not lead to his advocacy for U.S. military involvement when it seemed like it should, just as his emphasis on being above the battle following U.S. entry into the war did not keep him from countenancing dubious actions on the part of Allied powers. Acknowledging these specific limitations or, for that matter, the others that we have discussed in this study should not diminish Niebuhr's legacy.

The fact that Niebuhr's life was in many ways defined by the dialectic between his existence and his ideals is precisely why it is worthy of careful study and ongoing reflection. Niebuhr may not have fully articulated the exact nature of the meaning he derived from Christian beliefs, but his life serves as a compelling witness to the profound convictions that guided him. Niebuhr's own ability to avoid

---

[27] Lovin, "Reinhold Niebuhr: Impact and Implications," p. 465.

"sentimentality and despair" and maintain his "in the battle and above it" perspective during the trying years of the mid-twentieth century attest to a profound faith. Put simply, he lived his life as if he understood it "to be in the hands of a Divine Power . . . whose suffering love can overcome the corruptions of man's achievements without negating the significance of our striving."[28] Niebuhr's efforts to live out his theological vision evinces an intellectual courage that renders him one of the most indispensable figures of the twentieth century and offers important lessons for how we live out our beliefs today.

---

[28] Niebuhr, *The Children of Light and Darkness*, p. 128.

Bibliography

Reinhold Niebuhr

Papers
Reinhold Niebuhr's Papers are located at the United States Library of Congress in Washington, D.C. Full references have been provided in the body of the book.

Long works (arranged by date of publication)
Does Civilization Need a Religion? A Study in the Social Resources and Limitations of Religion in Modern Life (New York: Macmillan, 1927).

Leaves from the Notebook of a Tamed Cynic (Chicago: Clark & Colby, 1929).

Moral Man and Immoral Society (New York: Charles Scribner's Sons, 1932).

Reflections on the End of an Era (New York: Charles Scribner's Sons, 1934).

An Interpretation of Christian Ethics (London: SCM Press, 1936).

Beyond Tragedy: Essays on the Christian Interpretation of History (London: Nisbet, 1938).

Christianity and Power Politics (New York: Charles Scribner's Sons, 1940).

The Nature and Destiny of Man, Volume I: Human Nature (London: Nisbet, 1941).

The Nature and Destiny of Man, Volume II: Human Destiny (London: Nisbet, 1943).

The Children of Light and the Children of Darkness: A Vindication of Democracy and a Critique of its Traditional Defense (London: Nisbet, 1945).

Discerning the Signs of the Times: Sermons for Today and Tomorrow (London: SCM Press, 1946).

Faith and History: A Comparison of the Christian and Modern Views of History (London: Nisbet, 1949).

The Irony of American History (New York: Charles Scribner's Sons, 1952).

Christian Realism and Political Problems (New York: Charles Scribner's Sons, 1954).

The Self and the Dramas of History (New York: Charles Scribner's Sons, 1955).

Pious and Secular America (New York: Charles Scribner's Sons, 1958).

The Structure and Nature of Empires: A Study of Recurring Patterns and Problems of Political Order in Relation to Unique Problems of the Nuclear Age (New York: Charles Scribner's Sons, 1959).

Man's Nature and His Communities: Essays on the Dynamics and Enigmas of Man's Personal and Social Existence (New York: Charles Scribner's Sons, 1965).

A Nation So Conceived: Reflections on the History of America from Its Early Visions to Its Present Power, with Alan Heimert (New York: Charles Scribner's Sons, 1965).

The Democratic Experience: Past and Prospects, with Paul E. Sigmund (New York: Praeger, 1969).

The Irony of American History, ed. Andrew Bacevich (Chicago: University of Chicago Press, 2008).

Edited collections

The World Crisis and American Responsibility, ed. Ernest Lefever (New York: National Board of Young Men's Christian Associations, 1958).

Essays in Applied Christianity: The Church and the New World, ed. D. B. Robertson (New York: Meridian, 1959).

Young Reinhold Niebuhr: His Early Writings, 1911–1931, ed. William G. Chrystal (St. Louis: Eden Publishing House, 1977).

Articles (arranged by date of publication)

"The Present Day Task of the Sunday School," *The Evangelical Teacher*, 3:7 (1918), pp. 463–8.

"The Twilight of Liberalism," *New Republic*, June 14, 1919, p. 218.

"Henry Ford and Industrial Autocracy," *The Christian Century*, November 4, 1926, pp. 1354–5.

"How Philanthropic is Henry Ford?" *The Christian Century*, December 9, 1926, pp. 1516–18.

"What the War Did to My Mind," *Christian Century*, September 27, 1928, pp. 1161–2.

"Barth—Apostle of the Absolute," *The Christian Century*, December 13, 1928, pp. 1523–4.

"The Church in Russia," *The Christian Century*, September 24, 1930, pp. 1144–6.

"Must We Do Nothing?" *The Christian Century*, March 30, 1932, pp. 415–17.

"Eternity and Our Time," *The World Tomorrow*, December 1932, p. 596.

"Optimism and Utopianism," *The World Tomorrow*, February 22, 1933, pp. 179–81.

"After Capitalism—What," *The World Tomorrow*, March 1, 1933, pp. 204–5.

"A Reorientation of Radicalism," *The World Tomorrow*, July 1933, pp. 443–4.

"Marx, Barth and Israel's Prophets," *The Christian Century*, January 30, 1935, pp. 138–40.

"Radical Religion," *Radical Religion* (Fall 1935), pp. 4–5.

"Arrogance in the Name of the Church," *The Christian Century*, September 2, 1936, pp. 1157–8.

"The Blindness of Liberalism," *Radical Religion* (Autumn 1936), pp. 4–5.

"Fascism, Communism and Christianity," *Radical Religion* (Winter 1935), pp. 7–8.

"United Front," *Radical Religion* (Winter 1935), pp. 3–6.

"The Reality and Illusion of the Idea of Progress," *The Torch* (April 1937), pp. 3–6.

"The Truth in Myths," in *The Nature of Religious Experience: Essays in Honor of Douglas Clyde Macintosh*, ed. Julius Seelye Bixler (London: Harper & Brothers, 1937), pp. 117–35.

"Greek Tragedy and Modern Politics," *The Nation*, January 1, 1938, pp. 740–4.

"The *London Times* and the Crisis," *Radical Religion* (Winter 1938), pp. 30–2.

"Ten Years That Shook My World," *The Christian Century*, April 26, 1939, pp. 542–6.

"The British Conscience," *The New Statesman and Nation*, August 26, 1939, pp. 219–21.

"Synthetic Barbarism," *The New Statesman and Nation*, September 9, 1939, pp. 390–1.

"Idealists as Cynics," *The Nation*, January 20, 1940, pp. 72–4.

"The Christian Faith and the World Crisis," *Christianity and Crisis*, February 10, 1941, pp. 4–6.

"The Lend Lease Bill," *Christianity and Crisis*, February 10, 1941, p. 2.

"The Crisis Deepens," *Christianity and Crisis*, May 5, 1941, pp. 1–2.

"Just or Holy," *Christianity and Crisis*, November 3, 1941, pp. 1–2.

"A Faith for History's Greatest Crisis," *Fortune*, July 1942, pp. 99–100, 122, 125, 126, 128, and 131.

"In the Battle and Above It," *Christianity and Society* (Autumn 1942), pp. 3–4.

"Russia and the Peace," *Christianity and Society* (Autumn 1942), pp. 8–9.

"The Christian and the War," *Christianity and Crisis*, November 16, 1942, pp. 5–7.

"Christmas Light on History," *Christianity and Crisis*, December 29, 1942, pp. 1–3.

"Russia and the West," *The Nation*, January 23, 1943, p. 83.

"American Power and World Responsibility," *Christianity and Crisis*, April 5, 1943, pp. 2–4.

"Anglo-Saxon Destiny and Responsibility," *Christianity and Crisis*, October 4, 1943, pp. 2–4.

"The Bombing of Germany," *Christianity and Society* (Summer 1943), pp. 2–4.

"Christian Otherworldliness," *Christianity and Society* (Winter 1943), p. 12.

"The German Problem," *Christianity and Crisis*, January 10, 1944, pp. 2–4.

"The Christian Perspective on the World Crisis," *Christianity and Crisis*, May 1, 1944, p. 2.

"The Christian Faith and the German Problem," *The Student Movement*, October 1944, pp. 6–8.

"Soberness in Victory," *Christianity and Crisis*, May 28, 1945, pp. 1–2.

"Our Relations to Japan," *Christianity and Crisis*, September 17, 1945, p. 7.

"The Atomic Issue," *Christianity and Crisis*, October 15, 1945, pp. 5–7.

"The Vengeance of Victors," *Christianity and Crisis*, November 26, 1945, pp. 1–2.

"The Religious Level of the World Crisis," *Christianity and Crisis*, January 21, 1946, p. 5.

"The Conflict Between Nations and Nations and Between Nations and God," *Christianity and Crisis*, August 5, 1946, pp. 2–4.

"Will Germany Go Communist?" *The Nation*, October 5, 1946, pp. 371–3.

"Europe's Hope: (Dr. Niebuhr's Report)" *Life*, October 21, 1946, pp. 65–8, 70, 72.

"The Fight for Germany," *Time*, October 21, 1946, p. 31.

"The Fight for Germany," *Reader's Digest*, 50 (January 1947), pp. 69–72.

"Our Chances for Peace," *Christianity and Crisis*, February 17, 1947, pp. 1–2.

"The Organization of the Liberal Movement," *Christianity and Society* (Spring 1947), pp. 8–10.

"American Power and European Health," *Christianity and Crisis*, June 9, 1947, p. 1.

"Democracy as a Religion," *Christianity and Crisis*, August 4, 1947.

"The Marshall Plan," *Christianity and Crisis*, October 13, 1947, p. 3.

"Protestantism in a Disordered World," *The Nation*, September 18, 1948, pp. 311–13.

"We are Men and Not God," *The Christian Century*, October 27, 1948, pp. 1138–40.

"An Answer to Karl Barth," *The Christian Century*, February 23, 1949, pp. 234–6.

"Streaks of Dawn in the Night," *Christianity and Crisis*, December 12, 1949, pp. 162–4.

"The Hydrogen Bomb," *Christianity and Society* (Spring 1950), pp. 5–7.

"Utilitarian Christianity and the World Crisis," *Christianity and Crisis*, May 29, 1950, pp. 66–9.

"Editorial Notes," *Christianity and Crisis*, December 25, 1950, p. 170.

"Ten Fateful Years," *Christianity and Crisis*, February 5, 1951, pp. 1–4.

"Germany and Western Civilization," in *Germany and the Future of Europe*, ed. Hans Morgenthau (Chicago: University of Chicago Press), 1951, pp. 4–21.

"Our Relation to Asia," *Messenger*, October 23, 1951, p. 7.

"Editorial Notes," *Christianity and Crisis*, October 28, 1951, pp. 138–9. Review of Kennan, *American Diplomacy 1900–1950*.

"Coherence, Incoherence and the Christian Faith," *Union Seminary Quarterly Review*, 7 (January 1952), pp. 11–24.

"The 'Super-Theologians' Meet," *Union Seminary Quarterly Review*, 7 (January 1952), pp. 26–27.

"The Theologian and the Liberal," *New Leader*, 24 November 1952, pp. 23–24.

"Is History Predictable?" *Atlantic Monthly*, 94:1 (1954), pp. 69–72.

"The Theme of Evanston," *Christianity and Crisis*, August 9, 1954, pp. 108–11.

"The Peril of Sophistication," *Christianity and Society* (Autumn 1954), p. 29.

"Our Dependence is on God," *The Christian Century*, September 1, 1954, pp. 1034–7.

"Winston Churchill and Great Britain," *Christianity and Crisis*, May 2, 1955, pp. 51–2.

"Nullification," *The New Leader*, March 5, 1956, pp. 3–5.

"Not Argument but Witness is Required," *Messenger*, March 6, 1956, pp. 5–8.

"Seven Great Errors of U.S. Foreign Policy," *The New Leader*, December 24–31, 1956, pp. 3–5.

"Why is Barth Silent on Hungary?" *The Christian Century*, January 23, 1957, pp. 108–10.

"The Eisenhower Doctrine," *The New Leader*, February 4, 1957, pp. 8–10.

"Barth on Hungary: An Exchange," *The Christian Century*, April 10, 1957, pp. 453–5.

"Walter Rauschenbusch in Historical Perspective," *Religion in Life*, 27:4 (Autumn 1958), pp. 527–36.

"Lincoln and the Self-Image of America," *Berkshire Eagle*, February 12, 1959, p. A12.

"The Image of America," *The New Leader*, February 23, 1959, pp. 8–10.

"The Religion of Abraham Lincoln," in *Lincoln and the Gettysburg Address: Commemorative Papers*, ed. Allan Nevins (Urbana: University of Illinois Press, 1964), pp. 72–87.

"Some Things I Have Learned," *Saturday Review*, November 6, 1965, pp. 21–24, 63.

"Germany," *Worldview*, 16:6 (June 1973), pp. 13–18.

other sources

Book

Acheson, Dean, *Present at the Creation: My Years in the State Department* (New York: Norton, 1969).

Adams, James Luther, *Paul Tillich's Philosophy of Culture, Science and Religion* (New York: Schocken, 1965).

Bacevich, Andrew, *The Limits of American Power: The End of American Exceptionalism* (New York: Metropolitan Books, 2008).

Barth, Karl, *The Epistle to the Romans*, trans. E. C. Hoskyns (Oxford: Oxford University Press, 1933).

—— *Theological Existence To-Day! A Plea for Theological Freedom*, trans. R. Birch Hoyle (London: Hodder & Stoughton, 1933).

—— *Against the Stream: Shorter Post-War Writings, 1946–1952*, trans. E. M. Delacour (London: SCM Press, 1954).

—— *The Word of God and the Word of Man*, trans. Douglas Horton (New York: Harper & Row, 1957).

Biggar, Nigel, *The Hastening That Waits: Karl Barth's Ethics* (Oxford: Clarendon Press, 1995).

Biggar, Nigel, and Linda Hogan, eds., *Religious Voices in Public Places* (Oxford: Oxford University Press, 2009).

Bingham, June, *Courage to Change: An Introduction to the Life and Thought of Reinhold Niebuhr* (New York: Charles Scribner's Sons, 1972).

Bixler, Julius Seelye, ed., *The Nature of Religious Experience: Essays in Honor of Douglas Clyde Macintosh* (London: Harper & Brothers, 1937).

Bonhoeffer, Dietrich, *A Testament to Freedom: The Essential Writings of Dietrich Bonhoeffer*, ed. Geffrey B. Kelly and F. Burton Nelson (New York: Harper One), 1995.

Brown, Charles C., *Niebuhr and His Age: Reinhold Niebuhr's Prophetic Role in the Twentieth Century* (Philadelphia: Trinity Press International, 1992).

Brown, Robert McAfee, ed., *The Essential Reinhold Niebuhr* (New Haven, CT: Yale University Press, 1986).

Brunner, Emil, *Man in Revolt: A Christian Anthropology*, trans. Olive Wyon (London: R. T. S. Luttererworth, 1939).

Bury, J. B., *The Idea of Progress: An Inquiry into Its Origin and Growth* (New York: Dover, 1932).

Busch, Eberhard, ed., *Karl Barth: His Life from Letters and Autobiographical Texts* (London: SCM Press, 1976).

Butterfield, Herbert, *Christianity and History* (London: Bell, 1949).

Carter, Paul, *The Decline and Revival of the Social Gospel: Social and Political Liberalism in American Protestant Churches, 1920–1940* (Ithaca, NY: Cornell University Press, 1956).

Carwardine. Richard J., *Lincoln: A Life of Purpose and Power* (New York: Knopf, 2006).

Chambers, Whittaker, *Witness* (New York: Random House, 1952).

Charles, Evan, *The End of Darkness and Blackout* (London: F. A. Strauss, 1940).

Clark, Henry, *Serenity, Courage and Wisdom: The Enduring Legacy of Reinhold Niebuhr* (Cleveland, OH: Pilgrim, 1994).

Cook, Robert, *Troubled Commemoration: The American Civil War Centennial, 1961–1965* (Baton Rouge, LA: Louisiana State University Press, 2007).

Crouter, Richard, *Reinhold Niebuhr: On Politics Religion, and Christian Faith* (Oxford: Oxford University Press, 2010).

Dawson, Christopher, *Progress & Religion: A Historical Inquiry* (London: Sheed & Ward, 1929).

Denham, Robert D., ed., *Northrop Frye on Culture and Literature* (Chicago: University of Chicago Press, 1978).

Dewey, John, ed., *Creative Intelligence: Essays in the Pragmatic Attitude* (New York: Holt, 1917).

——*A Common Faith* (New Haven, CT: Yale University Press, 1934).

——*Freedom and Culture* (New York: G. P. Putnam's Sons, 1939).

Dibble, Ernest F., *Young Prophet Niebuhr: Reinhold Niebuhr's Early Search for Social Justice* (Washington, D.C.: University Press of America, 1977).

Diggins, John Patrick, *The Proud Decades: America in War and Peace, 1941–1960* (New York: W. W. Norton, 1988).

——*The Promise of Pragmatism: Modernism and the Crisis of Knowledge and Authority* (Chicago: University of Chicago Press, 1994).

——*Why Niebuhr Now?* (Chicago: University of Chicago Press, 2011).

Dorrien. Gary J., *The Making of American Liberal Theology, Volume II: Idealism, Realism, and Modernity* (Louisville, KY: Westminster John Knox Press, 2001).

Dreisbach, Donald F., *Symbols and Salvation: Paul Tillich's Doctrine of Religious Symbols and his Interpretation of the Symbols of the Christian Tradition* (Lanham, MD: University Press of America, 1993).

Duff, Edward, *The Social Thought of the World Council of Churches* (London: Longmans, Green, 1956).

Durkin, Kenneth, *Reinhold Niebuhr* (Harrisburg, PA: Morehouse, 1989).

Elshtain, Jean Bethke, *Just War Against Terror: The Burden of American Power in a Violent World* (New York: Basic Books, 2004).

Federal Council of the Churches of Christ in America, Commission on the Relation of the Church to the War in the Light of the Christian Faith, *Atomic Warfare and the Christian Faith* (New York, 1946).

Fousek, John, *To Lead the Free World: American Nationalism and the Cultural Roots of the Cold War* (Chapel Hill, NC: University of North Carolina Press, 2000).

Fox, Richard Wightman, *Reinhold Niebuhr: A Biography* (New York: Pantheon Books, 1985).

Gaddis, John Lewis, *The United States and the Origins of the Cold War, 1941–1947* (New York: Columbia University Press, 1972).

——*The Long Peace: Inquiries into the History of the Cold War* (Oxford: Oxford University Press, 1987).

—— *Strategies of Containment: A Critical Appraisal of American National Security Policy During the Cold War* (Oxford: Oxford University Press, 2005).

Gaddis, John Lewis, *George F. Kennan: An American Life* (New York: Penguin, 2011).

Gilkey, Langdon, *Gilkey on Tillich* (New York: Crossroad, 1990).

—— *On Niebuhr: A Theological Study* (Chicago: University of Chicago Press, 2001).

Gillon, Steven M., *Politics and Vision: The ADA and American Liberalism, 1947–1985* (New York: Oxford University Press, 1987).

Guelzo, Allen C., *Abraham Lincoln: Redeemer President* (Grand Rapids, MI: W. B. Eerdmans, 1999).

Gustafson, James, *Christ and the Moral Life* (Chicago: University of Chicago Press, 1968).

Halliwell, Martin, *The Constant Dialogue: Reinhold Niebuhr & American Intellectual Culture* (Lanham, MD: Rowman & Littlefield, 2005).

Hamby, Alonzo L., *Man of the People: A Life of Harry S. Truman* (Oxford: Oxford University Press, 1998).

Handy, Robert T., *The Social Gospel in America: 1870–1920* (New York: Oxford University Press, 1966).

Harland, Gordon, *The Thought of Reinhold Niebuhr* (New York: Oxford University Press, 1960).

Harries, Richard, ed., *Reinhold Niebuhr and the Issues of our Time* (London: Mowbray, 1986).

Harries, Richard, and Stephen Platten, eds., *Reinhold Niebuhr and Contemporary Politics* (Oxford: Oxford University Press, 2010).

Hauerwas, Stanley, *The Peaceable Kingdom: A Primer in Christian Ethics* (Notre Dame, IN: University of Notre Dame Press, 1991).

—— *With the Grain of the Universe: The Church's Witness and Natural Theology* (Grand Rapids, MI: Brazos Press, 2001).

Heclo, Hugh, and Wilford M. McClay, eds., *Religion Returns to the Public Square: Faith and Policy in America* (Washington, D.C.: Woodrow Wilson Center Press, 2003).

Hofstadter, Richard, *The American Political Tradition: And the Men Who Made It* (New York: Knopf, 1948).

Hook, Sydney, *Pragmatism and the Tragic Sense of Life* (New York: Basic Books, 1974).

Hopkins, Charles Howard, *The Rise of the Social Gospel in American Protestantism, 1865–1915* (New Haven, CT: Yale University Press, 1994).

Hulsether, Mark, *Building a Protestant Left: Christianity and Crisis Magazine, 1941–1993* (Knoxville, TN: University of Tennessee Press, 1999).

Hutchison, William R., ed., *Between the Times: The Travail of the Protestant Establishment in America, 1900–1960* (Cambridge: Cambridge University Press, 1989).

—— *The Modernist Impulse in American Protestantism* (London: Duke University Press, 1992).

Inboden, William, *Religion and American Foreign Policy, 1945–1960: The Soul of Containment* (Cambridge: Cambridge University Press, 2008).

James, William, *The Works of William James: Essays in Radical Empiricism*, ed. Frederick Burkhardt and Fredson Bowers (Cambridge, MA: Harvard University Press, 1976).

—— *The Varieties of Religious Experience: A Study in Human Nature*, introd. Reinhold Niebuhr (New York: Penguin, 1985).

Johnson, William Stacey, ed., *H. Richard Niebuhr, Theology, History and Culture: Major Unpublished Writings* (New Haven, CT: Yale University Press, 1998).

Kegley, Charles W., and Robert W. Bretall, eds., *The Theology of Paul Tillich* (New York: Macmillan, 1952).

—————eds., *Reinhold Niebuhr: His Religious, Social, and Political Thought* (New York: Macmillan, 1956).

Kierkegaard, Søren, *The Concept of Anxiety: A Simple Psychological Orienting Deliberation on the Dogmatic Issue of Heriditary Sin*, trans. and ed. Howard Hong and Edna Hong (Princeton, NJ: Princeton University Press, 1980).

—— *Sickness Unto Death: A Christian Psychological Exposition for Upbuilding and Awakening*, trans. and ed. Howard Hong and Edna Hong (Princeton, NJ: Princeton University Press, 1980).

Kennan George F., *American Diplomacy, 1900–1950* (Chicago: University of Chicago Press, 1951).

—— *Memoirs, Volume I, 1925–1950* (Boston: Little, Brown, 1967).

—— *Memoirs, Volume II, 1950–1963* (Boston: Little, Brown, 1973).

King, Martin Luther, Jr., *Stride Toward Freedom: The Montgomery Story* (New York: Harper Brothers, 1958).

Kirby, Dianne, ed., *Religion and the Cold War* (Basingstoke: Palgrave Macmillan, 2003).

Kissinger, Henry, *Diplomacy* (New York: Simon & Schuster, 1995).

Kleinmann, Mark, *A World of Hope, a World of Fear: Henry Wallace, Reinhold Niebuhr, and American Liberalism* (Bowling Green, OH: Ohio State University Press, 2000).

Kloppenberg, James T., *Uncertain Victory: Social Democracy and Progressivism in European and American Thought, 1870–1920* (Oxford: Oxford University Press, 1986).

LaFeber, Walter, *America, Russia, and the Cold War, 1945–1992*, 10th edn (New York: McGraw-Hill, 2008).

Landon, Harold R., ed., *Reinhold Niebuhr: A Prophetic Voice in Our Time* (Greenwich, CT: Seabury Press, 1962).

Leffler, Melvyn P., *The Specter of Communism: The United States and the Origins of the Cold War, 1917–1953* (New York: Hill & Wang, 1994).

Lemert, Charles, *Why Niebuhr Matters*, (New Haven: Yale University Press, 2011).

Lewis, R. W. B., *The American Adam* (Chicago: University of Chicago Press, 1959).

Loconte, Joseph, ed., *The End of Illusions: Religious Leaders Confront Hitler's Gathering Storm* (Lanham, MD: Rowman & Littlefield, 2004).

Lovin, Robin, *Christian Faith and Public Choices: The Social Ethics of Barth, Brunner, and Bonhoeffer* (Philadelphia: Fortress, 1984).

——*Reinhold Niebuhr and Christian Realism* (Cambridge: Cambridge University Press, 1995).

——*Christian Realism and the New Realities* (Cambridge: Cambridge University Press, 2008).

McCann, Dennis, *Christian Realism and Liberation Theology: Practical Theologies in Creative Conflict* (Maryknoll, NY: Orbis Books, 1981).

McClay, Wilfred M., *The Masterless: The Self and Society in Modern America* (Chapel Hill, NC: University of North Carolina Press, 1994).

McCormack, Bruce L., *Karl Barth's Critically Realistic Dialectical Theology: Its Genesis and Development, 1909–1936* (Oxford: Clarendon Press, 1995).

McDowell, John C., *Hope in Barth's Eschatology: Interrogations and Transformations Beyond Tragedy* (Aldershot: Ashgate, 2000).

McIntire, C.T., ed., *God, History, and Historians: An Anthology of Modern Christian Views of History* (Oxford: Oxford University Press, 1977).

Marty, Martin, *Modern American Religion, Volume I: The Irony of It All, 1893–1919* (Chicago: University of Chicago Press, 1986).

——*Religion and Republic: The American Circumstance* (Boston: Beacon Press, 1987).

——*Modern American Religion, Volume II: The Noise of Conflict, 1919–1941* (Chicago: University of Chicago Press, 1991).

——*Modern American Religion, Volume III: Under God, Indivisible, 1941–1960* (Chicago: University of Chicago Press, 1996).

Mattson, Kevin, " *What the Heck Are You Up To, Mr. President?" Jimmy Carter, America's "Malaise" and the Speech that Should have Changed the Country* (London: Bloomsbury, 2009).

May, Ernest R., ed., *American Cold War Strategy: Interpreting NSC-68* (Boston: Bedford Books, 1993).

——*Protestant Churches and Industrial America* (New York: Harper Brothers, 1949).

Mayers, David, *George Kennan and the Dilemmas of US Foreign Policy* (Oxford: Oxford University Press, 1990).

Mead, Sidney E., *The Lively Experiment: The Shaping of Christianity in America* (New York: HarperCollins, 1963).

Mead, Walter Russell, *God and Gold: Britain, America, and the Making of the Modern World* (New York: Knopf, 2007).

Menand, Louis, *The Metaphysical Club* (London: Flamingo, 2001).

Merkley, Paul, *Reinhold Niebuhr: A Political Account* (Montreal: McGill-Queen's University Press, 1975).

Miller, Randall M., Harry S. Stout, and Charles Reagan Wilson, eds., *Religion and the American Civil War* (New York: Oxford University Press, 1998).

Miscamble, Wilson D., *George F. Kennan and the Making of American Foreign Policy, 1947–1950* (Princeton, NJ: Princeton University Press, 1993).

Morris, Kenneth E., *Jimmy Carter: American Moralist* (Athens, GA: University of Georgia Press, 1996).

Neuhaus, Richard John, *Reinhold Niebuhr Today* (Grand Rapids, MI: Eerdmans, 1989).

Nevins, Allan, ed., *Lincoln and the Gettysburg Address: Commemorative Papers* (Urbana, IL: University of Illinois Press, 1964).

Niebuhr, H. Richard, *The Kingdom of God in America* (New York: Harper, 1937).

Niebuhr, Ursula, ed., *Remembering Reinhold Niebuhr: Letters of Reinhold and Ursula M. Niebuhr* (San Francisco: HarperCollins, 1991).

Noll, Mark A., *America's God* (Oxford: Oxford University Press, 2002).

Oates, Stephen, *With Malice Toward None: A Life of Abraham Lincoln* (New York: Harper & Row, 1977).

Ogletree, Thomas W., *Christian Faith and History: A Critical Comparison of Ernst Troeltsch and Karl Barth* (London: Westminster John Knox Press, 2003).

Oldham, J. H., *The Oxford Conference: World Conference on Church, Community and State (Official Report)* (New York: Willett, Clark, 1937).

Peterson, Merrill, *Abraham Lincoln in American Memory* (Oxford: Oxford University Press, 1995).

Rasmussen, Joel, *Between Irony and Witness: Kierkegaard's Poetics of Faith, Hope, and Love* (London: T&T Clark International, 2005).

Rasmussen, Larry, *Reinhold Niebuhr: Theologian of Public Life* (London: Collins Liturgical Publications, 1991).

Rauschenbusch, Walter, *Christianity and the Social Crisis*, ed. Robert D. Cross (New York: Harper & Collins, 1964).

——*A Theology for the Social Gospel* (Nashville: Abingdon Press, 1987).

Rawls, John *Political Liberalism* (New York: Columbia University Press, 2005).

Reinitz, Richard, *Irony and Consciousness: American Historiography and Reinhold Niebuhr's Vision* (Lewisburg, PA: Bucknell University Press, 1980).

Rice, Daniel F., *Reinhold Niebuhr and John Dewey: An American Odyssey* (Albany, NY: State University of New York Press, 1993).

Rice, Daniel F., ed., *Reinhold Niebuhr Revisited: Engagements with an American Original* (Grand Rapids, MI: Eerdmans, 2009).

Schlesinger, Jr., Arthur, *The Politics of Hope* (London: Eyre & Spottiswoode, 1964).

Schwartz, Barry, *Abraham Lincoln and the Forge of National Memory* (Chicago: University of Chicago Press, 2000).

Scott, Nathan A., ed., *The Legacy of Reinhold Niebuhr* (Chicago: University of Chicago Press, 1975).

Sharp, Joanne, *Condensing the Cold War: Reader's Digest and American Identity* (Minneapolis, MN: University of Minnesota Press, 2000).

Sifton, Elisabeth, *The Serenity Prayer: Faith and Politics in Times of Peace and War* (New York: Norton, 2003).

Stenger, Mary Ann, and Ronald H. Stone, *Dialogues of Paul Tillich* (Macon, GA: Mercer University Press, 2002).

Stone, Ronald H., *Reinhold Niebuhr: Prophet to Politicians* (Nashville, TN: Abingdon Press, 1972).

——*Paul Tillich's Radical Social Thought* (Louisville, KY: John Knox Press, 1992).

——*Professor Reinhold Niebuhr* (Louisville, KY: John Knox Press, 1992).

Stout, Jeffrey, *Democracy and Tradition* (Princeton, NJ: Princeton University Press, 2005).

Strauss, David Friedrich, *The Life of Jesus: Critically Examined*, trans. George Eliot, ed. Peter C. Hodgson (Philadelphia: Fortress Press, 1972).

Tanenhaus, Sam, *Whitaker Chambers: A Biography* (New York: Random House Modern Library, 1998).

Tillich, Paul, *The Religious Situation*, trans. H. Richard Niebuhr (New York: Henry Holt, 1932).

——*Systematic Theology*, 3 vols (Chicago: University of Chicago Press, 1951–63).

——*What is Religion?*, ed. James Luther Adams (New York: Harper & Row, 1969).

——*The Socialist Decision*, trans. Franklin Sherman (New York: Harper & Row, 1977).

——*Political Expectation*, trans. James Luther Adams (New York: Harper & Row, 1983).

U.S. Department of State, *Foreign Relations of the United States: Eastern Europe, the Soviet Union, 1946*, Vol. VI (Washington, D.C.: U.S. Department of State, 1969).

—— *Foreign Relations of the United States, National Security Affairs: Foreign Economic Policy* (Washington, D.C.: U.S. Department of State, 1950).

Wainwright, Loudon, *The Great American Magazine: An Inside History of Life* (New York: Knopf, 1986).

Warren, Heather A., *Theologians of a New World Order: Reinhold Niebuhr and the Christian Realists, 1920-1948* (Oxford: Oxford University Press, 1997).

West, Charles C., *Communism and the Theologians: Study of an Encounter* (Philadelphia: Westminster Press, 1958).

West, Cornel, *The American Evasion of Philosophy: A Genealogy of Pragmatism* (Madison, WI: University of Wisconsin Press, 1989).

White, Graham and John Maze, *Henry A. Wallace: His Search for a New World Order* (Chapel Hill, NC: University of North Carolina Press, 1995).

White, Morton G., *Social Thought in America: The Revolt Against Formalism* (Boston: Beacon Press, 1957).

White, Ronald C., *Lincoln's Greatest Speech: The Second Inaugural* (New York: Simon & Schuster, 2002).

Winnington-Ingram, A. F., *A Second Day of God* (London: Longmans, Green and Co., 1940).

Articles

Bacevich, Andrew, "Illusions of Managing History: The Enduring Relevance of Reinhold Niebuhr," *Historically Speaking*, 8:1 (January/February 2008), pp. 23-6.

Badham, Roger, "Redeeming the Fall: Hick's Schleiermacher versus Niebuhr's Kierkegaard," *Journal of Religion*, 78:4 (October 1998), pp. 547-70.

Baille, John, "Niebuhr's Gifford Lectures," *Union Seminary Quarterly Review*, 2 (March 1941), p. 8.

Barbour, John, "Niebuhr vs. Niebuhr: The Tragic Nature of History," *The Christian Century*, November 21, 1964, 1096-9.

Barth, Karl, "A Letter to Great Britain from Switzerland," *Christianity and Crisis*, October 15, 1941, pp. 6-7.

—— "No Christian Marshall Plan," *The Christian Century*, December 8, 1948, pp. 1330-3.

"Battle of the Theologians," *Time*, April 22, 1957, p. 72.

Beckley, Harlan, "Book Review," *Theology Today*, 42:1 (April 1985), pp. 123-5.

Bellah, Robert N., "Civil Religion in America," in *American Civil Religion*, ed. Russell E. Richey and Donald G. Jones (New York: Harper & Row, 1974), pp. 21-44.

Bennett, John, "Tillich and the Fellowship of Socialist Christians," *North American Paul Tillich Society Newsletter*, 16 (October 1990), p. 3.

Bennett, John C., "Human Destiny—Reinhold Niebuhr", *The Union Review*, 6:2 (March 1943), pp. 24–6.

Biggar, Nigel, "Saving the 'Secular': The Public Vocation of Moral Theology," *Journal of Religious Ethics*, 37:1 (March 2009), pp. 159–78.

Blake, Charles, "Obama and Niebuhr," *The New Republic*, May 3, 2009, p. 3.

Brinton, Crane, "The Problem of Evil in Human History," *New York Herald Tribune Book Review*, April 6, 1952, p. 5.

Brooks, David, "A Man on a Gray Horse," *The Atlantic Monthly*, September 2002, pp. 24–5.

—— "Obama, Gospel and Verse," *The New York Times*, April 26, 2007, p. A21.

Buehrer, Edwin T., "The Mythology of Theology," *The Christian Century*, March 2, 1938, pp. 277–8.

Calhoun, Robert L., "A Symposium on Reinhold Niebuhr's *The Nature and Destiny of Man*," *Christendom*, 6 (Autumn 1941), pp. 572–8.

—— "Review of *Human Destiny*," *Union Seminary Journal of Religion*, 24 (January 1944), pp. 59–64.

Coe, George A., "Two Communications," *The Christian Century*, March 15, 1933, p. 362.

Chambers, Whittaker, "Sin Rediscovered," *Time*, March 24, 1941, pp. 36–40.

—— "Faith for a Lenten Age," *Time*, March 8, 1948, pp. 68–72, 74–6, 79.

Chrystal, William G., "Reinhold Niebuhr and the First World War," *Journal of Presbyterian History*, 55:3 (1977), pp. 285–99.

—— "A Man of the Hour and Time: The Legacy of Gustav Niebuhr," *Church History*, 49 (1980), pp. 416–32.

Churchill, Winston, *The Sinews of Peace*, text in *The New York Times*, March 6, 1946, p. 4.

Cogley, John, "An Interview with Reinhold Niebuhr," *McCall's*, February 1966, pp. 90–91, 166–171.

Cremer, Douglas J., "Protestant Theology in Early Weimar Germany: Barth, Tillich, and Bultmann," *Journal of the History of Ideas*, 56:2 (April 1995), pp. 289–307.

Finstuen, Andrew, "This American Mess: Where is Reinhold Niebuhr When We Need Him?" *The Christian Century*, December 1, 2009, pp. 11–12.

Gardener, Neil, "Barack Obama Should Stop Apologizing for America," *The Daily Telegraph*, June 2, 2009, p. 14.

Gerson, Michael, "Obama Shows Maturity in Nobel Speech," *The Washington Post*, December 11, 2009, p. A23.

Gunton, Colin, "Reinhold Niebuhr: A Treatise of Human Nature," *Modern Theology*, 4:1 (1987), pp. 71–81.

Haas, Mark, "Reinhold Niebuhr's 'Christian Pragmatism': A Principled Alternative to Consequentialism," *The Review of Politics*, 61:4 (Autumn 1999), pp. 605–36.

Harbison, E. Harris, "The 'Meaning of History' and the Writing of History," *Church History*, 21 (1952), pp. 97–106.

Haroutunian, Joseph, "Review of *Human Destiny*," *Christianity and Society* (Spring 1943), pp. 36–39.

Hauerwas, Stanley, "The Search for the Historical Niebuhr," *The Review of Politics*, 38:3 (July 1976), pp. 452–4.

Hook, "A New Failure of Nerve," *Partisan Review*, 10 (January–February 1943), pp. 2–23.

Hume, Thomas, "Prophet of Disillusion," *The Christian Century*, January 4, 1933, pp. 18–19.

Jenkins, Daniel, "Review of *Faith and History*," *Union Seminary Quarterly Review*, 4 (May 1949), pp. 51–2.

Kennan, George F., "The Sources of Soviet Conduct," *Foreign Affairs*, 24:4 (July 1947), pp. 566–82.

—— "To Be or Not to Be a Christian," *Christianity and Crisis*, May 3, 1954, pp. 51–3.

Koshar, Rudy, "Where is Karl Barth in Modern European History?" *Modern Intellectual History*, 5:2 (2008), pp. 333–62.

Kristol, Irving, "The Slaughter-Bench of History," *Commentary Magazine*, July 1949, pp. 99–102.

Leuchtenburg, William, "Niebuhr: The Theologian and the Liberal," *New Leader*, November 24, 1952, pp. 23–4.

Loconte, Joseph, "The War Party's Theologian," *The Wall Street Journal*, May 31, 2002, p. A14.

—— "Obama Contra Niebuhr," *The American*, January 14, 2010, <http://www.american.com/archive/2010/january/obama-contra-niebuhr>.

Lovin, Robin, "Reinhold Niebuhr in Contemporary Scholarship: A Review Essay," *Journal of Religious Ethics*, 31:3 (2003), pp. 489–505.

—— "Reinhold Niebuhr: Impact and Implications," *Political Theology*, 6:4 (2005), pp. 459–71.

Luce, Henry, "The American Century," *Life*, February 17, 1941, pp. 61–5.

McCreary, David. "John Bennett on Oxford '37," *The Christian Century*, October 28, 1987, pp. 942–4.

Marty, Martin E., "Reinhold Niebuhr and *The Irony of American History*: A Retrospective," *The History Teacher*, 26:2 (February 1993), pp. 161–74.

—— "Citing Reinhold," *The Christian Century*, October 18, 2005, p. 71.

Murphy, Arthur E., "Niebuhr's Answer to a Loss of Faith," *The Christian Register*, November 1949, p. 2.

Murray, Wendy, "U.S. Delusions: An Army Man Changes his Mind," *The Christian Century*, August 11, 2009, pp. 26–29.

Niebuhr, H. Richard, "The Grace of Doing Nothing," *The Christian Century*, March 23, 1932, pp. 379–380.

—— "The Only Way Into the Kingdom of God," *The Christian Century*, April 6, 1932, p. 447.

Noll, Mark A., "'Both . . . Pray to the Same God': The Singularity of Lincoln's Faith in the Era of the Civil War," *Journal of the Abraham Lincoln Association*, 18:1 (1997), pp. 1–26.

Ogden, Schubert M., "Bultmann's Project of Demythologization and the Problem of Theology and Philosophy," *Journal of Religion*, 37:3 (July 1957), pp. 156–73.

Paeth, Scott, "Being Wrong and Right: A Response to Larry Rasmussen and Robin Lovin," *Political Theology*, 6:4 (October 2005), pp. 473–86.

Rasmusson, Arne, "Deprive them of their 'Pathos': Karl Barth and the Nazi Revolution Revisited," *Modern Theology*, 23:3 (July 2007), pp. 369–91.

Rees, Geoffrey, "The Anxiety of Inheritance: Reinhold Niebuhr and the Literal Truth of Original Sin," *Journal of Religious Ethics*, 31:1 (March 2003), pp. 75–99.

"Religion: Niebuhr vs. Sin," *Time*, April 29, 1946, p. 23. Review of Niebuhr, *Discerning the Sign of the Times*.

Rice, Daniel F., "Reinhold Niebuhr and Hans Morgenthau: A Friendship with Contrasting Shades of Realism," *Journal of American Studies*, 42 (August 2008), pp. 255–91.

Richardson, Cyril, "Review of *Beyond Tragedy*," *Review of Religion*, 2 (March 1938), pp. 331–338.

Schlesinger, Jr., Arthur, "Review of *Faith and History*," *Christianity and Society* (Summer 1949), pp. 26–27.

—— "Niebuhr and Some Critics," *Christianity and Society* (Autumn 1952), pp. 25–7.

—— "Prophet for a Secular Age," *New Leader*, January 24, 1972, pp. 11–14.

—— "God and the 1976 Election," *The Wall Street Journal*, April 28, 1976, p. 18.

—— "Reinhold Niebuhr's Long Shadow," *The New York Times*, June 22, 1992, p. A12.

—— "Forgetting Reinhold Niebuhr," *New York Times Book Review*, September 18, 2005, p. G12.

Sherlock, Richard, "Must Ethics be Theological? A Critique of the New Pragmatists," *Journal of Religious Ethics*, 37:4 (December 2009), pp. 631–49.

Stone, Ronald, "An Interview with Reinhold Niebuhr," *Christianity and Crisis*, March 17, 1969, pp. 48–52.

Thompson, Michael G., "An Exception to Exceptionalism: A Reflection on Reinhold Niebuhr's Vision of 'Prophetic' Christianity and the Problem of Religion and U.S. Foreign Policy," *American Quarterly*, 59:3 (September 2007), pp. 833–55.

Tillich, Paul, "Review of *Human Nature*," *Christianity and Society* (Spring 1941), pp. 34–37.

—— "The Religious Symbol," trans. James Luther Adams, *Daedalus*, 87:3 (Summer, 1958), pp. 3–21.

True, David, "Embracing Hauerwas? A Niebuhrian Takes a Closer Look," *Political Theology*, 8:2 (2007), pp. 197–212.

Van Dusen, Henry Pitney, "The 'Super-Theologians' Meet," *Union Seminary Quarterly Review*, 7 (January 1952), pp. 25–6.

Vann Woodward, C., "The Irony of Southern History," *Journal of Southern History*, 19:1 (February 1953), pp. 3–19.

Webber, David, "Niebuhr's Legacy," *The Review of Politics*, 64 (2002), pp. 339–52.

White, Morton, "Of Moral Predicaments," *The New Republic*, May 5, 1952, pp. 18–20.

Whitman, Alden, "Reinhold Niebuhr is Dead; Protestant Theologian, 78," *The New York Times*, June 2, 1971, pp. 1, 45.

Wieseltier, Leon, "Reinie and Woody," *The New Republic*, September 11–18, 2006, p. 38.

Wilkins, Burleigh Taylor, "Pragmatism as a Theory of Historical Knowledge: John Dewey on the Nature of Historical Inquiry," *The American Historical Review*, 64:4 (July 1959), pp. 878–90.

Unpublished theses

Brandt, Jonathan, "On the Possibility of Revelation Through Film: Paul Tillich's Theology of Revelation through Culture in Light of Original Research into the Experiences of a Group of Filmgoers," DPhil Thesis, University of Oxford, 2008.

Colaco, Nita, "The Anglo-American Council on Productivity: A Study of Industry, Labour Relations, and the Drivers of Productivity, 1948–1952," MPhil Thesis, University of Oxford, 2010.

Erwin, Scott, "'America's Greatest Theologian': Abraham Lincoln Through the Lens of Reinhold Niebuhr," MPhil Thesis, University of Oxford, 2008.

Index

Morrison, C. C.
The Christian Century 27
Murphy, Arthur E. 110
myths 37, 41, 44
Fall 46
Niebuhr on 46–7, 50

natural sciences 90–1
Nazi Germany 47, 56, 57–8, 66–7, 68,
83, 97, 103, 107, 108
Nazism 40, 41–2, 43, 57, 59, 74, 93,
96–7, 105, 148
New Republic 99
New Testament 109, 120–1, 142
Niebuhr, Elisabeth 123
Niebuhr, Gustav 5
Niebuhr, H. Richard 25, 31, 35–6, 50,
111, 112–13
comparison with brother 30, 153, 155
"ethically-driven coercion" 31–2
God in history 30, 36, 50
and God's grace 29
history 27
human nature 35
and redemption 30
"The Grace of Doing Nothing" 27
Niebuhr, Reinhold
on Abraham Lincoln 4–6, 17–18, 19,
20, 51, 71, 120, 138, 140–1, 146, 147,
148–50, 159–60
as advisor to U.S. State
Department 21
"in the battle and above it" 2, 3, 4, 5,
10, 17, 18–19, 21, 25, 29, 50, 51, 53,
54, 73, 75–6, 82, 83, 85–6, 87, 94,
105, 114, 120, 125, 137–8, 152,
160, 161
biblical faith 11, 15, 44
Christian beliefs 153, 155, 160–1
Christian faith 14, 48–9, 78, 79, 84,
88, 89–90, 91–2, 102, 106, 108,
109–10, 117–18, 119, 124–5, 127,
134, 136, 139–40, 142–3, 150, 154
Christian message 110, 120, 121,
153–4, 156
Christian witness 156, 157
on Germany 73–4, 95, 96
on God 13, 19, 20–1, 29, 30, 50,
74–5, 79
and health 141, 146–7
on history, Christian
interpretation 13, 14, 18, 76–7,

89–91, 106–9, 111, 113, 119, 120,
123–4, 129, 133, 153, 157
on history, tragic view 14, 25, 27, 30,
39, 76
and human brokenness 25, 49
on human nature 13, 19, 35–6, 38, 39,
44, 45, 52, 58, 59, 60, 62, 63–4,
130, 197
on irony/humour 127–8, 129, 130,
132, 133, 134, 135, 136, 137, 139,
140, 150
on liberalism 38, 39
moral accountability 67–8, 112
on morality 33
on myths 39, 44, 45, 46–7, 50, 145
and non-religious audiences 9
on orthodox Christianity 38, 39
as pastor in Detroit 6, 31
and patriotism 29
on politics 7–8, 9, 10, 54, 55, 56, 72,
84, 101, 117, 140
on Resurrection 13–14, 15
on sins/sinfulness 11–12, 35, 39,
48, 52, 56, 59, 63–4, 65, 66, 77,
82–3, 86
and symbols 15–16, 112–13, 144, 146
on theology 7–8, 9, 10–11, 14, 16–17,
18–19, 19–21, 33, 35, 44, 46, 48,
50–1, 52, 53, 56, 63, 66, 86, 101–2,
113, 118, 119–20, 121, 126, 129,
133, 136–8, 140, 141, 141, 148,
150–1, 152–4, 157, 160
on transcendent-immanent God
39, 42
on U.S. foreign policy 7, 20, 28–30
writings 2, 4, 6, 22, 29, 39, 50, 53, 54,
56, 58, 59, 70, 73, 75, 81, 85, 88, 90,
92, 98, 100, 106, 107–8, 110
Beyond Tragedy 11, 17, 25, 49–50, 51,
52, 76, 138, 149, 158
*The Children of Light and the
Children of Darkness* 14, 84
Discerning the Signs of the Times 21,
87, 90, 91–2, 101, 106–7, 119,
127, 129, 134, 136, 137, 140,
155, 158
Faith and History 19, 21, 88–9, 106,
107, 109–10, 112, 119, 120, 123–4,
128, 129–30, 133, 143, 154
Human Destiny 19, 20, 27, 53, 54–55,
56, 76–7, 79, 81, 82, 83, 84, 86, 87,
106, 109, 123, 137, 152, 153